INDUSTRIAL RELATIONS IN JAPAN

THE NISSAN INSTITUTE/ ROUTLEDGE JAPANESE STUDIES SERIES

Other titles in the series:

Industrial Relations in Japan

The Peripheral Workforce

NORMA J. CHALMERS

ROUTLEDGE
London and New York

First published 1989
by Routledge
11 New Fetter Lane, London EC4P 4EE
29 West 35th Street, New York NY 10001

Typeset by Pat and Anne Murphy,
Highcliffe-on-Sea, Dorset.
Printed in Great Britain by
Billing & Sons Ltd, Worcester

British Library Cataloguing in Publication Data

Chalmers, Norma J. *1924–*
  Industrial relations in Japan: the peripheral
  workforce. — (The Nissan Institute/Routledge
  Japanese studies series).
  1. Japan. Industrial relations.
  I. Title II. Series
  331′.0952
  ISBN 0-415-00008-4

Library of Congress Cataloging in Publication Data

Chalmers, Norma.
    Industrial relations in Japan: the peripheral workforce /
  Norma J. Chalmers.
        p.   cm. — (Nissan Institute/Routledge Japanese studies
  series)
    Includes index.
    Bibliography: p.
    ISBN 0-415-00008-4 (U.S.)
    1. Industrial relations — Japan. 2. Labor and laboring
  classes — Japan. 3. Contract labor — Japan. I. Title.
  II. Series.
  HD8726.5.C43 1989
  331′.0952—dc19   88-39843 CIP

Contents

Figures

Tables

Introduction

In downtown Tokyo in December each year, 47 masterless samurai re-enact the popular 280-year-old tale of a vendetta involving honour, revenge, and the samurai spirit. At the assembly point some score of spectators share rice biscuits and *sake* before travelling by subway across town in company with the samurai, splendid in their crêpe paper topknots and feudal regalia, complete with swords and lances. One lance bears the severed and bloody head of the hated enemy who had humiliated the warriors' lord and prompted his ritual suicide. Tens of thousands of people cheer the procession in its last stages, the short walk from the subway exit to the temple where the original 47 samurai and their lord were buried. Here the crowds burn incense before relaxing at the many food, drink, games, and souvenir stalls erected for the occasion.

Visitors at the festival, however, are not merely seeing one of Japan's fascinating celebrations. They are joining many workers who make up the statistics related to the Japanese workforce and who participate in some aspect of its complex labour-relations system. The leader of the 47 'modern' samurai is the president of a small wholesale textile factory and the lesser warriors are his factory workers. Independent proprietors, helped by their families, operate the many temple stores. Industrial homeworkers, mainly women, make souvenirs and goods for the stalls and artificial decorations for the temple; casual and day labourers, frequently part-time farmers, clean and maintain the subway and adjacent streets. Most of the parts for the popular brands of cameras and tape recorders carried by the people in the festival crowd are made and assembled by workers in very small firms. Many of the workers celebrating at the festival do not have regular jobs or belong to a labour union. Few have entered the closed world of the core workers in Japan's large private enterprises.

This book is about industrial relations and focuses on workers similar to many in the festival crowd. It looks at workers who are employed in medium and small firms or who work on a non-regular basis, such as the self-employed, seasonal workers, part-timers, temporary and day labourers, industrial homeworkers,

1

and agro-industrial workers. Such workers belong to Japan's peripheral workforce.[1]

Management and labour relations in this peripheral segment of the workforce is to a large extent controlled, directly and indirectly, through structures and processes in Japanese industry.[2] In addition, the smaller the firm and the lower the worker's employment status, the greater the likelihood for industrial relations to be informal and non-institutionalized.

This book will identify some of the salient features of Japan's peripheral sector. It will look at some of the effects of the structures and processes of industry on the relative strengths of checks and balances in industrial relations in this, the major sector of its workforce. It will examine how the distribution of power affects work behaviour and workers' access to effective organization and articulation, and proscribes the avenues through which peripheral workers can express their sectional interests. This approach assumes that industrial relations is concerned with power relations and, further, that there is an unequal distribution of power and access to power in Japan's industrial society. It is an approach that questions conventional perspectives of what industrial relations is all about. It challenges the pluralist assumption that relatively equal power relations exist among the actors. Industrial relations is therefore defined in this work, in a modification of Hyman (1977: 12), as the process within which relationships between management and workers operate. Checks and balances within this process, both direct and indirect, institutionalized and non-institutionalized, contribute to a complex web of controls over work behaviour and management and labour relations.

A power-relations approach to industrial relations is appropriate for three main reasons. First, it means that this study of the peripheral workforce does not exclude areas usually covered in the literature. Thus, it is valid to look at job regulation and systems of rules, the interactions between management, unions, and relevant government agencies, and procedures such as collective bargaining and dispute settlement. However, the analysis in this study concerns itself with control aspects of such phenomena and in this way differs from analyses in the conventional literature on industrial relations in Japan.

The second reason for favouring a power-relations approach is that factors that are usually omitted or marginalized in the literature come under scrutiny. These factors are the covert controls in the structure and processes of industry. No doubt such controls have an input into relations involving Japan's core workforce, however, in the peripheral workforce they are dominant factors that affect the distribution of power. Because the peripheral work environment is largely non-unionized and unregulated, formal and institutionalized aspects of industrial relations are to a large extent irrelevant.

The third main reason for adopting a power-relations approach to Japanese industrial relations is that it brings to the forefront a fundamental question. Is there a connection between power relations in Japan's predominantly regulated and organized sector and power relations in its predominantly unregulated and non-unionized sector? This question has explanatory force. It provides more insights into Japan's industrial-relations situation than emerge from looking at either institutionalized and formal controls, or at indirect and informal controls, though clearly there is a relationship between these two levels of interaction.

Little has been written about the issues raised by a power-relations approach to industrial relations in Japan, and, to a remarkable extent, research concerned with Japan's industrial society ignores the peripheral workforce. References to these workers are piecemeal or marginal, and industrial relations in their world of work tends to be seen as the passive residue of the mainstream of industrial relations in Japan's large enterprise sector. This neglect may have contributed significantly to biased perceptions of Japan's industrial relations. Unless the peripheral workforce *is* taken into account and recognized as part of the complex industrial-relations situation, the credibility of these perceptions is open to question. In this way, this study is exploratory. It fills part of an information gap, while at the same time arguing that industrial relations in the peripheral segment of the workforce is far from irrelevant.

Research for the study was conducted in Japan from September 1982 to March 1983, in Tokyo and in Chiba, Saitama, and Nagano Prefectures. The research included a search of the relevant literature but mainly relied on two primary sources. The first consisted of discussions with Japanese and non-Japanese actors and observers whose interests were in the industrial relations area, and through an examination of the data obtained from and discussed with them. More than 40 respondents co-operated actively in these discussions. Among these were key representatives of employer organizations, government agencies, unions, union federations, academics, and political parties with a predominantly rank-and-file base (see 'List of respondents', Appendix 1). The second source consisted of five case studies. The choice of plants was determined by three criteria: that the firms selected should vary in size, that they should vary in location so that both rural and urban environments would be included, and that they should be connected with the two industries on which the research tended to concentrate — manufacturing and construction. In the event, these criteria were satisfied. Each case study provided opportunities for observation and discussion with plant management and staff in five different but relevant environments. More importantly, this fieldwork included a rank-and-file input.

Whereas interviews with respondents were arranged personally, visits to five plants were organized in collaboration with Professor Masuo Ikeda (Chuo University), whose area of interest is labour market segmentation. Interpreter assistance was used in these case studies and also during three of the interviews. Some interviews involved non-Japanese respondents. Among these were labour counsellors from the United States and Australian Embassies in Tokyo, American and Australian expatriates operating in relevant areas of interest in Japan, authors, and journalists from major Australian and British media.

Interviews and discussions were unstructured, and although the substance of each discussion was similar, the order of priority of questions was rearranged to make the first question of intimate and controversial interest according to the individual respondent. For example: differentials in wages and conditions were the initial points raised with the Director of the International Section of Japan's Federation of Employers' Organizations (Nikkeiren); low or non-existent unionization rates in small and medium enterprises were the key issues in discussions with leading officials in union federations (Sohyo and Domei); relatively high levels of industrial disputation among workers in the medium range of firms in contrast to relatively low levels in the large and small enterprises was a central issue in talks with the Director of the Disputes Adjustment Section of the Central Labour Commission.[3] Not all interviews involved controversial issues. In several, the purpose was to gather information about specific aspects of Japan's working population. Respondents in these situations explained and discussed the significance of the material they supplied. For example, at the Prime Minister's Office, the Director of the Labour Statistics Division explained his department's methodology and its categorization of the workforce in Japan's census data; the Deputy Director of the Trade Union Section of the Ministry of Labour (MOL) outlined methods of tabulating industrial dispute statistics and the operation of her department; the Director of the Women and Youth Bureau, MOL supplied and elaborated on data on the female workforce; and the Director of the Industrial Home-workers Section of the same ministry discussed these nominally 'self-employed' workers.

Two industries — manufacturing and construction — came under closer scrutiny than others in the analysis of data, discussions, and case studies. There were three reasons for this choice. First, these industries operate in different economic contexts, one primarily export-oriented and the other primarily a domestic industry. It was expected this difference might produce different findings. Second, both were useful in any examination of the peripheral workforce because each has a wide although not identical base in the small and medium enterprise sector[4] — 74 per cent of employees in manufacturing and 95 per cent in construction work in small and medium firms (Ministry of International Trade and Industry (MITI), White Paper, 1982).[5] The third reason for selecting these industries was that the use of sub-contractors and contract labour — crucial processes in Japanese industry — is very prevalent in both, and these work practices intimately affect the peripheral workforce.

The scope of the research strongly suggests that findings should not be extrapolated beyond the areas dealt with in this book. Other areas in the private sector receive only general treatment although they also have a high percentage of non-regular workers and firms are predominantly small in scale. In the service and wholesale/retail industries, for example, 69 per cent and 74 per cent of workers respectively work in small and medium enterprises (MITI, White Paper, 1982). Documentation and sources of information on these two industries were not readily available at the time of the research, and for similar reasons some categories of non-regular labour, such as *arubaito* (students working part-time), receive little attention. Further studies in Japan that look at other specific industries and other categories of peripheral workers will complement the aim of this study — to extend the range of perceptions of Japanese industrial relations. However, gathering information about the peripheral environment is of itself not the main objective, which is to examine the significance of this information in the context of the industrial-relations area of study.

For those interested in industrial-relations theory, the relevant literature is discussed in Chapter 1. This chapter looks at a range of perspectives as to what constitutes the industrial relations area. It considers how these approaches have been used to interpret Japanese industrial society, and how they may have contributed to popular and academic perceptions of a Japanese industrial-relations 'model'. It also discusses the existence of a research and information gap in so far as the peripheral workforce is concerned, and possible reasons for this gap.

The main body of the work, Chapters 2 to 7, examines aspects of the peripheral working environment. It evaluates ways in which characteristics of that environment control work behaviour and affect the checks and balances in communication and conflict between management and workers. What is then at issue is whether and in what way this environment affects power relations in Japan's industrial relations process.

Chapters 2 and 3 look at the peripheral workforce in terms of structures of Japanese industry: working conditions, employment status, type of industry, establishment size, and the urban or rural location of the workplace. Chapter 2 is a profile of workers in small and medium enterprises. Chapter 3 is a profile of the environment of non-regular workers. Chapter 4 turns to the effects of some of the processes of industry. It looks at the use of contract and sub-contract labour and other production techniques, particularly the just-in-time (*kanban*) system, the micro-electronic revolution, and rationalization of the workforce.

Chapter 5 consists of case studies of five medium and small firms. Two are medium-sized urban firms (one a machinery manufacturer and one a steel fabrication construction company). The other three firms (each in the electrical manufacturing industry), are located in rural areas; one rural-based firm is a large enterprise and is the parent company of one of the remaining two firms, both small sub-contractors. This chapter concludes with an evaluation of these case studies in the light of earlier analyses.

Chapter 6 examines the enterprise union system and its

relevance and implications for the peripheral workforce. It looks first at the differences between union organization and informal associations of workers, and then assesses the power relations between core unions and peripheral unions. Chapter 7 turns to an examination of mechanisms of communication and conflict: collective bargaining, work rules, joint consultation, unfair labour practices, formal and informal disputes, dispute settlement and manifestations of conflict. In this way, Chapters 6 and 7 deal with the effects of the working environment on power relations and the articulation of the interests of peripheral workers within the management and labour dichotomy.

In a brief conclusion, Japan's management and labour relations are considered in three ways: first, in the light of the initial discussion of the literature; second, in the context of the argument that structures and processes of industry are major controls in the power relations process; and finally, the relevance of the analyses for the fundamental question posed at the outset, whether there is a connection between the industrial relations situation in Japan's core, organized sector of the workforce and the situation in its peripheral, largely non-organized sector.

Although this fundamental question cannot be answered definitively, there are strong indications that the apparent stability of Japan's industrial relations stems in part from two related processes. First, the relative powerlessness that characterizes the majority of workers, those in the peripheral segment of the workforce. Second, the ability of management in the large-enterprise sector to shift the burden of their problems onto smaller firms, via, for example, the contract system. As to other questions concerning the distribution of power, this book throws some light on ways in which this varies from sector to sector, and offers some explanations.

NOTES

1. The term 'peripheral' is borrowed, particularly from Friedman (1977) and Paci (1981).
2. 'Industrial relations' and 'management and labour relations' are regarded in this work as areas of study, and as such each is treated as singular.
3. The term 'adjustment' is not an error in translation. The Director of the Disputes Adjustment Division of the Central Labour Commission

(interview 8 March 1983) insisted on its use in preference to 'settlement', as did respondents from other government departments. With its more positive connotations, 'adjustment' is also used in official translations of relevant laws and publications by such agencies as the Japan Institute of Labour.

In a similar way, the practice of referring to sub-contractors as 'co-operating firms' avoids the negative implications of exploitation often associated with sub-contracting.

4. Small and medium in the statistics cited here refer to enterprises with fewer than 300 employees, or fewer than 50 in retail and service industries.

5. 'Statistics on places of business', Prime Minister's Office, in *White Paper on Small and Medium Enterprises in Japan*, MITI, 1982. White Papers published by MITI are frequently cited in this book. Hereafter they will appear in the text in parentheses as: (MITI, White Paper) followed by the year of publication.

1

Perspectives of industrial relations in Japan: in search of the peripheral workforce

The search for Japan's peripheral workforce takes as its point of reference the literature on industrial relations, particularly the literature concerning Japan. Clearly there are many perceptions of what constitutes the industrial relations area of study and diverse theoretical approaches to the subject. Before proceeding with the specific concerns of this study, therefore, this chapter will look at the range of approaches to industrial relations research. Discussion will then turn to ways in which these approaches have been applied to the Japanese situation and an assessment of the literature's influence on perceptions of a Japanese 'model' of industrial relations.

PERSPECTIVES OF INDUSTRIAL RELATIONS

The range of approaches to industrial relations is dealt with here in two broad categories, the unitary and pluralist perspectives. Both are concerned with power relations but a major distinction between them concerns the locus of power.The unitary view according to Fox (in Child 1973: 185–233) vests sole legitimacy in management, asserting that common values and objectives unite and bind both management and the managed. Given this assumption, Fox (1973: 188–9) reasons that unitarists tend to deny the right of any challenge to management authority, and have little trouble in justifying management exercise of power to meet any perceived challenge. This use of power, moreover, is seen by the unitarists to be for the common good, so that:

management may have to be cruel to be kind by overriding what it asserts to be 'irrational' beliefs, purely short-term pre-occupations, and limited perspectives produced by ignorance. Still more is it disposed to feel justified in coercing subversives who would otherwise destroy the system.

(Fox 1973: 187–8)

There are two main sub-groups within the unitary perspective according to Palmer (1983: 6–7, 10–11). One, along the lines suggested by Fox, takes a simple approach that conflict is unnatural and dissidents must be suppressed. The second and more sophisticated group accepts that conflict in industry is inevitable but can be controlled through careful management. The unitary good management approach is clearly illustrated in some thinking about Japan's industrial relations. For example, Ouchi (1981) asserts that 'a new generation of business consultants prescribes Japanese managerial techniques . . . and claims that the right technique will eliminate all the problematic conflicts of employment relations' (cited in Palmer 1983: 11).

The pluralist perspective, however, dominates the industrial relations literature. In contrast to unitary perspectives, sub-groups in this mainstream of thinking accord legitimacy to a plurality of interest groups and assume relative equality between them in their ability to influence the industrial relations agenda. Adherents of the pluralist approach, of whatever variety, also recognize that the relative power of the major interest groups comes into play in the resolution of conflict. Fox argues that in general terms pluralist thinking sees the enterprise as:

a complex of tensions and competing claims which have to be 'managed' in the interests of maintaining a viable collaborative structure within which all the stakeholders can, with varying degrees of success, pursue their aspirations.

(1973: 193)

With regard to the eruption of conflict within the coalition of these stakeholders, according to Fox, the pluralist would see conflict as an indication that the relative norms require a negotiated reconstruction or adjustment. The pluralist approach assumes that 'the normative divergencies between the parties are not so fundamental or so wide as to be unbridgeable by compromise or new syntheses which enable collaboration to continue' (Fox 1973: 195–6). There is thus an underlying assumption that both parties to the conflict accept (or should accept) the same basic ground rules and are willing to compromise (Fox 1973: 197–8). This attitude stems from a shared morality, through which the parties accept the sanctity of agreements 'freely and honourably undertaken' (Fox 1973: 197–8).

On the specific question of power relations, Fox's summation is that pluralism is often linked with the view that 'there can and should be, or indeed even is, a balance of power as between the principal interest groups of society' (1973: 198–9). In this way, the centres of power in the pluralist perception move from final and definitive authority, the unitary position, to the principal interest groups in society. Within the pluralist school, however, there are many variations. In the light of interpretations and emphases concerning conflict, the distribution and balance of power and the range of actors involved, Palmer (1983) suggests four main sub-groups: liberal collectivist, corporatist, liberal individualist, and marxist variations.

The liberal collectivist approach within pluralism, according to Palmer, endorses a form of industrial democracy in which collective bargaining is a primary element. This perspective accepts the legitimacy of employee organizations and their right to make contractual arrangements with management. There is a limited role for government in this perceived industrial democracy, and at the same time, freedom for a plurality of interest groups to negotiate solutions to conflict, primarily economic conflict.

The dominant stream is systems analysis, which is closely associated with Dunlop's institutions and 'web of rules' model. Varieties of the systems-analysis school have been prominent in industrial relations enquiry for the past three decades (for example Dunlop 1958, 1971; Dunlop *et al.* 1975; Flanders 1975; Donovan 1968; Clegg 1970, 1976; Kerr *et al.* 1960). It is appropriate therefore to look more closely at this approach before proceeding with a summary of other varieties of pluralism.

In the late 1950s, a watershed occurred. The industrial relations area of study moved from description, mainly dealing with the development of unions, towards analysis within a theoretical framework. Dunlop (1958) saw industrial relations as a closed system within which a network of rules was central. For Dunlop, industrial relations concerned the way rules were formulated, administered, and modified over time, and the way in which these rules, legitimized by a shared ideology, governed the workplace and workforce. Flanders (1975) modified Dunlop's model. Flanders' focus remained on the institutions of job regulation and institutionalized processes such as collective bargaining, but he added an informal factor — custom and practice (see also Clegg 1970). Dunlop's perspective was also later reformulated in the 'pluralist industrialism' of Dunlop *et al.* From this perspective, government, management, unions, and other interest groups interact and counterbalance each other's power, and the market exerts substantial influence (Dunlop *et al.* 1975: 14).

Fox (1973: 230–1) criticized aspects of the systems-analysis approach. He argued that, as an analytical tool, it tended to obscure more than it revealed about the distribution (or maldistribution) of power. Although Fox gave entrenched institutions a central role in industrial relations, he saw a need to appraise them in terms of the distribution of power in a wider social context. For example, Fox (1971) opted to examine problems in the industrial relations area in a sociological framework. Looking at attitudes to work in terms of intrinsic or extrinsic rewards, he examined the emergence of privilege for a minority of workers. He argued that the majority tended to be subject to the influence of a variety of socializing agencies to uncritically accept that, intrinsically, work could be expected to be 'burdensome, restrictive and often irksome, involving subjection to the control of others and often proving monotonous and stultifying into the bargain' (1971: 14). Fox maintains that although the pluralist perspective is a vital mechanism in determining public policy, the realities of social power are obscured when appraisals are made in accordance with the 'noble' myth of a rough balance of power (1973: 231).

In arguments such as those raised by Fox, Dunlop, Kerr *et al.*, and their followers, concepts with a universal application tend to emerge, showing a strong relationship between systems analysis and support for the convergence hypothesis. This is explicit in their reiterated arguments that there is an internal logic in the process of industrialization which overrides differing culture-specific aspects of the process (for example, Dunlop *et al.* 1975: 6). Since the 1960s, arguments in support of either universalism (convergence) or cultural specificity have tended to be prominent in the industrial relations literature. This debate dominates the literature on Japan either explicitly or implicitly.

Returning to Palmer's assessment of pluralist approaches to industrial relations, the second sub-group she identifies is the corporatist approach. Followers of this school assume that 'there is a sufficiently complex balance of power to ensure that no group dominates, and that the state will adopt a neutral "umpire" role between competing interests' (Palmer 1983: 19). This legitimizes the state's active participation in an institutionalized triumvirate, on the assumption that it has a vested interest in relations in industry.

The third sub-group within the pluralist school, the liberal-individualist perspective, holds that the key to the control of conflict lies in a free market in the buying and selling of labour (Palmer 1983: 20–21). This belief is based on the premise that a free labour market is a viable concept. Concerted action by group interests is anathema, because it represents intervention that only serves to upset the otherwise natural balance. A balance is assumed to exist in management and labour relationships, and the individual contract contains mutually agreed terms of employment. A one to one contract is established after which the relationship should be free of conflict.

Liberal-individualist perspectives are based on neo-laissez faire, nineteenth-century assumptions of a society composed of relatively equal people capable of making the free market — the contract concept — workable. This approach is reflected in the election of President Reagan in the USA and Prime Minister Thatcher in the UK — both of whom rely on neo-laissez faire economic policies and adopt anti-union stances in liberal-individualist terms. In the USA, the concept has encouraged management's opposition to trade unionism and is the ideology that supports the 'right to work' laws that prohibit union shops in many American states.[1]

The final sub-group of pluralist thinking covers marxist perspectives. These approaches are interpretations of the same phenomena examined by adherents of other sub-groups but within the framework of antagonistic class relations. (See, for example: Edwards 1979; Edwards *et al.* 1975; Piore 1975; Friedman 1977; Gordon *et al.* 1982; Edwards and Scullion 1982).

Whether marxist perspectives of industrial relations come within the pluralist stream is open to debate. The inclusion of some marxist thinking may be valid if industrial relations is seen to concern an inevitable and continuing conflict of interests in relations between power groups, and that issues can be resolved and reforms achieved within the industrial contract. The inclusion of other marxist thinking may not be valid if conflict in industrial relations is seen to be the inevitable outcome of antagonistic relations. In this case, the resolution of issues in conflict is an interim condition that in no way negates the continuing polarity of interests of the parties to the conflict. For example, Miliband rejects industrial relations as a valid area of study — the mere assumption of a 'relationship' suggests that the concerned parties share the same ground rules. He dismisses industrial relations as the 'consecrated euphemism for the permanent conflict, now acute, now subdued, between capital and labour' (cited in Hyman 1975: 12). On the other hand, Hyman (1975), who declares his unqualified marxist approach, accepts industrial relations as a valid research area. He nevertheless rejects the pluralist assumption that stability and regularity in industry can be maintained through institutionalized methods of conflict resolution. He also rejects the pluralist working hypothesis that there is an equality of power between the parties. Admittedly, Hyman looks at the ground rules and the relations in industry that are rejected out of hand by Miliband. However, Hyman does so from the perspective that industrial relations concerns the study of processes of control over work relations that are inextricably linked with social relations (1975: 11–12). Hyman then argues that ideology generates and perpetuates controls inherent in social values, expressed, for example, in notions of 'a fair day's pay for a fair day's work' (Hyman and Brough 1975).

It is clear from the foregoing discussion, that there are significant differences between and within the unitary and pluralist perspectives of industrial relations. Despite these differences, the dynamics of power and legitimacy, and the problematic of control over conflict underlies the literature written from all of these perspectives. Of greater significance for this study is the fact that, common to all perspectives, is the neglect of the role of the peripheral sector within the 'managed' segment of the workforce.

IN SEARCH OF THE PERIPHERAL WORKFORCE

In this search for the peripheral workforce, the literature, dominated by the pluralist approach, gives rise to three main and interrelated problems. The first problem stems from placing perspectives of industrial relations into categories such as unitary or pluralist groups and sub-groups. Admittedly, 'ideal types' help to clarify an otherwise bewildering array, but the divisions between them are not discrete. For example, the unitarist argument that common values and objectives bind management and the managed is frequently put forward in the Japanese context by followers of pluralist sub-groups. To some extent, marxist variants of the pluralist school also put forward the 'shared goal' perspective. A case in point is the relatively powerful association of managers in Japan's small and medium sector, which lobbies the government on behalf of management and labour in this sector in line with a left to left-liberal philosophy (Kobayashi in Itō 1973: 49–87; see Chapter 5).

The second problem stems from the dominance of pluralism in the literature. This means that research is generally confined to a focus on those who make, administer and adjust the rules and who define the issues of concern. However, neither management nor labour is a homogeneous entity. The rule-making process is beyond the power of some management and workers, and ground rules and agendas of industrial relations are settled without them. In this way, pluralism lends itself to elitist and therefore limited interpretations of industrial relations.

Elitist tendencies in pluralism lead to a third and fundamental problem. The distribution of power in industrialized societies receives scant attention, and neglect of this aspect of industrial relations emerges consistently in the Japan-related literature. Yet the importance of looking at power relations and the distribution of power cannot be overstated. For example, Clegg (1975: 309–10) argues that pluralist thinking looks at mechanisms of coalition, concession, and compromise, but that it is the powerful interest groups with resources and potential that are heard. Clegg then makes the point that powerful interest groups are heard at the expense of those without. The implications of this bias are crucial in any industrial relations situation.

Despite these problems, the evaluation of industrial relations perspectives discussed thus far lays the basis for examination of studies with a more specific focus. Among these are studies that deal with the central concerns of this book — the distribution of power, the segmentation of labour and the peripheral workforce.

SEGMENTATION IN THE WORKFORCE

Stratification in the workforce, conflict, class relations, and ideology as a control mechanism are areas that have attracted a considerable amount of research, particularly in the American context (Edwards, Reich and Gordon 1975; Piore 1975). Much of this work is in the marxist tradition. Of specific relevance is the centre-periphery concept of divided labour and divided workers (Gordon *et al*. 1982), and the centre-periphery dichotomy (Friedman 1977).

Friedman looks at managerial strategies of labour-cost minimization and labour control, and at methods to overcome manifestations of inflexibility imposed by technological and social factors. Friedman argues that there is a close relationship between the core and peripheral sectors. Firms and their workers not only exist and work in very different circumstances and in close proximity to one another, but:

> The steady profits of large firms and the steady, high wages of privileged workers depend on the instability of profits and wages of small firms and unprivileged workers in an unplanned system such as capitalism.

> (Friedman 1977: 105)

Friedman also discusses centre-periphery relations within and between firms, particularly in the sub-contracting practice. With regard to centre-periphery relations within the firm, Friedman (1977: 10) argues that management strategy is to isolate its central (core) workers, whose loss or resistance would be the more disruptive. Management then provides security for these core workers, often with their collaboration, at the expense of the more expendable peripheral workers. Turning to centre-periphery relations between firms, Friedman (1977: 115) maintains that peripheral workers may be, first, peripheral within the firm where they work, and second, peripheral because they are employed in a peripheral firm. They are in this way doubly insecure and doubly restrained in their resistance to authority.

In identifying the more important characteristics of the peripheral workers, Friedman emphasizes their relative expendability as contributors to the work effort and their relative inability to pose a threat to order and authority:

Expendability is really a continuum. Whether any particular worker or group of workers will be laid off depends on both *relative* expendability and *relative* severity of top managers' need to reduce costs. Nevertheless it is possible clearly to identify categories of workers which are significantly more at risk than others. Generally these will be workers who:

1 Perform work which can easily be carried out by the remaining workers.
2 Perform work which is not necessary for the output which top managers desire to be produced after demand has fallen (i.e. work at jobs which are duplicated).
3 Perform work for which replacement workers are readily available when top managers want them.
4 Will not cause disruption among the remaining workers when laid off because of lack of solidarity with them.
5 Do not contribute to the maintenance of managerial authority.

(Friedman 1977: 110)

Friedman's model provides insights into relationships at work in industrial societies in general, and it is also clearly useful in this analysis of the peripheral continuum in the Japanese workforce. First, Friedman clarifies the core-periphery interpretation of segmentation in the workforce. Second, he clarifies the process within the peripheral workforce that is expressed as a 'continuum'. He suggests a continuous scale in terms of expendability within the workforce and also in terms of power relations in the peripheral segment of the workforce *vis-à-vis* not only management but core workers in the total workforce.

Paci (in Pinto 1981: 211–12) adopts a similar approach in the Italian context in his discussion of the peripheral workforce and dualism in industry. Paci (1981: 10) argues that the proliferation of small businesses is a specific feature of the Italian situation and is found in no other advanced capitalist country with the possible exception of Japan. In his view, the most important aspect of industrial dualism lies in the large and small firm dichotomy. This consists of a central industrial proletariat made up of workers in large industrial firms with relatively high wages and good conditions, and:

[a] large mass of workers in the small factories, artisan workers and industrial homeworkers, often in 'irregular'

work conditions, tied to 'part-time farming' situations, hardly ever protected by the trade unions.

(Paci 1981: 210)

Paci's emphasis is less on the role of the core segment of the labour force than on the crucial function of the peripheral sector. In his words, the 'surplus population [has] an important productive function, contributing in a far from irrelevant way to the mechanism of national accumulation' (Paci 1981: 217).

Paci (1981) also extends Friedman's argument concerning core-peripheral relations within and between firms, and looks at the concept of relative expendability in the framework of dependency theories. He argues that there are centre and peripheral societies, that centre-peripheral relationships operate between industrial and developing societies and between advanced and less advanced industrial societies. In this context, Russett, writing on resource dependency, makes an apposite comment: dependency theories are typically concerned with 'the degree to which asymmetric relations lead to conditioning or control — power over decisions — in the dependent state' (1984: 484).

Paci's reference to core and peripheral societies raises the question of the international division of labour, and in so doing adds a further dimension to the concept of expendability. This dimension is highly relevant to Japan in view of the economic advantage to management of employing lower-wage peripheral labour outside Japan, for example, in South Korea, Taiwan, and the Philippines. While theories of dependency and the international division of labour are not pursued in this study, they are nevertheless significant in later discussion, notably on control mechanisms in Japan's sub-contracting relationships and in workers' perceptions of threats to their job security.

Core-periphery models, although they provide valuable insights, do not clarify the distinction between core workers in Japan's major enterprises and core workers in smaller firms. (Nor does Paci's reference to peripheral firms address the question of core and peripheral management in the workforce — though characteristic differences could be inferred from his analysis.) There is, of course, a sharp difference in privilege between core workers in Japan's large enterprises and those in its small and medium firms. But it can also be demonstrated that the small/medium core workers are not expendable, at least not

Figure 1.1 Core-peripheral segmentation structure, Japan

	Regular workers	Non-regular workers
	A	B
Large-enterprise sector workers	core workers	temporary and day labour, contract labour
	C	D
Small and medium-enterprise sector workers	core workers in dependent or sub-contract firms	temporary and day labour, family workers, aged and female workers, contract labour, self-employed

Source: Modified from Craig R. Littler, 'Japan and China', in S. Feuchtwang and A. Hussein (eds), *The Chinese Economic Reforms*, Croom Helm, London, 1983, p. 131.

to the extent that they can be classified as peripheral in Friedman's terms. These core workers in the secondary sector 'move' into peripheral status if their firm is peripheral, that is, if it operates in a dependent or sub-contract relationship. In that case, no matter how essential a worker's labour effort is to the firm, the firm's degree of expendability or dependence becomes a decisive factor. Figure 1.1 illustrates this core-peripheral concept of segmentation of Japan's workforce. Peripheral workers (boxes B, C, and D) are those who lack the security and privilege experienced by core workers (box A), and their degree of expendability, as noted, is contingent on employment status and the dependent or sub-contract status of the firm in which they work.

A recent analysis of the Japanese labour market by Littler (1983a: 130–31) goes a long way towards explaining this complexity. Based on his perception of internal and external labour-market segmentation, Littler developed a four-sector model of employment and production systems which he then linked to Japan's primary- and secondary-firm sectors and characteristics of job level. Littler does not develop his analysis of the external labour market and non-regular workers in depth, nevertheless, he stresses the importance of understanding the secondary sector in order to understand the primary sector. In this context, he criticizes the narrow perceptions that flow from standard descriptions of the Japanese employment system, arguing that these descriptions focus exclusively on regular workers in Japan's

19

large enterprises. It is this segment of the workforce that reflects the 'half-truths' evident in popular Anglo-American perceptions and most modern Anglo-American academic literature on Japanese industry (Littler 1983a: 129).

THE ENGLISH-LANGUAGE LITERATURE AND JAPAN'S INDUSTRIAL RELATIONS

The following discussion of the literature, concerned specifically with Japan, clearly shows a concentrated focus on three related areas. First, the elite workforce in firms at the apex of Japanese industry; second, the institutions of industrial relations; and third, the principal pressure groups in the interplay of coalition, compromise, and conflict control. This focus is determined in part by the parameters set by the dominant pluralist approach to industrial relations, but it also stems from an abiding interest in two related and ongoing debates that dominate research initiatives. The first debate revolves around whether there is a continuity of 'tradition' in Japanese industrial relations, the second, on whether industrial relations in Japan has special or unique characteristics. The issue which brings about the relationship between these questions is the possible, even probable, connection between industrial relations in Japan and its economic successes, particularly since the 1970s following Japan's high growth period.

In these debates, two underlying trends emerge in approaches of researchers and observers. First, they have looked for causes in traditional and cultural factors when conventional perspectives fail adequately to explain aspects of Japan's industrial relations. Second, they have extrapolated almost exclusively from interpretations of the situation in Japan's major enterprises as both the source and the confirmation of their 'explanations'. There is little doubt that these trends have provided the grounds at the theoretical level for a continuing confrontation between the advocates of convergence and divergence hypotheses. There are those who perceive industrial relations in Japan as having a cultural and traditional base (Benedict 1946; Abegglen 1958; Nakane 1970; Vogel 1979). There are others who look at the same phenomena and take an 'internal logic of industrialism' approach (Dunlop *et al.* 1975; Kerr *et al.* 1960). Variants of the convergence school can also be found in the functional-equivalence approach (Cole 1971); the 'Japan is not unique' approach (Levine 1958, 1982; Levine and Taira 1977, 1979, 1980); or a 'late-development' hypothesis and intimations that other industrial societies may be 'converging' towards Japan (Dore 1973).

An important sub-theme to emerge from the convergence problematic is the transportability of aspects of Japanese industrial relations. That is, assuming a relationship between Japan's style of industrial relations and its economic successes, is the Japanese formula transportable? If Japan's industrial relations is culture-based and unique, clearly such an idea is not viable. From the logic of industrialism or functional equivalent perspectives, however, aspects of industrial relations, styles of control over work behaviour and relations at work are amenable to transfer to other societies.

Underlying all these concerns lies the basic question posed by Shimada (in Shirai 1983), who looks at the sustained interest in such concerns and asks 'whether we Japanese have a clear-cut model of our industrial relations to present to the world' (1983: 5). Shimada's theoretical approach is that industrial relations is a sub-category of social relations, and within this framework, he discusses representative examples of English-language literature dealing with Japan. He argues there are four major schools of thought: classical culturalist, descriptive institutionalist, functional analysis, and neo-culturalist synthesis. Significantly, Shimada points out that these approaches are not exclusive to the large body of English-language literature but 'to some extent' also reflect trends in Japanese thinking (1983: 6).

The substance of Shimada's four schools clearly illustrates the comparative trend in research in the Japan stream:

- *Classical culturalism:* aspects of industrial relations in Japan are different, they reflect its unique cultural legacy, the base for a popular model emerges.
- *Descriptive institutionalist:* aspects of industrial relations, claimed to be unique, are explored and questioned and the convergence hypothesis is reinforced.
- *Functional analysis:* degrees of cultural specificity are accepted but assumed to function according to universal concepts, thus supporting the convergence hypothesis.
- *Neo-cultural synthesis:* aspects of industrial relations in Japan may resemble the situation in other advanced

21

societies but there is a strong Japanese identity which con-
vergency cannot obscure.

The classical culturist school stems largely from the early
anthropological work of Benedict (1946). It is exemplified in
Abegglen's (1958) analysis based on a survey of two large
Japanese plants. He found notable differences between Japanese
and American practices, particularly with regard to terms of
employment and wage determination. Abegglen's perspective
and a 'lifetime commitment concept' rapidly became hallmarks
of a widely accepted Japanese stereotype in which consensus and
the resolution of conflict in industry owe much to hierarchical
relationships, acceptance of authority, and the legitimacy of
managerial wisdom. In this sense, the classical culturists adopt a
unitarist perspective. Some marxist perspectives also come
within this school; authoritarianism and control of conflict in
industrial relations are the social and cultural legacy of
antagonistic class relations that existed in pre-industrial Japan.

The descriptive institutionalist school, Shimada's second
category (1983: 10–13), involves the study of structures and
institutions perceived to be peculiar to Japan, primarily within
the pluralist parameters established by Dunlop. The value of
studies such as these is undeniable. However, they do not
provide a theoretical framework within which to explore the
largely non-institutionalized segment of the workforce. For
example, the work of Marsh and Minnari (1976) was based on
large firms in leading industries, and Cook's (1966) study was
based on interviews with the leadership of major unions and
union federations, and although Levine stresses the necessity of
looking at the secondary-sector workforce, he does not do so,
like others who make this same point.

The third school defined by Shimada is functional analysis,
which emerged in the 1960s and 1970s. In an advance on the
impressionistic and deductive evaluation in descriptive research,
this approach requires a more disciplined collection of data to
test working hypotheses based on specified theoretical models.
At the same time, as Shimada argues, functional analysis:
'seems to have an inevitable methodological bias; that is, the
technique has an unavoidable inclination to imply a universal
commonality or convergence' (1983: 13–14).

Adherents of the functional analysis school are then impelled
to debate aspects of industrial relations that are in the main

concerns of the classical culturalists: some see contemporary Japanese industrial relations as a rational economic choice of management rather than a legacy of feudal society: others challenge cultural explanations for lifetime commitment and length-of-service wage systems; and still others put forward a 'micro-economic rationale' to explain bonus payments and the operation of Japan's internal labour market (Shimada 1983: 14–16). Cole (1971), in his study of blue-collar workers, describes relations quite unlike the hierarchical family concept of management and, within a modified Dunlopian framework, finds functional equivalents that indicate convergence despite cultural differences.

While comparative studies tend to use Anglo-American experiences as standards, this west-to-east direction is partly reversed in Shimada's fourth and final category of perspectives — neo-cultural synthesis. This approach in the English-language literature emerged recently from increasing interest in a genuinely Japanese type of industrial development 'while at the same time trying to be as free as possible from a priori theoretical assumptions and methodological restraints' (1983: 20–23).

In his discussion of some contributors to the neo-culturist school, Shimada pays little or no heed to the restricted bases of their research. For example, Dore (1973) studied four large plants in the same industry, two in Britain and two in Japan; Rohlen (1974) looked at white-collar workers in a Japanese bank; Vogel (1971, 1979) described the community life of the salaried worker and the operation of only major social, economic, and industrial organizations. There are others that Shimada includes in this school whose base is less confined. Hanami's work (1979, 1981), primarily descriptive and concerned with labour law, nevertheless looks outside the regulated segment of the workforce. Cole (1971) looks beyond the large-enterprise sector and assumes an interaction between the industrial and social environments.

The neo-culturalist school stresses a particular Japanese identity; nevertheless it differs from classical culturism, which assumes that Japan's unique industrial relations is viable only in its indigenous cultural environment. As noted earlier, Dore (1973) suggests that industrial societies are tending to grow more towards Japanese-style relationships in industry. Vogel (1979) recommends that they should; Cole (1971) argues the differences are cosmetic; Hanami (1979) infers that strong historical, cultural, and social inputs into industrial relations would make transportability of Japan's experience difficult though not impossible. Approaches such as these accept two possibilities. First, there are degrees of transportability of Japanese-style industrial relations, and second, that convergence can occur without loss of national identity.

It could be argued that variants of the neo-culturalist perspective endeavour to establish a Japan-centric convention to substitute for Anglo-American-based standards. In so doing, neo-culturalism challenges the dominance of western perceptions of industrial relations, particularly American, against which Japan's industrial relations has continuously been evaluated. The neo-culturalist synthesis is becoming increasingly popular. Its followers challenge some of the myths associated with industrial relations in Japan, but, comparing Japan with other industrial societies, are clearly committed to the preservation, and projection, of a new-style 'Japanese-ness'.

COMPARATIVE STUDIES

In the area of comparative studies, the treatment of the peripheral sector has significant implications. It raises the question of what is to be compared. There is of course the obvious problem of comparing data based on different criteria. There is also the problem of interpretations being made on culture-bound value judgements. However, a major problem is the tendency to compare and contrast long-standing perceptions of industrial relations that are undifferentiated or based on limited samples. The following discussion looks at some of these problems.

Shalev argues that comparative analyses have tended to be used as a means of supporting a priori hypotheses or 'to produce abstract generalizations derived from research findings in a variety of national contexts' (Shalev 1980: 26). His argument is that comparative study should not be dismissed out of hand because of the absence of explicit theory, nor should its role in the discipline be one of confirmation or rebuttal of conventional theories such as those of Dunlop and his imitators.

Dore broke with convention. When he looked at reasons for the striking differences that he found in employment systems in Britain and Japan, he did not follow the usual convergence interpretation — a progression from backwardness to industrialism. Dore arrived at a type of convergence: in this case, convergence towards Japan. Dore argued:

Why should 'rationality' have pointed to one kind of managerial policy in capitalist Japan *in 1900–20 when the 'Japanese system' was becoming institutionalized*, and to quite different kinds of policies in capitalist Britain *in the mid-nineteenth century when British employment institutions and industrial relations were becoming institutionalized*?

Because between, say, 1850 and 1920 the world had changed in significant ways; because the objective structure of opportunities and constraints, and hence the means by which profits and growth can be maximized can never be the same for the late developer as they were for the early developer.

(1973: 403)

Although Dore broke with convention, he used conventional research tactics to arrive at his findings. On the basis of his study of just two large Japanese enterprises (Hitachi), he developed the concept of 'welfare corporatism'. The progression in his argument moves from *the* modern enterprise system of permanent employment, to *the* modern system of industrial relations; finally, Dore's 'welfare corporatism' becomes *the* system. *The* system becomes a significant element in his 'late development' hypothesis. Like others who preceded and followed, such as Abegglen (1958) and Rohlen (1974), Dore used the inductive process to arrive at generalities from restricted samples.

The attitudinal survey conducted by Whitehall and Takezawa (1968), is a case in point. Their questionnaire covered approximately one thousand workers in Japan and in the US. Their samples came from industries of relative importance in the economy, that is, from large, 'pace-setting' firms, and covered only rank-and-file workers. The Japanese sample specifically excluded temporary workers. In the event, Japanese female workers in the sample were skewed to young women workers, and the American sample turned out to consist of mostly white respondents.

A second example of problems inherent in comparative analysis occurs in Cox (1971), whose work has particular relevance for the 'compare what?' question asked above. Cox's approach is allegedly free from a priori theoretical constraints, and indeed, at the outset Cox makes his advocacy of freedom from industrial relations conventions explicit:

> there is a merit in retaining a term [industrial relations] which has been widely used in scientific literature, but in order that the concept of industrial relations be valid for a global study, it must be shorn of any ideological affiliation with the particular historical development which gave rise to the term itself.
>
> (Cox 1971: 140–42)

Cox (1971: 146) postulated nine ideal types of industrial relations systems: peasant-lord, primitive market, small manufacturing, lifetime commitment, bipartite, tripartite, corporatist-bureaucratic, mobilizing, and socialist. With one exception, each of these nine systems is defined in universal terms, the exception being the lifetime commitment system. Far from being universal, this system as defined by Cox is an adaptation of the requirements of long-term industrialization in Japan.

Unlike Dore, who used conventional research tactics, Cox adopted conventional assumptions about industrial relations in Japan. Cox then incorporated these assumptions into his construction of a futurology chart of industrial relations, which is thrown into disarray should this characterization of the Japanese system be questioned or discredited. Cox's perception that *the* Japanese system is an adaptation to the requirements of industrialization endorses the Dunlopian view of the inherent logic of industrialism, and his contribution to the convergence hypothesis becomes increasingly obvious as his argument develops. It reflects Cox's affiliation to theoretical concepts — a commitment he claims to eschew.

The most telling implication in Cox's study, however, arises from the way in which he isolates the Japanese system and gives no cultural specificity to any of his other ideal types. As a result, Japan's industrial relations is presented as having a particular identity in which lifetime commitment is sanctified. In this way, Cox sustains assumptions that are reinforced by their uncritical repetition and contributes to the subliminal acceptance of a particular model of Japanese industrial relations.

As to Dore, his work continues to have a strong influence in the Japanese studies area. As a result, his approach and his conclusions are particularly significant. His analysis suggests a dynamic in industrial relations in Japan, not a closed-ideal type, and, because he imbues the industrial relations process with ongoing potential for change, there is good reason why his approach has replaced Abegglen's fixed classical culturalism as the source of industrial relations wisdom. Dore has contributed valuable insights into the origins of some institutions and elites and given vitality to the picture of workers attached to the enterprise community. However, his approach falls short of providing a general framework for comparative analyses of Japan's peripheral firms and peripheral workers, and workers of this status in other societies. Whether his conclusions with respect to Japan-specific studies provide any insights into Japan's industrial relations outside its institutions and beyond its elite workforce is open to question. In the case of Japan, variations in the industrial relations situation are very acute and discernible.

Research initiatives into internal variations within a society and attempts to account for them have an important contribution to make to cross-cultural comparisons. They also make an important contribution to understanding the industrial relations process in the particular societies concerned. The following section of this chapter will consider examples in the Japan-related literature that deal with Japan's labour-market segmentation and then turn to micro-studies of particular aspects of the industrial workforce.

These are areas of the literature that appear to have the potential to contribute to questions raised in this book, yet this expectation, as will be shown, is not fully satisfied. The peripheral sector of the workforce remains 'peripheral' in the majority of Japanese studies, which give their priorities to examining lifetime employment, seniority-based wages, enterprise unionism, a unique work ethic, consensus, and loyalty. In research concerned with labour-market segmentation, analyses of the peripheral sector tend to take the form of generalizations, research into particular aspects of the industrial workforce is piecemeal, and attempts to place the peripheral sector in a theoretical framework are minimal.

JAPAN'S LABOUR MARKETS AND THE LABOUR PROCESS

Research concerned with labour-market segmentation and the labour process in Japan tends to be pursued, as with more general research, within the framework of a systems-and-institutions, rules-and-regulations approach. It is not surprising that the main focus is on the large-enterprise sector and the internal labour markets. While the contribution of this literature is obvious, the question to be addressed is the way dualism in the labour market and possible relationships between sections of Japan's segmented workforce have been dealt with. This line of enquiry raises the issue of the distribution of power, both within and between the two sectors. For example, Dore's 'welfare corporatism' may apply to a small segment of the workforce but in addition may be dependent upon other types of power relations, namely those involving the workforce in the peripheral sector.

In studies of the dynamics of the labour market or the labour process, examples are legion in which priority is given to the large-enterprise sector of Japanese industry at the expense of the external market and the small and medium sector. For example, Gospel (1983), in a comparative study covering Britain, USA, Germany, and Japan, approaches industrial relations in the Dunlop/Flanders tradition. He is concerned with the central role of elites, the interaction of management and unions, and the rules controlling regulated labour (1983: 12–18). He looks at managerial structures and strategies and focuses on internal labour markets in large-scale industry, and his concern with power relations is confined to these dimensions. Of the situation in the US, Gospel suggests that there is historical evidence that management in some large firms has 'more or less consciously developed internal labour markets as part of a control strategy' (1983: 15). Of the Japanese situation, he writes that, 'at least in the big-firm sector, the system of lifetime employment and seniority wages can be tracked back to employer initiatives in the early period of industrialization' (1983: 15). When Gospel differentiates between kinds of work relations and ways in which management exercises its policy options, his interpretation does not take into account the options facing peripheral management.

The proclivity for Japanese studies to focus on Japan's modern and large-scale industry is further illustrated in Littler's (1982) study of the development of internal labour markets in Japan and the evolution from indirect to direct systems of employment and labour control. In this analysis, Littler, with acknowledgements to Dore, examines the development in the late 1920s and early 1930s of a distinctive Japanese employment system, which he calls corporate paternalism (1982: 154–6). Littler argues that the change from indirect to direct systems of employment and control stemmed from this development.

The transition did not take place in a vacuum. It was related to transitions that were also occurring in the nature of indirect systems of employment and control — a development deserving of closer analysis. Elsewhere, however, Littler (1983a) looks beyond corporate paternalism. He discusses dualism in the labour market in Japan and characterizes the differences between the two sectors in the following general terms (1983a: 130). The large (primary) sector consists of enterprises that are oligopolistic and capital-intensive. They are able to pay high wages and offer considerable job security. In addition:

[they] exercise control over the product market and help to structure the labour market itself . . . training and job advancement systems are incorporated within the body of the enterprise such that an internal labour market is formed. Thus most jobs in an organization, especially the higher, better-paid jobs are shielded from the direct influence of competitive forces in the external labour market. Instead positions are filled by the promotion and transfer of workers who have already gained entry to the firm.

(Littler 1983a: 130)

Littler then turns to the secondary sector, which consists of smaller and more labour-intensive enterprises. In this sector, jobs tend to be low-paying with poorer working conditions. Moreover:

[these smaller firms] have to face frequent instabilities in the product market and, consequently, there is considerable insta-bility of jobs, little training or prospect of advancement, and a high turnover among the labour force.

(Littler 1983a: 130)

Littler then looks at the connection between labour-market segmentation and production processes in the large- and small-firm sectors. In this context, he develops a model of labour-

29

market segmentation (1983a: 131), a modification of which was used earlier in this chapter to clarify the core-peripheral dichotomy concept. The significance of Littler's model lies in the linkages not only between the internal and external markets but between the segmented market and production and employment systems. A vital element in these linkages, as Littler (1983a: 130) emphasizes, is that secondary firms frequently function as sub-contractors for the primary sector. This phenomenon is widely recognized in the general literature on industrial relations, particularly by writers discussed previously (for example Paci 1981 and Friedman 1977) who deal with dualism in the labour market, labour-market segmentation, the peripheral economy, power relations, and systems of control. Few writers look at the situation in Japan within such frameworks. Littler is one of these exceptions, but his treatment of the peripheral sector and sub-contract labour is nevertheless a sub-theme of his main concern — the internal labour market and primary firms. Despite this priority, Littler raises the significance of the relationship between the secondary labour market and control strategies and looks at interrelationships between the primary and secondary sectors, and between primary and secondary production and processes of control.

Others have written on the interdependence within Japan's labour-market segmentation, but like Littler, the peripheral sector is a sub-theme of their main arguments. For example, Palmer (1983: 41) argues that the distinctions Dore found from his case studies are still relevant and have been supported by Clark's (1979) research. However, Palmer then turns to look at reward systems in large Japanese firms and asks how employers, 'operating with a fixed and increasingly costly labour force, respond to market fluctuations and the need to cut labour costs?' (1983: 43–4). She finds some answers in Japan's dual economy and the protection that the secondary economy supplies to the regular employee in the primary economy.

Crawcour (1977) also refers to the interdependence between the modern large-scale sector and the small-scale sector. Again, the reference is brief, but it introduces an important dimension — the significance of the linkage between the sectors for industrial relations. Crawcour (1977: 14) writes that management and labour relations in modern business and industry profited relative to other sectors as a result of the dual nature of the economy. He then argues that this advantage and the persistence of the dual structure led to a 'comfortable relation-ship' between management and labour at the modern firm level. Crawcour's assessment clearly implies that the efficiency of segmented systems of deployment of labour is related in large degree to 'comfortable' industrial relations within the modern firm. What is not yet sufficiently clear in Crawcour or elsewhere is the reverse — the extent to which the secondary sector is affected by the comfortable industrial relations in the primary economic sector. This issue will be expanded upon in an analysis of the effects of sub-contracting and the just-in-time (*kanban*) production process (Chapter 4), and an examination of union-ization, communication, and conflict (Chapters 6 and 7).

What emerges from these examples and other brief references to the peripheral workforce is its 'buffer' role. This role is generally acknowledged, though there are variations of the theme and the context varies. For example, Kōshiro (in Shirai 1983: 83–7) looks at the *nenkō* system (wages based on age and length of service). He points out that the workforce in most industries generally consists of an upper one-third of regular workers with job security, good wages and safe working con-ditions, and the majority who are relatively poorly paid, have less job security and are more subject to work-related accidents (Kōshiro 1983a: 83). However, Kōshiro then rationalizes this situation, arguing that, in one sense, the dual structure is an indispensable supplement to the lifetime commitment system; the gap between regular and sub-contract workers may seem unfair but many workers retire from parent companies and are then employed by related or co-operating firms.[2] He argues that:

> hasty criticism of the dualistic employment system would not serve to stimulate positive reforms. There can be no free enter-prise that has no buffer against business fluctuations. At the same time, the system of dual employment itself, supported by 'related' subsidiaries, is an integral part of the 'lifetime employment' system.
>
> (Kōshiro 1983a: 85)

Tokunaga (in Shirai 1983), writing from a marxist perception, also briefly notes the buffer role of the peripheral workers. His concern is with the relationship between conditions for regular employees in large firms and those for other workers. Tokunaga argues that the lifetime employment system (and by inference, the contrasting situation of the non-regular workforce in the secondary sector) is a legacy of traditional relationships:

> the 'lifetime employment system' for regular workers depends upon the existence of a corps of part-time workers, workers on sub-contract (*shagaiko*) or employed by sub-contracting enterprises, and seasonal labourers from the country (*dekasegi*). However, the system exists only as traditional practice, and there is no rule, like the American seniority principle, written into collective agreements in Japan.
>
> (Shirai 1983: 322)

Koike (in Shirai) also refers to the buffer segment of the workforce; the role and function of workers' associations, the career patterns of female workers and employees in small firms, and the entrepreneurial opportunities available to such workers. Koike questions the widespread belief (based on the dual labour market hypothesis) that workers in Japan's small firms and female workers suffer from low wages and inferior working conditions, and are generally exploited (Koike 1983: 89). He draws attention to the lack of evidence to support these perceptions, which stem in part from insufficient observation and scrutiny of the secondary segment of the workforce, and insufficient communication about this sector to non-Japanese audiences. Koike's research has led him to conclude that differentials are not as great as believed and that the dual labour market explanation is misleading (1983: 89–115).

Shirai (1983) examines characteristics of Japanese management, primarily management in the large-scale enterprise sector, but also management in the small-enterprise sector. More importantly, Shirai deals to some extent with interaction of managerial attitudes in both sectors. Shirai (1983: 377–9) notes, for example, the tendency for management in large firms to rate non-union suppliers and sub-contract firms above unionized firms, and he elaborates on the control mechanisms inherent in these attitudes.

Literature dealing with Japan's internal labour markets and the labour process thus generally acknowledges that Japan's economy depends to a considerable extent on its secondary sector. With regard to the workforce in these sectors, this section of the literature also accepts that the privileges enjoyed by workers in Japan's closed internal labour markets depend on the buffer role consigned to workers in the volatile external market. It is further acknowledged that, in the past, expanding industries depended on the growth of internal work teams. As industries expanded, however, they also depended on 'outside' work. In a similar way, interdependence characterizes modern industry, conditioned by developed techniques and innovations in production processes.

What should be called the '25 per cent model' has emerged from Japan's large firms and internal labour market. In the manufacturing industry, for example, giant firms assemble components of a modern car (ash-trays, radios, tyres, engine parts) that have been produced elsewhere. A considerable amount of materials and components upon which assembly workers operate already contains a value-added component that has been produced by labour power external to the company. The smallest contribution to the finished unit comes from workers in the internal market — estimated to be around 25 per cent (see Chapter 4). Around 75 per cent of materials and components in each car are the result of a variety of work organization schemes, job designs, and various sub-markets for the purchase of labour power. From this perspective, Japanese industrial relations can be seen as a synthesis of a variety of relationships of production. In the literature on labour-market segmentation and the labour process, with rare exceptions, this synthesis is bypassed and the role of workers in the external labour market is accorded background status. As a result, perceptions of industrial relations in Japan to a large extent remain undifferentiated.

In most western reports, the concentration on the internal labour market in large companies has led to an oversimplified characterization of Japan's industrial relations. Littler (1983a: 129–30) suggests that, at the popular level, the perceived characteristics are: hierarchical family-style relationships, lifetime employment, worker participation through Quality Control Circles (QCs), company involvement in providing sport, and recreation facilities, assistance with housing, and daily life centring around the firm. Perceptions are more sophisticated at the academic level, but the conclusions are that 'the essential elements of Japanese work organizations are the lifetime employment system, wages determined by length of service rather than type of work, and the ideological concept of the firm as a community' (Littler 1983a: 129–30).

From such perceptions, stereotypical models of Japan's

industrial relations are sustained. They are closely related to the debate on the continuity of value systems, in which hierarchical relationships and the enterprise as a community are seen to be crucial elements. As has been noted, the debate pervades Japanese studies, although the question of 'tradition' is also raised in other culture-specific and comparative studies. In the Japan-related literature it is evident in the good management (unitary) school, and to an extent in variants of the compromise, consensus and coalition (pluralist) school. It is also evident in the approaches of the classical culturalists, descriptive institutionalists, functional analysts, and contributors to the neo-cultural synthesis school.

The dominance of cultural explanations in the debate is epitomized in the words of Yanagita Kunio who wrote that there is 'an abiding indigenous tradition that [underlies] superficially modernized forms of social life [because] the past [is] pendant "like circles" in the present' (in Gluck 1978: 43). In Japanese industrial-relations research, the cultural explanation is most clearly expressed, as has already been pointed out, in the work of writers in the classical culturalist school, ideally illustrated in the work of Abegglen (1958). Although Levine (1982) takes a different perspective, he argues that Japan's smooth transition to industrialization retained pre-existing patterns, and that traditional paternalism in industrial relations combined feudalism with deep national consciousness. Continuity (in terms of antagonistic class relations) is evident in variants of the marxist school, illustrated in Tokunaga's (1983) acknowledgement of the traditional legacy in the lifetime employment system.

Jacoby (1979: 195) maintains that the emphasis on cultural uniqueness has been misplaced. In a study of Japan's internal labour markets, he argues that classical culturalist interpretations of the development of the labour market tend to stress continuity in values, and this is of itself a problematic. Jacoby is also critical of the descriptive institutional approach and proposes an alternative that gives greater emphasis to structures of production, the organization of labour, and management's desire to forestall unionization (Jacoby 1979: 196). For Jacoby there is a causal connection between these factors and the emergence of strategies aimed at achieving stability and control in the labour markets and at cultivating new pressures to maintain employee effort and loyalty. From this perspective, Jacoby looks at the determinants of power relations between different groups of employees within and across firms, and the possible effect of these relationships on the development of internal labour markets. In his assessment, management is continually concerned with maintaining discipline, continuity of output, and avoidance of strikes, and in this way the control of labour effort is a fundamental element in personnel policies (1979: 196).

Jacoby's alternative framework raises several important questions concerning power relations and ideological control. First, whether management production and employment policies involve the maintenance of differences in group bargaining power. Second, whether constraints on management exist as a result of a perceived need to avoid unionization or militancy. Third, with regard to the continuity of values, whether it is part of management strategy to reinforce the values of the past to legitimize authority and buttress pressures to ensure continued effort, loyalty, and discipline. What Jacoby is arguing is that there is no natural continuity of traditional values but they are reproduced as part of the overall control strategies with pragmatic motivation.

Brecht (in Bix 1978) expresses a similar view of the continuity of ideas and its relationship to mechanisms of control. According to Brecht, revolt is 'unnatural':

> Think how reluctantly men decide to revolt! It's an adventure for them: new paths have to be marked out and followed; moreover the rule of rulers is always accompanied by that of their ideas.
>
> (Bix 1978: 243)

Moore (1966) raises the issue of ideological control in his analysis of Japanese totalitarianism. He notes the inclination of some people to include continuity as a factor in the Japanese system of values, particularly the warrior tradition of the samurai. Moore asserts that there was continuity, but:

> one has to explain why the tradition continued. Human sentiments do not persist of their own momentum. . . . They have to be drilled into each generation anew and kept alive.
>
> (1966: 291)

Control may in this way be a latent function of the stereotypical models of Japanese industrial relations that beatify many of the values ascribed to industrial relations and sanctify them with an aura of tradition. The values attributed to Japan's industrial relations do not persist of their own momentum but are drilled into popular and academic perceptions by means of 'the company is a family', or the 'Japan-is-Hitachi' syndrome.

This line of thought has to a large extent stemmed from the foregoing examination of the literature concerned with comparative analysis, labour-market segmentation, and the labour process. These contributions to the Japan-related literature were analysed with power relations in mind, and it is also from this perspective, that discussion turns finally to look at micro-studies — research into particular aspects of Japan's workforce. The question is whether micro-studies conform to trends already discussed and contribute to this search for the peripheral workforce.

MICRO-STUDIES OF THE JAPANESE WORKFORCE

There is a continuous stream of literature that deals with specific areas or processes in Japanese industry. Among this mass of descriptive material there is a section, which, though small in the total body of the literature, adds to an otherwise limited store of available information about Japan's peripheral sector. This relevant section of micro-studies can be usefully considered in three broad groups. The first and by far the largest group includes research in response to dynamic changes in the workforce and emerging social and economic problems related to these changes. High on the agenda, for example, are discussions on the ageing of the workforce, increasing female participation in industry, the spectacular rise of part-time employment, and the impact of high technology on the workforce.

The second and smallest group of relevant micro-studies is concerned with describing specific categories of workers and less well documented aspects of industrial relations. Research in this group is less a response to changes and contemporary problems than a response to a perceived need to fill some information gaps. For example, there are studies of the rural-industrial workforce, day labourers in specific industries, unemployed workers, sub-contract labour, and industrial conflict in the non-unionized segment of industry. Within this group are the 'myth-busters'. These contributions form a sub-group that challenges specific assumptions and aspects of the mythology about Japan's work-force. The third group of micro-studies includes a small but growing amount of empirical research on the social, industrial, and political situation of Japan's minority groups such as the Korean minority, the Ainu population, descendants of the *eta*, and Japan's atomic bomb victims.

The literature in the first and second groups will be discussed below. Although these contributions do not address the peripheral sector in a cohesive or comprehensive sense, they expand on some of the generalizations and fragmentary references that appear in the literature discussed so far. In this way, they help to bring the peripheral world out of relative obscurity. The third group of micro-studies, which deals with minority groups of workers, is beyond the scope of this work despite the possible relevance of employment patterns in this area. Nevertheless, the existence of a body of literature on these minorities should be noted.

The first group looks at current developments in Japanese industry and changes in the workforce such as ageing and increasing female participation. (These areas are dealt with later in a profile of the small and medium sector, Chapter 2.) The greying of the workforce is frequently linked with analyses of changes in the *nenkō* system (wages tied to length of service). This linkage is in turn associated with predictions and specula-tions about the possible replacement or modification of the *nenkō* system by a merit-based system. The problem of increasing numbers of women entering the workforce, particu-larly part-timers, late-entries and the re-entry of older women is also frequently linked with the length of service aspect of the *nenkō* system to explain male-female differentials in wages and conditions. For example, Sano (in Hancock, Sano *et al.* 1983: 435−57) suggests that an internal labour-market model can provide a key to understanding labour-market segmentation and differentials. Length of service may be the most important factor in determining differentials, but in addition, females are excluded from jobs that require in-house training (the expecta-tion is that females will not work as long as males), and are crowded into specific low-skill jobs. Sano (1983: 454) also looks at the greying of the Japanese population and how this change affects the female segment of the workforce. Female workers' retirement from the workforce has in the past been more or less related to marriage, childbearing, and child care. This is changing now Japan is facing a rapidly ageing society, with many women retiring to nurse and tend aged people at home (1983: 454).

Sano brings another and most important situation out of obscurity — discrimination. According to Sano (1983: 453), there are significant limits in Japan's Labour Standards Law in that it offers little protection for part-time and other non-regular workers and does not properly regulate working hours and other working conditions for part-timers or temporary workers. She points out (1983: 453) that the law protects only people who are already employed and is not concerned with recruitment, screening, or hiring — there is no legal provision that can fully control management's differentiated employment policies concerning sex, age, and other characteristics. (As will be briefly discussed in a profile of non-regular workers, Chapter 3, characteristics discriminated against in Japanese management's employment policies, as in other societies, may include a worker's membership of a minority group, or a trade union or political involvement.) Sano also draws the connection, although without elaboration, between problems faced by female workers and activities of Japan's labour unions. She believes unions should diversify their activities and it should be easier for female part-timers to participate — a comment that is but a part of her package of prescriptions (1983: 454).

The significance of Sano's argument increases when her criticism of union activities is considered in conjunction with her criticism of the Labour Standards Law. There is then a clear inference that some problems associated with female workers reflect their relative powerlessness. Female workers tend to lack power *vis-à-vis* the power of the state (the law) and the power of management (regulations and policies). At the same time, female workers tend to lack power as a result of their limited access to organized or institutionalized forms of articulation and the means of finding redress (the unions).

Sano's paper is an illustration of ways in which foraging in the abundance of material on specific problem areas can throw some light on aspects of the peripheral working environment. At the same time, micro-studies of this first group suggest possible relationships between the problems and changes they deal with and Japan's industrial relations situation. It should be noted, nevertheless, that a diligent and often frustrating search is involved. For example, in analyses of the effects of the micro-electronic revolution (see Chapter 4), there is very little material that refers to, much less documents, its flow-on effects on peripheral workers. There is also very little information and analysis of the trade-offs for these workers, which follow the rationalization of the workforce that accompanies that revolution.

The second and smaller group of relevant micro-studies includes those that aim to fill perceived information gaps and others that challenge assumptions. It is not surprising that this group, like the first, provides a considerable amount of information relevant to the peripheral workforce. Some examples will illustrate this value, first from the information gap sub-group, then from the 'myth-busters'.

At a recent conference on Japanese studies (1985),[3] two papers merit mention. Tanaka looked at day labourers, specifically, day labourers engaged by large firms that operate nuclear reactors. Tanaka examines the problems of these workers: in his words, Japan's 'nuclear gypsies'. He describes their extreme difficulty in establishing a satisfactory relationship with management and their relative impotence in the bargaining game. Tanaka dealt with a small area, from which extrapolation would be unwise, nevertheless, his descriptive work, backed by data and case studies, provided some insights into a relatively unknown segment of the non-regular workforce. The second paper delivered at the conference was by Matsuzawa, who also dealt with day labourers, in this case, those who are involved in Japan's *yoseba*, street labour markets. The poverty and squalor at the *yoseba* in Tokyo's Sanya district is relatively well known. It has attracted the attention of the media on several occasions and has been treated as a piece of exotica. Matsuzawa's approach is also exotic in that his description of the conditions of the day labourers of the Sanya slum dormitories is in highly emotive terms. This being said, Matsuzawa's background summary is more objective, and raises an interesting historical perspective. Like many marxist analysts of the labour process in Japan, Matsuzawa sees continuity in the development of Japan's industrial workforce, but he departs from conventional wisdom with regard to the role of *oyakata* (labour bosses) during the period of early industrialization in Japan. It is generally proposed that the *oyakata* of the 1910s to 1930s were the controllers of skilled workers (see for example: Ujihara 1965; Crawcour 1977; Littler 1980, 1983a). This skilled labour force was eventually absorbed into the internal labour market and came under the control of a direct system of employment. In contrast to this focus, Matsuzawa looks at another *oyakata* role — to recruit and supply the unskilled, flexible and expendable source of labour for the growing *zaibatsu* (industrial cartels) of that time.

In less academic style, two recent publications of the descriptive and 'myth busting' school are worth noting. The first, by Kamata (1982), highlights the situation of Japan's seasonal workers. He produces a vivid case study of non-regular work in a giant enterprise, and writes in a style that humanizes abstract data. Kamata's account of his experiences as a non-regular worker for Toyota throws serious doubts on the accepted image of the Toyota worker. Kamata's work is reminiscent of that by Haraszti (1978). Haraszti's personal and political documentary describes and analyses his experience as a worker in a Hungarian metal factory. He communicates clearly the alienation of assembly line work and the we-and-they contradiction in a socialist state. In the context of casual work in a large Japanese enterprise, Kamata portrays this contradiction no less vividly and from a similar political perspective, albeit in a different social context.

The second illustration in this sub-group is the work of Jon Woronoff (1982a, 1982b). Woronoff also sees contradictions in the organization of work in Japan, but from his observation, the contradiction has few political connotations. Woronoff's approach is an explicit challenge to Vogel's *Japan as Number One*.[4] Woronoff argues that in some areas Japan could be number 16. He offers profiles of Japan's 'wasted' workers, questions the credibility of official statistics (particularly data on the workforce), and analyses particular concerns such as 'real' unemployment in Japan and the exploitation of women workers. In addition, Woronoff attributes pragmatic reasons for workers' apparent 'company loyalty'.

There are many others who challenge aspects of the popular, stereotypical image of Japan, but Kamata and Woronoff are mentioned here because the work of both has received wide circulation. It should be noted, however, that both Kamata and Woronoff are journalists for Japanese and foreign media, and tend to attract academic criticism. For example, Dore's introduction to Kamata's (1982) book is paternal, and faint praise indeed. In a similar vein, Hanami's reaction to Woronoff is that 'his work is interesting but he knows nothing about industrial relations' (Hanami, interview, 22 December 1982). The consensus of critics of Woronoff is that his work is negative. To some, his contribution is provocative, to others, his credibility is destroyed by the range of 'unprofessional' works he has produced. However, Kamata and Woronoff deal with areas that academics, including their critics, tend to neglect or minimize. Their contributions have a place in the literature, and, irrespective of their styles, their studies confirm the potential for micro-studies to be sources of communication about the environment in the little-known peripheral area.

To turn to other research in this second group of relevant micro-studies, a useful contribution is the work of Kato (1980a). Like Matsuzawa (1985), Kato examines day-labour markets such as those in Sanya, Yokohama, and Hokkaido. Kato points out that the construction industry includes a large number of day labourers, but only a very small percentage operate from the so-called street markets. More importantly, Kato places these day labourers in the context of the wider picture of workers in the construction industry, about which he has written extensively.[5] Kato's focus leads him to look at under-employment and unemployment and the relationship between non-regular labour and industrial relations.

Kato's analysis (1980a) of patterns of labour use in Japan is very relevant. He looks at connections between internal and external labour markets and relationships between enterprise unions and the non-unionized workforce. Together with other writers noted earlier, he argues that the dual nature of the economy is to a large degree linked through the sub-contracting system, and is characterized by the wide gap in working conditions for workers in the two sectors. Like Sano's (1983) prescription with regard to correcting conditions for working women, Kato is critical of the unions' lack of response to this situation. More importantly, he points out that official and management sources continue to minimize the significance of the gap between the sectors by emphasizing the widespread middle-class perceptions of the Japanese people (Kato, interview, 13 January 1983).

Kato's most relevant contribution is that he examines the inequalities between the internal and external labour markets and the unionized and non-unionized sectors within a particular theoretical framework (Kato 1980b: 17−24). In addition, unlike the conventional marxist perspective, Kato does not stress a continuity of past employment patterns. In the place of the surplus unskilled labour force of the pre-war period, he argues that in contemporary Japan there is an accumulation of a relatively surplus population, which is a phenomenon of post-war monopoly capitalism, and that during the period of Japan's high economic growth, catch-cries of 'labour shortage' and 'full employment' obscured the growth of this unstable stratum.

This perception derives from a three-tiered model of stratification developed by Eguchi (interview, 2 February 1983). Eguchi and a team of colleagues conducted surveys in the mid-1960s from which it was hypothesized that the working population consists of three main sections: the stable stratum, the unstable stratum, and the protected stratum. Workers in the unstable stratum are those who exist precariously between employment and under-employment. They are always vulnerable and on the verge of joining the totally surplus ranks of the workforce under direct government assistance. Eguchi and his research team continued field studies of segmentation in the workforce, and found that population growth in the relative surplus workforce occurred even during Japan's high-growth period (cited in Kato 1980b: 22–3).

The importance of the research by Eguchi and his colleagues is two-fold. First, it fills a significant information gap, particularly with regard to low-income sections of the workforce. Second, and more importantly, the three strata model suggests a process within Japan's segmented labour market. This process concerns the dynamics of power relations beyond the relatively stable core stratum, and in this way, places the core sector of the workforce in a broader context.

CONCLUSION

Gaining insights into Japan's peripheral workforce has been frustrated to a large extent by the dominant focus in the literature on the large-enterprise sector. It is not surprising that references to the peripheral workforce are fragmentary, in view of the overwhelming importance given to relations between major interest groups and the rules and regulations that institutionalize the interaction between them. The pluralist approach in general theories of industrial relations affects the outcome of comparative studies and is replicated in the Japan context where it is translated into an almost exclusive focus on the internal labour market, and management and unions in the large-enterprise sector. The importance of the secondary sector to the economy and its buffer role in production and employment patterns are acknowledged, and ignorance about this sector is deplored. However, this has not led to a cohesive and documented examination of the sector, or, with some notable exceptions, its inclusion in an overall theoretical analysis.

A further feature of studies in the Japan area is that relationships are frequently seen to be the legacy of traditional value systems, and in this continuity lie the factors that 'explain' its industrial relations 'system'. This perception constantly stimulates debate on Japan's uniqueness or otherwise.[6] Yet the convergence problematic and its sibling — the debate on the transportability of Japan's industrial relations 'system' — remain largely within the boundaries of the large-enterprise sector.[7] This strong bias overwhelms the small input of contributions that would invite the peripheral workforce into the industrial relations game, at least to sit on the reserve benches.

Trends in the literature summarized above have led to the perpetuation of interest in factors that are central to generally accepted models of Japan's industrial relations. Even when these models are challenged, the same factors remain the focus of attention. Significantly, this phenomenon also exists in the Japanese community outside the world of research and analysis. Japanese government, management, and union philosophies constantly emphasize concepts such as: management and labour have a shared goal; we sink or swim together; we are all in the same boat; the enterprise is a family (even a sub-contracting network is like a family with the contractor as the parent company); welfare corporatism, the enterprise, the firm — they are like a community; we have an abiding tradition of consensus. Thus philosophies of the unitary 'good management' and pluralist 'liberal collectivist' approaches are espoused by the actors, and serve to complement the 'model'.

When this shared approach on the part of the major actors is considered in conjunction with trends in the literature, a series of questions arises. Does the prevailing ideology among the main actors confirm conventional perceptions of industrial relations in Japan, or does it contribute to their creation? More importantly, does the constant reiteration of this ideology by major organizations of management, unions, and relevant

43

agencies of the state influence expectations and in some measure control relationships within Japanese firms and in the wider society? Even more importantly, does the restatement of these concepts serve to legitimize employment practices and industrial structures and procedures, and justify the core-peripheral dichotomy? These questions are inescapable.

To pursue such questions is to digress from the primary purpose of this book, which is to explore two main concerns: the core-peripheral dichotomy and relationships between management and labour in the peripheral sector. Clearly, fragmentary references and scattered sources in the search of the literature are inadequate and insufficient to achieve this purpose. The main body of this work will, therefore, look at the peripheral workforce in detail in an attempt to understand its place in Japan's complex relations of production.

NOTES

1. Liberal individualist attitudes are not confined to the US or British situations. A similar, almost classical, contemporary exercise in combined unitary and laissez faire approaches to industrial relations is unfolding in Australia, institutionalized in Queensland and proposed by strong business lobbies and conservative parties on the federal opposition benches. The trend is associated with deregulation of the labour market, extension of the system of direct contract negotiation, the de-politicizing of union activity and a minimization of government intervention.

2. According to Kōshiro (1983a: 87), 'co-operating' and 'related firms' are standard euphemisms for sub-contractors.

3. Conference, Japan Studies in Australia Association, La Trobe University, Australia, 1985.

4. Neither Kamata nor Woronoff has gained the spectacular and continuing popularity of Vogel. Vogel's bestseller sold 500,000 copies in the first year of publication. Written in the culturalist genre and in highly positive terms, Vogel's work is not dealt with here, because clearly it does not come within the classification of micro-studies, nor does it concern itself with the issues addressed in this book.

5. During an interview (13 January 1983), Kato Yūji elaborated on his research findings in the construction industry. For those interested in the methodology used in the research for this book, the interview with Kato was based on debating controversial points in his published work. A similar procedure was followed in interviews with other respondents such as Hanami Tadashi (law), Ikeda Masayoshi (sub-contracting), Eguchi Eiichi (national and local labour-market hypothesis), Thomas Nevins (management and human resources), Kato Masuo (unemployed

workers and low-income earners).

6. The lines of the debate are clearly set out in Cole (1971: 17).

7. There are exceptions. Since the early 1980s there have been conferences in Japan involving businessmen from countries such as South Korea, Malaysia, and the Philippines at which the export of strategies in the small-firm sector, particularly sub-contracting, have been on the agenda. See also Hanami 1983b.

2

Japan's peripheral workers: a profile of the small and medium sector

For a fortunate few there is a once in a lifetime opportunity at graduation to join a prestige company in Japan's large-enterprise sector and hopefully to join its elite of regular workers. If this opportunity is missed, there remains the possibility of obtaining regular work in a smaller, less prestigious firm. Other than entrepreneurship, an alternative is to work on a non-regular basis. The majority of Japanese workers in the private sector, who work in small or medium size firms or on a non-regular basis, are Japan's peripheral workers. For these workers, firm size and employment status are two aspects of work that have a major effect on working conditions and relationships between management and labour.

The working environment for the peripheral majority is qualitatively distinct from that of Japan's elite workers, the core or regular workers in large enterprises. In quantifying the differences between the two segments of the workforce, four brief points need to be made. First, some statistics refer to 'people engaged'. This covers all members of the workforce, from company directors to unpaid family members. Second, 'employee' is a specific term in Japanese statistics that covers employees of two kinds: first, regular employees,[1] and second, temporary or day-labourers. Third, the term 'non-regular workers' in this book includes not only the temporary and day-labour category of employees but those who are engaged on a casual, contracted, or unpaid basis and who are *not* classified as 'employees'. The fourth point to note is that the use of the term 'worker' throughout, unless qualified, refers to the managed members of the workforce as distinct from management.[2]

46

Before dealing with non-regular status of employment, this chapter will explore the working environment in Japan's small and medium sector. This includes firms that employ fewer than 300 workers regularly, and, in the case of small firms, less than 20. These are the common though not universal criteria.[3] The extent of this sector and some of its salient features will be examined, and the implications of some of these features in the industrial relations context will be discussed.

THE SMALL AND MEDIUM SECTOR

More than 80 per cent of all Japanese employees work in privately owned, non-primary businesses in the small- and medium-enterprise sector (MITI, White Paper 1982: 3). Of the 51.5 million people engaged in Japan's non-agricultural workforce, 88 per cent work in this sector. Over 50 per cent work in firms with fewer than 30 regulars on staff, and, significantly, 42 per cent work in firms with fewer than ten regular employees (Table 2.1). Japan's triennial census of establishments (PMO 1982a) gives a detailed picture of the distribution of establishments and workers. Of 6 million privately owned businesses (excluding primary industry), 97 per cent are small firms, over 2 per cent are medium, and far less than 1 per cent are large enterprises.[4] Figures in Table 2.1 concerned with the distribution of the workforce show that almost 48 per cent of all privately owned businesses employ no regular workers at all. These small firms are individually operated or use only family members or temporary and day labour. In addition, the census found that more than 11 per cent of all establishments had 'the ordinary outlook of an ordinary dwelling place', employing 4 per cent of the non-regular workforce. (The census statistics exclude the nominally self-employed housewives working part-time without special equipment, an important segment of the peripheral workforce whose role will be discussed later in the context of non-regular and sub-contract labour.)

As might be expected, there are variations in the percentage of small and medium firms within and between industries. The difference is not significant in the case of percentage share of establishments, but there are some distinct differences in the distribution of employees (Table 2.2). For example, 74 per cent of employees in manufacturing work in the small and medium

47

Table 2.1 Labour force by sector, persons engaged, employees, by establishment size, all industries (privately owned, non-primary), 1981 (%)

Size (regular employees)	Number of establishments	Number of persons engaged	Persons engaged of which employees		
			Total	Regular	Temporary and day labour
Total	100.0	100.0	100.0	100.0	100.0
0^1	47.8	12.6	1.7	—	18.4
Small					
0−4	80.4	30.3	16.2	13.1	45.9
5−9	9.4	11.4	12.2	11.9	14.8
10−19	5.4	12.0	13.8	14.0	12.3
20−29	1.9	7.1	8.5	8.7	5.9
Medium					
30−49	1.4	8.3	10.2	10.6	6.1
50−99	0.9	9.3	11.6	12.2	6.0
100−199	0.4	7.2	9.1	9.7	4.2
200−299	0.09	3.2	4.1	4.4	1.5
Large					
300−499	0.06	3.2	4.1	4.4	1.2
500−999	0.03	3.2	4.1	4.5	1.1
1,000 or more	0.02	4.7	6.1	6.6	3.2
Small/medium	99.89	88.8	85.7	84.6	96.7
Large	0.11	11.1	14.2	15.5	3.2

Source: Establishment Census 1981, Statistics Bureau, Prime Minister's Office, Tokyo, 1982.

Note: 1 Establishments with no regular employees, labour force in firms with a sole proprietor, employing only temporary and day labour, or engaging unpaid family members or other non-regular workers such as contract labour.

sector, compared with 95 per cent in construction. The census shows that in the construction industry, almost 70 per cent of all firms are very small, with fewer than five employees, while 33 per cent have no regulars. The distribution of very small firms varies within the manufacturing industry. For example, very small firms account for 42 per cent of establishments in electrical machinery and equipment, compared with 56 per cent in the transport, automobiles, and parts segment.

Table 2.2 Relative share of industry by sector, establishments, and employees, private, non-primary industries, 1981 (%)

Industry	Employees small/medium	Establishments small/medium
Mining	75.9	99.5
Construction	95.3	99.9
Manufacturing	74.3	99.5
Wholesale/retail	87.4	99.5
Finance/insurance	85.9	99.5
Real estate	97.6	100.0
Transport/communications	88.8	99.6
Utilities	66.5	97.3
Services	69.2	98.5

Source: 'Statistics on places of business', Prime Minister's Office, in *White Paper on Small and Medium Enterprises in Japan*, Ministry of International Trade and Industry, Tokyo, 1982.

Note: Small/medium — less than 300 employees (less than 100 for wholesale, less than 50 for retail and services).

In view of the dominance of small and medium firms, it is not surprising that workers in this segment make a major contribution to the Japanese economy. In the case of the manufacturing industry — the core of Japan's export economy — the majority of firms are small and medium in size and the majority of workers in this industry are engaged in such firms. This labour-intensive sector of manufacturing is responsible for the greater value of shipments relative to the capital-intensive large-firm sector. For example, in 1980, small and medium establishments accounted for 52 per cent of shipments (MITI, White Paper, 1982:112).

Over time, the percentage of small and medium firms across industries has not changed appreciably, but the percentage of employees in the small and medium sector has increased. Between 1972 and 1981 the proportion of employees in this sector rose from 78 per cent to 81 per cent (Table 2.3). Firm by firm, size does not always remain static. This is particularly so in the case of smaller businesses, which are the more sensitive to changes in production technology and business fluctuations. They are also operating in strong competition with each other as well as with larger enterprises. In the process, some firms grow larger and others smaller. Irrespective of whether upward or downward trends are due to business success or failure, rationalization or

Table 2.3 Number of places of business and number of employees, privately owned, non-primary industry, 1972–81 (%)

	Small/medium-scale sector				Large-scale sector			
	Number of places of business		Number of persons employed		Number of places of business		Number of persons employed	
	(000)	%	(000)	%	(000)	%	(000)	%
1972	5,083	99.4	30,400	78.4	30	0.6	8,393	21.6
1975	5,358	99.4	31,530	79.5	31	0.6	8,111	20.5
1978	5,815	99.4	34,289	81.1	34	0.6	8,006	18.9
1981	6,230	99.4	37,206	81.4	39	0.6	8,514	18.6

Source: 'Statistics on places of business', Prime Minister's Office, in *White Paper on Small and Medium Enterprises in Japan*, Ministry of International Trade and Industry, Tokyo, 1982.

Note: Small and medium places of business — less than 300 employees (less than 100 for wholesale and less than 50 for retailing and services).

expansion in the firm, or other reasons, the change can bring into play the 'size effect' on the material environment of the workers involved.

A significant implication of changes in firm size is its effect on communication and conflict at the job site (see Chapters 6 and 7), however, in this profile of the small and medium sector, it is the material environment that is of immediate concern. To this end, it is important to consider some of the variations in the job environment by firm size.

SIZE, WAGES, AND BENEFITS

Differentials are not peculiar to Japan. However, according to Hanami (interview, 22 December 1982), the dual labour market hypothesis of exploitation in the case of Japan is an over-simplification. It is argued by many — for example, by key figures in Nikkeiren (interview, 6 December 1982) and the Japan Productivity Centre (interview, 10 January 1983) — that differentials are quite compatible with differences in length of service and, in particular, productivity levels. Nevertheless, a recognition that the vast majority of Japanese workers are employed in small and medium firms, and that wages and benefits decrease markedly with firm size, underlines the importance of examining 'size' as an indicator of differences between the core and peripheral sectors.

An elite of regular workers is employed in Japan's high-wages-and-benefits brackets. The extent of differentials in average cash earnings (private sector) by firm size is shown in Table 2.4. Employees in firms with between 5 and 29 on staff rate 60 on an index that assigns 100 to earnings in firms with over 500 employees. The higher wage rate applies to firms employing 8 per cent of the total number of regular employees and the lower rates to 57 per cent (MOL 1983). There are, of course, wage differences by age within each size category. For example, in each category, wages for males increase until around age 40 to 50, after which they decline. Wage levels for female workers in large firms peak when these workers reach the mid-50s, and at two points if they work in medium and small firms — around ages 30 and 55. The wage/benefit gaps are at their greatest at these points of maximum earnings despite the fact that starting wages are comparable irrespective of firm size.

Table 2.4 Index of average monthly cash earnings per regular employee, by industry and size of establishment (employees), privately owned, non-primary (assigning a value of 100 for establishments with 500 regular employees or more), 1981

Size	All industries
5–29	61.2
30–99	76.7
100–499	84.8

Source: Compiled from *Year Book of Labour Statistics 1981*, Statistics and Information Department, Minister's Secretariat, Ministry of Labour, Tokyo, 1983.

Note: Cash earnings include contractual and special cash payments.

Pay hikes (so-called base-up rates) and bonuses are higher in large firms (MITI, White Paper, 1982). In fiscal 1981, base-up increases averaged 5.5 per cent in the large firm sector and 4.1 per cent in the small and medium firm sector where obviously the base wage rate is lower. At the same time, bonuses in the small and medium sector averaged 33 per cent less than those paid in the large firm sector (MOL, 1983 and interview, Small and Medium Enterprise Agency, MITI, 8 March 1983).

Non-obligatory welfare allocations are similarly graded. A Labour Ministry survey of welfare facilities (MOL 1983) found that in 1981 these allocations accounted for 2 per cent of average total labour costs in firms with 30–99 regular employees as compared with 3 per cent and 4 per cent of total labour costs in firms employing 1,000 to 4,999 and 5,000 or more respectively. In terms of actual outlay in welfare facilities, the amount paid out in the smallest firms is 31 per cent of amounts set aside by the largest firms. Firms with less than 30 employees, not covered in the published results of the survey, can with reasonable certainty be assumed to outlay a far lower percentage.

Productivity levels also decline in parallel with levels of wages and benefits. It can be clearly shown that productivity levels also decrease with firm scale or size (Table 2.5). The large gaps in wages and productivity have continued despite efforts to improve efficiency since the oil crisis. Indeed, the gap has increased since 1975 although with respect to capital investment, the gap has narrowed (MITI, White Paper, 1982: 34–5). MITI analysts argue, however, that 'the expansion in differences in wages and productivity (competitiveness) between corresponding occupations and industries is not as large as that shown by the indicators as a whole' (MITI, White Paper, 1982: 34–5). This, according to MITI, is due to two main features of the industrial structure. First, there are significant changes occurring in the workforce of the large-scale enterprises. The average age of employees is rising so that there is an increase in high-wage labour as a result of incremental wage increases with age and length of service — a trend for workers to about age 50 — particularly in large enterprises.

At the same time, the number of 'production labourers' is declining in these large businesses due to rationalization, so that there is a decrease in relatively low-wage labour. MITI analysts then point to a second feature of the industrial structure that renders the gaps in wages and competitiveness more apparent than real. This lies in the difference in capital intensity between those industries composed primarily of small and medium enterprises and those comprised mainly of larger enterprises. It is in such a context that a causal connection is made between the decline in levels of wages and benefits and the decline in levels of capital investment and productivity.

A different interpretation of the relationship, however, is that the decline in levels of wages and benefits coincides with the

Table 2.5 Index of gap in value-added productivity, manufacturing industry, enterprises employing less than 300 regularly (large enterprises with more than 300 persons engaged = 100), 1974–80

| | Enterprise size | | | |
	1–9	10–19	20–99	100–299
1974	32.6	48.5	57.8	73.7
1975	36.3	51.3	58.2	75.1
1976	33.5	47.3	53.9	70.2
1977	33.4	48.0	54.2	70.9
1978	32.6	46.9	53.5	72.1
1979	30.4	43.7	49.2	66.7
1980	30.1	44.1	50.0	68.1

Source: 'Industrial statistics table', in White Paper on Small and Medium Enterprises 1982, Ministry of International Trade and Industry, Tokyo, 1982.

Notes:
1 Based on places of business.
2 For scale of business 1–9 persons, rough added value.
3 1980 figures are preliminary.

organization of labour effort into the more labour-intensive areas of industry by using people assumed to be less productive, such as female, aged, and less well educated members of the workforce. Bearing in mind arguments that emphasize the productivity/capital-intensive approach, it is nevertheless apparent that the majority of workers is to be found in lower-income and benefit categories, and that the numbers of workers in these categories are increasing. The following examination and analysis of trends in the workforce structure relevant to age and sex, and then in education, expands on this conclusion.

SIZE OF THE JOB: AGE, SEX, AND EDUCATION

In the core-periphery distribution of the workforce, variations according to age, sex, and education level are highly visible, particularly towards the outer limits of the peripheral sector. There are also changes over time to take into consideration. The smaller the firm by numbers of regular employees, the greater the tendency for its workers to be in older age brackets, for the proportion of female workers to increase, and for education levels to be lower. Changes in the structure of the workforce since 1974 as shown in the triennial *1979 Employment Status Survey* (PMO 1980) indicate an increasing gap between the large- and the small- and medium-firm sectors with regard to these variables.

The age factor

In the overall greying of the workforce, the employment of older workers is increasing more rapidly in the small and medium sector. According to MITI (White Paper, 1981: 69–70), by 1979 more than 75 per cent of all workers aged 45 years or more were employed in small and medium firms in the private sector. The percentage distribution of workers in this age bracket is considerably higher in the smaller sector (36.9 per cent) than in the larger sector (25.4 per cent). A continuing shortage of young workers is a characteristic of the small and medium sector, despite a tendency for large firms to reduce their intake of graduates since the oil crisis of 1973–4. While the ratio of older to younger workers increases in firms as they become smaller, the trend is particularly noticeable in firms in which less than 100 people work. Approximately 14 per cent of employees in small firms (1–29 persons engaged) are 55 years of age or more, but this drops to between 5 per cent and 8 per cent in large firms (300 or more persons engaged). The higher rate applies to over one-third of people with a job (1979 statistics in PMO, 1980). Retirement at ages 55 or 60 is common in large firms, and the higher rate in small firms is also due to the entry of retired workers into these firms. As pointed out by Kōshiro (1983a: 83–5), such workers frequently move from large parent companies to associated sub-contract firms.

Within the general ageing of the workforce, a MITI analysis (MITI, White Paper, 1981: 68–9) in part attributes the high percentage of older aged workers in the small and medium sector to patterns of mid-career hiring. In the MITI analysis, three significant points emerge. First, the rate of new entries into the workforce by older people is higher in small and medium enterprises than in large. Second, a large proportion of older workers who change jobs — almost 70 per cent — do so within the small and medium sector. Moreover, 80 per cent of them change jobs in firms employing 100 workers or less. MITI's third point is that:

As a trend of the whole working population of middle and advanced ages, 'downward movement', in which workers move from enterprises of a larger scale to enterprises of a smaller size, far exceeds 'upward movement', and this tendency intensifies as the age bracket increases.

(MITI, White Paper, 1981: 69)

This downward mobility means that there is a tendency for workers, particularly older workers, not only to move to smaller enterprises, but to lower wage brackets.

Female workers

The proportion of women in the workforce is increasing across all sectors. The annual rate of increase is clearly higher in the small and medium sector, where, between 1974 and 1979, the rate increased by 3.8 per cent compared with 1.7 per cent in large enterprises (MITI, White Paper, 1981: 71). (The increase in the ratio of female to male workers is particularly high in the manufacturing industry.) A major factor affecting the increased ratio of female workers to males is the growing number of female part-time workers (35 or less hours per week). Many of these part-timers are married women re-entering the workforce, though frequently they are not re-employed in jobs they previously held. According to MITI (White Paper, 1981: 72), of the 2 million or more female part-timers in 1979, 73.7 per cent worked in enterprises at the small end of the scale, that is, in firms with a workforce of 100 or less.

By sector, women workers comprise 40.1 per cent of the workforce in small and medium enterprises compared with 30.2 per cent in large enterprises (MITI, White Paper, 1981: 70–71). By firm size, the proportion of women workers on staff increases as firms become smaller. The *1979 Employment Status Survey* (PMO 1980) illustrates the pyramid structure of this phenomenon. Women workers make up almost 46 per cent of all persons with a job in firms that engage 1–9 persons; 33.5 per cent in firms with 100–299; and from 26.6 per cent to 29.6 per cent in large firms with 300 or more engaged (Table 2.6).

Wages for female workers are markedly less than wages for male workers within each category of firms by size (Table 2.7). On an index that assigns 100 to firms with more than 30 on staff,

Table 2.6 Persons with a job, female component by enterprise size (number of persons engaged), percentage of all persons with a job, 1979

Enterprise size (number of persons engaged)	Females with a job, percentage of total of females engaged all enterprises (%)	Females with a job, percentage of total of persons engaged in each category (%)
Total	100.0	100.0
1–9	49.4	45.9
10–19	7.4	37.4
20–29	4.1	36.1
30–49	4.5	35.8
50–99	5.7	34.9
100–299	6.9	33.5
300–499	2.2	29.6
500–999	2.2	27.3
1,000 or more	9.7	26.6
(Government)	(7.7)	(37.9)

Source: 1979 Employment Status Survey, Prime Minister's Office, Tokyo, 1980.

Table 2.7 Index of average monthly cash earnings (contractual) by establishment size (number of regular workers) and sex, non-primary industries, excluding government (assigning a value of 100 to average earnings, all employees in firms employing more than 30 regulars), 1981

Size	Total	Male	Female
500 or more	114.6	205.3	70.1
100–499	99.3	116.7	61.6
30–99	92.4	109.7	62.6
5–29	80.5	98.1	54.6
1–4[1]	63.7	83.8	44.6

Source: Year Book of Labour Statistics 1981, Ministry of Labour, Tokyo, 1983. Establishments with 5 or more regular employees, pp. 76–83. Establishments with 1–4 regular employees, p. 102.

Note: 1 The survey of firms with 1–4 regulars is carried out separately from the survey covering larger firms. Any comparison of figures in the two surveys should therefore be treated with caution.

the earnings of female workers in small firms (5–29 employees) rate less than 55 compared with the male rate of over 80. Figures in Table 2.7 also show a marked increase in the male rate of earnings compared with that of female workers as firms increase in size.

The difference between male and female wage rates and the decline in workers' wages in the older-age cohort are due in part to the tendency for women and older workers to be employed in lower-wage small and medium firms and lower-status occupations. The downward trend, the 'mid-career' re-employment of workers from firms of one size to firms of a smaller size, from one wage bracket to a lower, is also a significant factor affecting the working and earning environment of women and older workers. As noted earlier, this downward mobility is particularly prevalent in smaller firms. It has also been pointed out that rates of employment of lower-wage female and older workers is increasing in this sector.

Education levels

A further factor to be considered is the distribution of workers by education level — the third variable dealt with in this profile of the small and medium sector. While it is clear that Japanese workers are moving towards higher education levels, this change is unevenly reflected in the employment structure. The smaller the size of the employing firm, the lower the level of education of its workforce. This trend is confirmed by MITI, based on firm scale (MITI, White Paper, 1981: 73–4), and also by the *1979 Employment Status Survey*, based on firm size by numbers of regular employees (PMO 1980). It is also clear from both sources that the lower range in education levels applies to the largest number of working people (Table 2.8). Forty-one per cent of all persons with a job are employed in small firms (1–9 regulars) and 53 per cent of this segment of the workforce did not attend senior high school or a tertiary institute.

The percentage of workers in the non-primary, private sector who have completed high school, university or college is not only greater in large-scale businesses, 26 per cent compared with 13.5 per cent in smaller firms (1979), but the rate of improvement is faster. Between 1974 and 1979, the number of workers in large-scale firms to reach tertiary level increased by 5 per cent

57

Table 2.8 Persons with a job, levels of education, by enterprise size (number of persons engaged), all persons with a job, 1979 (%)

Size	Percentage of all persons with a job %	Of those completed school		
		Total %	Never attended, elementary, junior high %	Senior high %	Junior college, technical school, college, university %
1–9	41.0	100.0	53.0	36.0	9.0
10–19	7.0	100.0	42.0	42.0	15.0
20–29	4.0	100.0	43.0	43.0	14.0
30–49	5.0	100.0	41.0	43.0	15.0
50–99	6.0	100.0	38.0	43.0	18.0
100–299	8.0	100.0	32.0	46.0	21.0
300–499	3.0	100.0	26.0	47.0	26.0
500–999	3.0	100.0	22.0	48.0	29.0
1,000/more	14.0	100.0	21.0	53.0	25.0
Government	9.0	100.0	17.0	41.0	42.0
Total	100.0				

Source: 1979 Employment Status Survey, Prime Minister's Office, Tokyo, 1980.

compared to an increase of less than 3 per cent in small and medium firms (MITI, White Paper, 1981).

It is not surprising that the higher the level of education, the greater the access to higher job opportunity and levels of earnings. Beyond this general pattern, trends in earnings within each education level vary according to workers' sex and age and the size of the employing firm. For example, the labour ministry survey of wage structures in the manufacturing industry (firms with 10 or more employees) found that wages for graduates rise with age irrespective of firm size, and large enterprises pay up to 20 per cent more than small- or medium-size firms (MOL 1983). The numbers of female graduates are far fewer than male graduates and they earn a considerably lower income than their male colleagues. According to the labour ministry, wages of standard workers[5] aged 30 or more with university education are higher than wages for high school graduates in enterprises of all sizes. The gap widens with age, and exceeds 20 per cent for the

45 to 49 age group — the period of maximum earnings. The size of the firm has a substantial effect on male graduates' wage rates but wage levels of female graduates tend to be less affected (MOL 1983), reflecting other general trends in male/female differentials. The effects of firm size on female workers who have reached only lower secondary school level is considerable and has wide implications: the numbers of female workers exceed males in this lower education level; their earnings are markedly less than males; and those who work in small firms are clearly averaging a lower wage compared with female workers of the same education level in larger firms (MOL 1983).

Characteristics of the workforce structure with regard to age, sex, and education level discussed thus far help to identify some of the differences between the core and peripheral sectors and illustrate differentials along the peripheral continuum. More-over, changes in the workforce structure suggest the gaps between the elite and other workers relative to these factors is increasing. Nevertheless, it is important to bear in mind that the picture that has emerged has internal variations with respect to segments of the workforce by industry.

Differentials by industry

As in most industrialized countries, wage levels vary from industry to industry. This can be illustrated by making a comparison of regular earnings in three industries by age and sex. According to the survey of wage structures (MOL 1983), up to 70 per cent of Japan's small businesses (1981) operate in the wholesale, retail, and service industries. These are acknowledged to be labour-intensive areas, whereas the manufacturing industry covers a range of capital-intensive and labour-intensive firms. In the manufacturing segment of industry, the ratio of small/medium to large firms, while similar to the situation in wholesale and retail, is greater than that found in the service sector (Table 2.2 above). Yet manufacturing workers despite the higher incidence of capital-intensive firms, average the lowest regular contractual earnings of workers in the three industries (MOL 1983: 122–47).

Inconsistencies in the earnings of workers across different industries and within them may or may not be partly explained in terms of productivity or capital- versus labour-intensity. This question has already been raised and, as was pointed out, is one which is outside the scope of this book. Within industries, however, patterns in wage levels follow a consistent trend in that earnings decrease with diminishing firm size. The situation for manufacturing and construction workers, shown in Table 2.9, reflects this trend. It should also be noted that average monthly cash earnings in 1981 for workers in these two major industries were always below the average for workers in all industries.

Table 2.9 Index of average monthly cash earnings per regular employee, by industry, size of establishment (number of regular employees) privately owned, non-primary industries, assigning a value of 100 to establishments with 500 or more regular employees, 1981

Size	All industries	Construction	Manufacturing
5–29	61.2	58.5	56.9
30–99	76.7	67.1	65.1
100–499	84.8	80.9	79.9

Source: Compiled from *Year Book of Labour Statistics 1981*, Statistics and Information Department, Ministry of Labour, Tokyo, 1983.

Note: Cash earnings include contractual and special cash payments.

WORKING HOURS

An examination of differentials can be approached from many directions, some of which will be looked at in the following chapter dealing with working status. One aspect relevant to this profile of the small and medium sector is the trend in the workforce continuum for working hours to increase the smaller the size of the employing firm. This presents a contradiction — longer hours exist in parallel with lower wages — which will be looked at in terms of age, sex, and education level with firm size as the reference point.

The Japanese government, through its 'administrative guidance' mechanism,[6] has applied pressure on Japanese business firms to 'internationalize' working hours. In the government's view, it is desirable to bring Japan more in line with conditions in other advanced industrial societies. The campaign for shorter hours is even more strongly advocated by leading sections of the union movement. Despite strong resistance in some areas of the economy (Nikkeiren, interview,

6 December 1982), major firms have moved noticeably toward this goal. Labour ministry statistics for 1981 (confined to firms with 30 or more regular employees) show that 32 per cent of firms with over 1,000 regulars have introduced a five-day week (MOL 1983). The data also show that the larger the firm, the greater the incidence of a staggered two-days-off system. That is, two days off fortnightly or once, twice, or three times a month.

In contrast to the moves towards a shorter week in Japan's relatively few large firms, most Japanese firms work a six-day week and the smaller the firm, the less likely that a shorter week is practised. The MOL survey showed that 57.4 per cent of firms employing 30–99 regular employees practise the longer, six-day week, compared with 33.5 per cent in firms employing 100–999, and 7.1 per cent in the largest firms employing 1,000 or more (MOL 1983). The survey also showed that variations in the 'average hours worked per day' were insignificant, a matter of minutes (between 7.47 hours for the smallest firms and 7.35 hours in the largest). This suggests that workers in the majority of firms are not only likely to be in a lower wages and benefits bracket, but are likely to work a longer week to earn that lower income.

A less truncated picture emerges from other official data. A report on the labour force (PMO 1982c) includes data for 1981 on firms with less than 30 on staff, and therefore looks beyond the MOL study, at almost 40 per cent of all employees (Tables 2.10 and 2.11). This wider survey shows two size-related trends in the distribution of employees and the hours they work. The first trend indicates that the smaller the firm, the greater the tendency for employees to work for less than 35 hours a week — the usual criterion for the classification of part-time work. In all enterprises employing under 30 persons, 13.7 per cent are part-timers compared with 7 per cent to 8 per cent in larger firms. A second and even stronger trend concerns hours worked per week. Data in this area indicate that the smaller the firm, the greater the tendency for some full-time workers to work considerably more than the average hours for all workers. Again looking at the workforce segment in the smallest category of enterprises, 21 per cent of persons engaged averaged 60 hours or more in their working week. This is significantly more than the 16 per cent to 13 per cent who work such long hours in larger-firm categories (Table 2.10).

Table 2.10 Weekly hours of work, employees, by size of enterprise (persons engaged), non-agricultural industries, excluding government (numbers in parenthesis represent percentages of all persons at work), 1981

Size (persons engaged)	Persons at work (million)	Average hours worked	Hours worked			
			Less than 35 hours		35 hours or more	
			1–14 %	15–34 %	Total %	Of which 60 hours or more %
1–29	13.5 (39.0)	47.9	2.2	11.5	86.0	21.0
30–99	6.1 (18.0)	48.8	1.1	6.9	91.8	16.4
100–499	5.7 (17.0)	48.5	0.9	6.1	92.7	15.8
500/more	9.3 (27.0)	46.6	0.8	7.6	91.2	12.7

Source: Annual Report on the Labour Force Survey, Prime Minister's Office, Tokyo, 1982.

Differences in hours worked are even more apparent in the case of the female component of the workforce. This is particularly so in the category of firms with less than 30 people engaged (PMO 1982c). Again, this is a significant segment of the female workforce — small firms of this size employ 44 per cent of female workers. According to the survey, 26 per cent of females engaged work less than 35 hours a week compared with between 13 per cent and 16 per cent in larger firms. As to long hours of work, 10 per cent of female workers in the smaller firms work 60 hours or more per week compared with 4 per cent to 5 per cent in the larger size categories of firms (Table 2.11).

In the Japanese working and earning experience, the size of the firm has a greater input into variations in working conditions than factors that are singular to each worker, such as age, sex, and education level. Of course, it is popularly argued that other factors, such as productivity and capital output ratios (themselves related to firm size), are the primary determinants of these variations. With due regard to debates over causes, patterns in the numbers of hours worked, nevertheless, further illustrate the differences between the core and peripheral sectors. One inference to be drawn from the size-related differences in hours worked, male and female, is that the smaller the firm the greater the extremes in hours of paid work. In other words, working and

Table 2.11 Weekly hours of work, employees, female, by size of enterprise (persons engaged), non-agricultural industries, excluding government (numbers in parenthesis represent percentages of all females at work), 1981

			Hours worked			
			Less than 35 hours		35 hours or more	
Size (persons engaged)	Persons at work (million)	Average hours worked	1–14 %	15–34 %	Total %	Of which 60 hours or more %
1–29	5.3 (44.0)	41.3	4.0	22.3	73.3	10.1
30–99	2.2 (19.0)	43.8	1.8	13.4	84.3	5.3
100–499	1.9 (16.0)	43.9	1.5	11.9	86.1	4.8
500/more	2.6 (21.0)	41.8	1.6	14.8	83.2	3.8

Source: *Annual Report on the Labour Force Survey*, Prime Minister's Office, Tokyo, 1982.

earning for a significant segment of the workforce takes place either under short-term employment or is characterized by very long hours of work per week. Part-time employment, more common in the smaller firm environment, nevertheless attracts a larger income in large firms. Because wage rates vary so consistently with firm size, time spent at work bears less relationship to wage differentials than firm size and other factors. Indeed, dissatisfaction with wage levels and long working hours figures largely in job mobility — in workers' reasons for changing jobs and wanting to quit their company.

JOB MOBILITY

Within Japan's workforce, changing jobs is less common than in most advanced industrial societies. Where job mobility occurs, it is significantly higher among older workers generally, among young workers in the peripheral sector, and is found more among blue- than white-collar workers.

Data from the Labour Ministry (MOL 1983), reveal some interesting aspects of job mobility. Newly hired workers (excluding construction workers) numbered 3.8 million in 1981. Of these new entries, 50 per cent had previous job experience, including school leavers and new graduates who changed their occupations during the year. Of the other new entries, 25 per cent were employed straight from school or tertiary institutions. The remaining 25 per cent were entries to the workforce without previous work experience, presumably mature-age entries.

MOL statistics also show that members of the workforce who changed jobs (separations) numbered 3.6 million. Of these, 4 per cent were new graduates/school leavers and the balance were experienced workers. Young workers outside the elite workforce in major companies are particularly prone to job change. One observer comments that:

> young workers in small plants move from one firm to another so frequently that the annual separation rates are more than 30 per cent. Although these rates drop to about 15 per cent when these workers are in their thirties and forties, they are still about 10 percentage points higher than the rate of Japanese workers in large enterprises.
>
> (Koike 1983: 97)

Reasons for changing jobs are varied. A 1979 survey of employment status (PMO 1980) shows that, of 1.8 million workers who changed jobs during 1979, 1.4 million (80 per cent) were in what could be called a 'steady job' (working more than 200 days per year). Their numbers were greater in the younger-age cohorts, that is, workers between 15 and 35 years of age. The two most frequently given reasons for changing jobs were 'not sufficient income' and 'bad labour conditions' (Table 2.12).

In addition to those who changed jobs, 4.7 million workers wanted to change (Table 2.13). Numbers were greater in the middle- and older-age cohorts — workers aged between 25 and 54. Blue-collar workers (miners, quarry workers, craftsmen, production workers, and labourers) wanting to change jobs were noticeably in the oldest-age cohorts. As to reasons for wanting to change jobs, these were similar to those given by workers who actually changed jobs. The two most frequent reasons were 'long working hours or heavy physical burden' and 'not sufficient income'. Blue-collar workers were fairly evenly divided in the weight they gave to these two reasons. White-collar workers, on the other hand, were more dissatisfied with long hours and the heavy physical burden of work than with the problem of low incomes.

Table 2.12 Persons who changed jobs, reasons for having changed jobs, by number of days working annually (excluding persons attending school), 1979 (%)

Total %	By annual working days	
	200 days or more	Less than 200 days
(1.8 million) 100.0	(1.4 million) 100.0	(0.4 million) 100.0
Personnel reduction, dissolution, or bankruptcy of company 9.5	9.3	10.3
Job was temporary or unstable 10.4	9.9	12.5
Income was not sufficient 14.4	14.6	13.6
Bad labour conditions 17.8	18.5	15.0
Better use of skill or knowledge 8.4	9.2	5.6
Family member in new job, changed job, firm transferred 3.4	3.5	3.1
Retirement 4.5	4.3	5.0
Illness, old age 3.8	3.0	6.7
Marriage 3.4	3.1	4.4
Taking care of children 0.9	0.6	1.9
Others, and not reported 23.5	23.8	21.7

Source: Constructed from *1979 Employment Status Survey*, Statistics Bureau, Prime Minister's Office, Tokyo, 1980, pp. 292–3.

The data in Tables 2.12 and 2.13 indicate these workers' perception of their unstable employment as well as their dissatisfaction with low incomes and burdensome working conditions. A significant percentage of the workers who had changed jobs gave as their reasons: their jobs were unstable; the workforce on the job was being rationalized; or the company had gone out of business. Those working on a part-time basis were more affected

Table 2.13 Persons wishing to change jobs, reasons for wishing to change jobs, by occupation (excluding persons attending school), 1979 (%)

	Total %	By occupation		
		Professional, technical, managers, officials, clerical and related workers	Workers in mining and quarrying, craftsmen, production process workers, labourers	Other workers
	(4.7 million) 100.0	(1.0 million) 100.0	(1.9 million) 100.0	(1.7 million) 100.0
Poor future promise	13.7	10.6	12.7	16.4
Temporality of present job	10.1	10.1	9.6	10.6
Income not sufficient	24.3	18.0	29.7	22.2
Long working hours or heavy physical conditions	29.8	24.0	30.6	32.3
Better use of skill or knowledge	6.9	13.1	5.1	5.0
Utilization of spare time	1.7	2.9	1.2	1.7
Coming to retirement age or the like	3.1	4.8	2.7	2.4
Incompatibility with housekeeping	4.2	5.0	3.7	4.2
Others, and not reported	6.3	11.3	4.6	5.0

Source: Constructed from *1979 Employment Status Survey*, Statistics Bureau, Prime Minister's Office, Tokyo, 1980, pp. 292–3.

by these factors. Similarly, a significant percentage of those wishing to change jobs gave as their reasons: poor future prospects; the temporary nature of their present jobs. By occupation, blue- and white-collar, the percentages were higher for blue-collar workers.

A REGIONAL FACTOR

The preceding discussion on working and earning in Japan's small and medium firms has highlighted salient features of this sector of industry. To a large degree, these features represent the basis of the difference between the core and peripheral segments of the workforce. If the situation is weighted, that is, if the vast numbers of people working in Japan's smaller firms are taken into account, then the difference between core and peripheral workers assumes not only quantitative but qualitative proportions. The difference is even more obvious in the light of the constraints — material and social — that restrict articulation of their concerns. To a significant extent, features of the urban/rural dichotomy contribute to this qualitative difference.

Japan's privately owned, non-primary industries tend to be concentrated in its major metropolitan areas. Moreover, 26 per cent of establishments and 31 per cent of the workforce are located or work in Japan's eleven major cities. Statistics in the 1981 census of establishments (PMO 1982a) show that almost 55 per cent of establishments are located in urban areas and that such firms account for 60 per cent of the workforce. The census also shows that it is more likely that businesses will operate with a small number of people on the payroll in firms outside Japan's metropolitan areas. For example, less than 30 per cent of the workforce in large firms (1,000 or more regular employees) work outside the metropolitan area compared with 45 per cent of the workforce in very small firms (less than five employees).

Management can count on some economic benefits from the lower wages that are paid to workers in less heavily industrialized prefectures. This represents a pragmatic reason for large firms to establish plants outside the major centres, though workers also benefit from the saving in living costs, particularly housing.[7] More importantly, management has access to a local labour market of full-time industrial workers (many from farming households), seasonal industrial workers who are

67

farmers for part of the year, and part-time workers who share their time between industry and agriculture (agro-industrial workers). In short, management has a ready source of both regular and intermittent contract labour in the regional labour markets (see Chapter 3).

According to a MITI report on regional small and medium industries (MITI, White Paper, 1982: 80–3), the expansion of some segments of industry into rural and semi-rural areas has been very rapid in the decade after 1970. The highest rate of growth has occurred in key processing industries, namely the manufacture of electronic equipment and integrated circuits, and businesses related to these so-called 'front-line industries' (see Figures 2.1 and 2.2).

The MITI report attributes this development to two main factors. First, large-scale enterprises have expanded into regional areas due to the advantages to be gained; a local labour force is readily available, industrial sites are cheap and spacious, and the infrastructure has been improved. The second major factor affecting this development is that smaller manufacturing firms have accompanied the growth of large-scale regional operations. This is partly due to the growth of businesses supplying ancillary services, but the major impetus has come from the development of local sub-contracting relationships.

According to the MITI report, the process has had a far-reaching result in that it has exacerbated the social division of labour in Japan.

> The share of small manufacturing industries participating in subcontracting deals has become large in the metropolitan regions and has been increasing in other regions as well. This reflects the movement toward processing industries in the other regions and the accompanying deepening social division of labour.
>
> (MITI, White Paper, 1982: 93)

The local population, however, is not only the source of a flexible labour force for industry. Like the small and medium workforce generally, the regional labour market is also acknowledged to be a rich source of entrepreneurship (MITI, White Paper, 1982; Koike 1983: 102). Sixty per cent of regional small business owners establish their operations spontaneously rather than through inheritance (White Paper, 1982: 90). Firms of this

Figure 2.1 Regional growth in processing industries: trends in shipments of integrated circuits, 1970–80

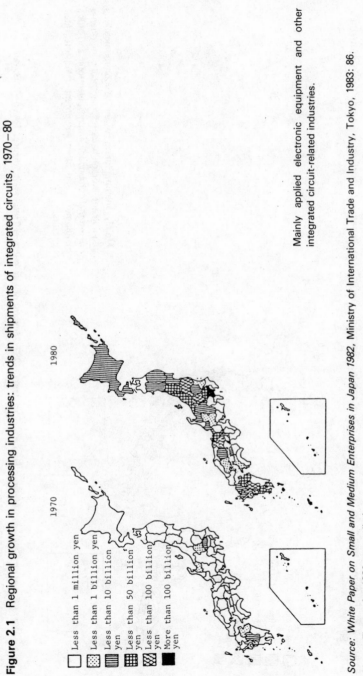

1970   1980

Less than 1 million yen
Less than 1 billion yen
Less than 10 billion yen
Less than 50 billion yen
Less than 100 billion yen
More than 100 billion yen

Mainly applied electronic equipment and other integrated circuit-related industries.

Source: White Paper on Small and Medium Enterprises in Japan 1982, Ministry of International Trade and Industry, Tokyo, 1983: 86.

Notes: Figures for 1980 are preliminary.

Figure 2.2 Regional trends in shipments of other applied electronic equipment: small and medium manufacturing industries, 1970–80

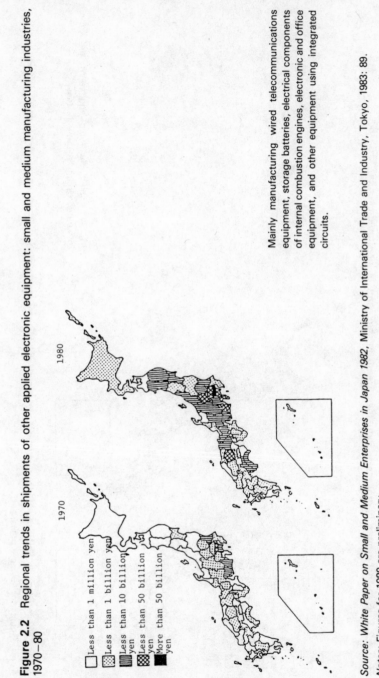

1970   1980

Less than 1 million yen
Less than 1 billion yen
Less than 10 billion yen
Less than 50 billion yen
More than 50 billion yen

Mainly manufacturing wired telecommunications equipment, storage batteries, electrical components of internal combustion engines, electronic and office equipment, and other equipment using integrated circuits.

Source: White Paper on Small and Medium Enterprises in Japan 1982, Ministry of International Trade and Industry, Tokyo, 1983: 89.
Notes: Figures for 1980 are preliminary.

order are also acknowledged to be the first to suffer from the effects of an economic downturn, the last to show signs of recovery. MITI (White Paper, 1982: 12) reports that 17,567 small and medium enterprises — the third highest number since 1977–8 — went bankrupt in 1981. According to the report, business failures were particularly prevalent among smaller firms (especially those in construction-related and retail industries), and firms in the less economically advanced prefectures in the Hokkaido, Tohoku, Shikoku, and Kyushu regions (see Appendix 2: 'Japan: regions and prefectures').

The percentages of the local workforce who are employed in the small and medium private sector varies by region. For example, small and medium enterprises account for 70 per cent of such workers in Hokkaido and Kyushu, but about 60 per cent in Kanto and Chubu (MITI, White Paper, 1982: 17). Thus there is an uneven regional distribution of peripheral industrial workers that adds further complexity to any national profile of the small and medium sector.

The fact that these regional workers are drawn from Japan's local labour markets introduces a rural, local community factor into relationships on the job. Unlike workers in the national labour market, rural, semi-rural, and agro-industrial workers are tied not only to the fortunes of local entrepreneurs of paddy field factories, but to the pervasive pressures of a social context where home, factory, family temple, and shrine are part of the same community.[8] Working and earning, presented in personal rather than statistical terms, entails a short walk through the paddy fields, not one or two hours travelling by commuter train. Factory hands and owner are likely to belong to the same sports club and to be members of the local festival organizing committee, and industrial homeworkers and an entrepreneur's wife may go to the same *ikebana* class; workers and management will meet at ceremonies such as the funerals and weddings of mutual friends and relatives. Such community relations meld with relations on the job — a process through which the intimacy of the smaller-firm environment is reinforced by the intimacy of the integration of factory with village (see Ikeda, 1979, and case studies, Chapter 5).

As reported by MITI (White Paper, 1982: 80–93), small firms in the metropolitan areas tend to be more of the enterprise type, consisting of owner and employees (22.9 per cent) compared with small firms in other areas (19.3 per cent). In addition, small

71

firms in the metropolitan areas are less likely to be owner operated with a staff confined to family members (57.5 per cent) compared with similar small firms outside the metropolitan areas (60.7 per cent). As to regional entrepreneurs in small firms, 60 per cent work full-time in their firms, the majority have their wives working with them, they depend almost totally on the revenue from the firm, and conduct their business within the prefecture (White Paper, 1982: 80–93). In a large number of these enterprises, it is impossible to separate the household from the business:

> The average small enterprise at the prefectural level has its own store or factory (82 per cent), generally within the owner's own residence or on the same grounds as his residence (69 per cent). . . . The self-employed entrepreneur is, in most cases (84 per cent), a person born in the area who plays a large role as a resident in the region through positive participation in the region's cultural activities.
>
> (MITI, White Paper, 1982: 90)

In the rural and semi-rural labour market, it is extremely difficult, if not impossible, to separate the community from the business — to separate labour relations from social relations. The meld of industrial and community relations reinforces hegemonic acceptance of informal forms of control over work behaviour and exists to a far greater extent in the rural or semi-rural areas than in the more impersonal urban industrial environment. This factor has particular significance with respect to issues to be discussed later, particularly unionization, communication, and conflict.

CONCLUSION

This chapter has identified features of working and earning in the small- and medium-firm environment. In this, by far the largest segment of the workforce, the scale of the employing firm is critical. It is increasingly likely that unstable employment, longer hours of work, lower levels of wages, benefits and facilities, and vulnerability to economic change will escalate as fewer people make up the workforce of progressively smaller and smaller firms. At the same time, lower wage earners such as the aged, female workers, and workers with lower education levels are swelling the numbers of workers in smaller firms. Relatively low-wage production labourers are being rationalized out of large-scale enterprises, moving to smaller firms and to even lower wage and benefit brackets.

The working and earning environment in the small and medium sector decisively affects the industrial relations situation, contributing to the relative powerlessness of the workers concerned. This problem is dealt with in later chapters, (Chapters 6 and 7), nevertheless, it is appropriate to conclude this profile by foreshadowing an assessment of the constraints on organization in the small and medium sector that inhibit the articulation of workers' concerns. First, the practical problems in forming a viable union are formidable. Second, under the enterprise union system, each union in each firm must be self-supporting; its officers must be employees of the firm; to leave the firm is to leave the union; to close a firm is to de-unionize its employees; to establish a union is to begin again in the face of these practical difficulties that overlay negative social attitudes. It is not surprising that the further from the elite workforce, the lower the frequency of unionized enterprises (the unionization rate is less than 1 per cent in over 89 per cent of establishments).

The following chapter will examine the place of non-regular labour in Japan's peripheral workforce and some of the outcomes of non-regular status for its industrial-relations situation. The non-regular workforce includes temporary and day-labour employees and contract workers who form an adjunct to the employed staff of most firms. Moreover, of Japan's 6 million establishments, about half employ only family members, temporary, and day-labour employees or contract labour. These very small firms, in the aggregate covering over 30 per cent of people engaged, provide an environment in which unionization is impracticable but which, moreover, is not socially viable. In a broader sense, and irrespective of whether non-regular workers are engaged in a large or small firm, their status affects their relations with management and in addition their relationship with fellow workers and employees.

NOTES

1. Regular employee: one engaged regularly (continuously), including

apprentices, but if a temporary or day labourer was contracted with an employment period of one month or more, or employed for 18 days or more in each of the past two months, he is included as a regular employee. Family workers and managers and directors who work regularly and receive remuneration are classed as regular employees.

2. Different definitions of worker status in official data can have significant implications. Status and problems of definition will be discussed in Chapter 3.

3. Definitions of the small and medium sector are at times conflicting. Legally, enterprise scale is determined by numbers of employees regularly engaged, type of industry and capital investment (the Small and Medium Enterprise Basic Law 1963). Small and medium places of business are those with less than 300 employees but with less than 100 in the wholesale industry, and less than 50 in retail and services. In addition, small and medium businesses are those with not more than ¥100 million capital, but not more than ¥30 million for wholesale firms, and not more than ¥10 million for retail firms. Small enterprises are those with not more than 5 employees in commerce and service industries, and not more than 20 in others. The Small and Medium Enterprise Agency of MITI follows the legal definition internally, but frequently cites data based on other criteria which depart from the legal definition.

Government ministries and agencies and employer and union organizations are neither unanimous nor internally consistent in their cut-off points. The small and medium sector, according to many sources, covers establishments with less than 500 employees, but the most common cut-off point is firms with less than 300. Variations in criteria will be noted where they affect tables or calculations used in this work.

The Director, Statistics Department, Prime Minister's Office (interview 17 January 1983) commented that a reassessment of size criteria is being considered. In some cases, very large-scale operations were being carried out by very few personnel.

4. The establishment census (1981) defines 'establishment' as a single physical location where goods are produced or services rendered, for example store, shop, factory, office, school, hospital, mine, cinema, etc.

5. 'Standard workers' are defined as those who enter their jobs immediately after graduation and continue to work in the same firm without interruption. *Wage Structure of the Manufacturing Industry: Summary of Findings of the 1981 Survey, Ministry of Labour*, Japan, Foreign Press Centre, June 1982a: 25.

6. 'Administrative guidance', as the name suggests, contains strong guidelines that emanate from the Japanese government from time to time on issues deemed to be in the national interest. 'Administrative guidance' can serve to place the government's stand on public record and air sensitive issues for debate as a prelude to legislative action. On issues such as the desirability of reducing working hours, 'administrative guidance' allows management room to protest, consider, implement, or reject. Sometimes backed up by heavy lobbying and worked over with an eye to trade-offs, the mechanism has too much

social impact for it to be completely ignored in the long term, at least in front-line industries.

7. For data on variations in income by enterprise size and prefecture, see *Year Book of Labour Statistics 1981*, Ministry of Labour, 1983, pp. 100–101, 103. For data on household wages and other income and household expenditure (excluding farming and fishing households), by major and minor cities, villages and districts, see ibid., pp, 260–61.

8. National and local labour market segmentation was discussed extensively with Eguchi Eiichi during an interview, Chuo University, 16 February 1983. In extremely simple terms, the national labour market consists of workers in large enterprises employed in their research and development centres in major industrial areas, and in their large plants, mainly in regional areas. The local labour market consists of local workers who are attached to regional plants and who are involved in contract labour arrangements or work in small and medium firms under sub-contract or ancillary relationships. Workers in the local labour market are a significant element in the unstable stratum of the work-force — a concept discussed in Chapter 1.

3

Japan's peripheral workers: a profile of non-regular labour

Workers employed on a non-regular basis tend to work and earn under the least-privileged conditions in the peripheral segment of the workforce. Because the vast majority of non-regular workers operate in the small and medium sector of industry, salient features of this sector also affect them. In this way they are subject to the impact of two factors acting in conjunction: industrial structures and employment status. With regard to working and earning, non-regular workers are vulnerable on two counts. On the one hand, there is the tendency for firms in the small and medium sector to be unstable and, on the other hand, non-regular employment within these firms is the more insecure. Small firms that are expendable, particularly those in a sub-contract relationship, in turn have their own expendable work-force of non-regular workers on term contracts and piecework. Non-regular workers thus protect the more privileged position of regular workers in the small and medium sector who may be employed in a more regulated and unionized milieu. While the small- and medium-sector workforce provides a buffer for the large enterprise sector, within a firm, non-regular workers provide a buffer for the firm's regular employees. The availability and expendability of these workers, euphemistically designated as their 'flexibility', is an economic advantage to their employees but enhances their degree of relative dependency (see Friedman 1977). Moreover, in the industrial-relations context, their status divides them from other workers in the workplace.

This chapter will look first at the niche in the workforce occupied by some of those who work for specified periods of time or, as 'self-employed', supply goods or services under a written or verbal contract: temporary and day-labour employees, family workers, agro-industrial workers, industrial home-workers and the unemployed. It will then examine briefly some of the implications of Japan's labour laws in the context of regulated and unregulated labour.

EMPLOYEES: TEMPORARY AND DAY LABOUR

There are problems in identifying different types of non-regular workers. Official statistics tend to gloss over ambiguities and definitions of 'employees', and there are variations in the defini-tions of other categories of employment. This means that while the relevant statistics are useful, it is necessary to be aware of this problem at the outset. For example, according to some definitions of status in the *Establishment Census 1981* (PMO 1982a), the numbers of regular employees may be inflated. In these statistics (on which the following analysis of non-regular workers is based), proprietors and family workers are classed as employees if they are on the firm's payroll. In addition, they are classed as regular employees if they work on terms or conditions similar to those applying to regular workers in the firm. Temporary workers and day labourers are also classed as regular employees if, in the two months prior to the census, they worked for over a month or for more than the equivalent of three working weeks. It should thus be borne in mind that an unknown number of temporary and day-labour employees and other non-regular workers may be obscured in the data.[1]

The census of establishments (PMO 1982a) shows that there are 35.5 million employees working in over 6 million privately owned establishments (non-primary industry), and 3.3 million of these employees have, by definition, temporary or day-labour status. The distribution of non-regular employees shows that the majority are concentrated in small and very small firms (see Table 2.1 above). Almost 80 per cent of temporaries and day labourers and almost all unpaid family workers are employed in firms employing fewer than 30 regulars. As has been noted, 3 million establishments, almost half of Japan's private-sector businesses, employ no regular workers at all. These are very small firms that are independently operated or which use only unpaid family workers, temporary or day labour. As could be expected, Japan's large firms do not use working family

77

members, but they employ 3.2 per cent of the total number of temporaries and day labourers.

Temporary and day labour: deployment by firm size and industry

The use of temporary and day-labour employees relative to regular employees increases as firm size decreases (PMO 1982a). In Japan's 1,021 major establishments (with 1,000 or more regular employees), there are 67 regular employees for each temporary and day labourer. This high ratio of regular employment applies to only 6 per cent of workers classified as employees. As figures in Table 3.1 show, the fall in the proportion of regular workers is dramatic as the workforce in firms drops below 1,000, with ever-widening involvement in percentages of the workforce. Calculations from these figures indicate that there are 4 regular employees to each temporary and day-labour employee in small firms (less than 10 regulars), affecting 28 per cent of all private-sector employees.

From industry to industry the ratio of regular to temporary and day-labour employees varies considerably. Three examples, from construction, electrical machinery and equipment, and transport equipment/automobile and parts manufacture, show this diversity. There are no regular employees in 30 per cent of establishments in the construction industry. These very small firms employ 15 per cent of temporary and day-labour construction workers. Eighty per cent of firms employ fewer than 10 regular workers, where the ratio of regular to temporary and day-labour employees averages less than 3 to 1. Thirty-four per cent of construction workers are employed in this segment of construction. Looking at large firms — those with more than 300 regulars — the ratio of regular to temporary and day labour is by no standard high, but rises to an average of 43 to 1. However, there are few such enterprises (0.04 per cent of the total) and this rate of regular employment affects only 5 per cent of construction employees.

With regard to electrical machinery and equipment, the ratio of regular to temporary and day-labour workers in the small-firm sector (fewer than 30 regulars) is similar to the situation in the construction industry, that is, almost 3 to 1. This low rate of regular employment, however, affects a smaller percentage of

Table 3.1 Ratio of regular employees to temporary and day-labour employees, by sector, establishment size (number of regular employees), privately owned (excluding agriculture, fishing, and forestry), 1981

Size (regular employees)	Number of regular employees to each temporary/ day labour employee	Percentage of all employees %
Total	9.6	100.0
Small		
0–4	2.7	16.2
5–9	7.7	12.2
10–19	10.9	13.8
20–29	14.2	8.5
Medium		
30–49	16.8	10.2
50–99	19.4	11.6
100–199	22.0	9.1
200–299	28.3	4.1
Large		
300–499	34.9	4.1
500–999	38.8	4.1
1,000 or more	66.9	6.0

Source: Establishment Census 1981, Statistics Bureau, Prime Minister's Office, Tokyo, 1982.

Notes: Individual proprietors operating on commission, as side work of housekeeping without particular equipment, are excluded from coverage in this Census.

'Establishment': a physical location where production, service, etc. are carried out.

Persons in receipt of remuneration in the form of wages are classed as 'regular' employees.

If contracted to work for more than one month or if engaged more than 18 days in the two months preceding the Census, day labourers and temporary workers are classed as 'regular employees'.

the workforce than is the case in the construction industry. Only 16 per cent of firms have no regular workers at all, compared with 30 per cent in construction. Furthermore, only 6 per cent of employees work in small firms employing fewer than 10 regulars compared with 80 per cent in the construction industry. Forty-six per cent of electrical machinery employees work in large firms (more than 300 employees). In these large firms, the rate of regular employment is high, ranging from 60 to 70 regulars for each temporary or day labourer.

In transport machinery/automobiles and parts, 65 per cent of employees work in the large-firm sector. Forty-seven per cent work in the largest enterprises with more than 1,000 regulars on staff. The rate of regular employment rises sharply within the large-enterprise sector. In large firms that employ between 300 and 500, there are 48 regulars for each non-regular employee. In larger firms that employ between 500 and 1,000, the ratio is 52 to 1. In the largest firms employing more than 1,000 the ratio is 80 to 1. Only 11 per cent of transport/automobile workers are employed in its small-enterprise sector. In the smallest firms, there are 2 regulars for each non-regular employee but 19 to 1 in firms employing between 20 and 30 regulars.

Of the three industries looked at above, regular employment is clearly more infrequent in the construction industry. This is to be expected considering the nature of the industry — not only in Japan. However, a cursory examination of the situation in other industrialized countries suggests the employment of non-regular labour in the Japanese construction industry is exceptionally high.

Allowing for statistical problems that might arise through survey criteria, and given that the picture varies considerably within Japanese industry as a whole, the effects of the firm-size factor on employment patterns are clear. The extent of these effects is also obvious — 79 per cent of all temporary and day-labour employees work in firms with fewer than 30 regulars on staff. Of these non-regular employees, 46 per cent work in the smallest firms that employ fewer than 5 regulars.

As pointed out earlier (Chapter 2), the constraints on labour organization in small and medium firms, particularly small firms, are almost overwhelming. The practicality of union organization becomes even more remote when the percentage of regular employment decreases as firms decrease in size. Of the workforce on each site, the percentage of workers unable to join any proposed union increases. While it is extremely difficult under the enterprise union system to form a union when there are few employees on the site, the difficulty is compounded when significant numbers of workers on the job are unable to participate should they wish to do so. Whether such non-regular workers become members of workers' associations is unknown. As will be shown later (Chapter 6), workers' associations are more common than unions in smaller firms, but there are indications that membership is restricted to permanent and regular workers.[2]

FAMILY WORKERS

Another dimension of the non-regular workforce concerns unpaid family workers. They do not come under the classification of 'employees', but are tabulated in the workforce data as 'persons engaged' or 'people with a job'. The presence of family workers in a firm, whether they are paid or unpaid, is also relevant to the question of organization. Family members work in the firm alongside the owner or proprietor and at times alongside regular and non-regular workers. Their presence underscores the strong possibility of informal relations on the job. Familial relationships become more likely as the firm becomes smaller in operation or more interwoven into a rural community and rural environment (see Chapter 2). The frequency with which paid family members occur in some workforce data is not precise, because they are classed as employees. However, some information is available with respect to those who are unpaid.

Frequency in the use of unpaid but working family members is affected by the firm-size factor. They generally work in smaller firms, and the smaller the firm, the more likely they will form all or part of the staff. Unpaid family workers make up a relatively small segment of the workforce, 6.5 per cent (PMO 1982a). This varies by industry: 4 per cent in construction, 6 per cent in electrical machinery and equipment, and 1 per cent in transport machinery, automobiles and parts. A higher proportion are engaged in some other industries, for example, the figure is 11 per cent in wholesale/retail (PMO 1982a). More important than the smallness of their number, however, is the fact that they are almost completely confined to working in very small businesses (Table 3.2).

The distribution of types of non-regular workers discussed so far, given variations between industries and the rural–urban dichotomy, in each case involves more of their numbers along the peripheral continuum. In this context, it will be recalled from earlier discussion (Chapter 2) that a similar continuum characterizes working and earning in the small and medium sector. As firms become smaller, workers are increasingly in the

Table 3.2 Unpaid family members by establishment size, selected industries, non-primary industry, excluding government, 1981 (%)

Size	All industries	Construction	Electrical	Autos, parts
0–4	93.9	83.6	74.6	85.9
5–9	4.2	11.3	14.1	9.6
10–19	1.4	4.1	8.0	3.5
20–29	0.3	0.7	2.2	0.6
30 or more	0.2	0.2	1.1	0.3

Source: Compiled from *Establishment Census 1981*, Prime Minister's Office, Tokyo, 1982, pp. 448–503.

low income and benefit bracket; mobility is greater and job security less. The percentages of older workers and female workers, and workers of lower education levels tend to increase. These trends accelerate towards the outer limits of Japan's peripheral firms. These small firms, with fewer than 10 regulars, account for 90 per cent of all establishments, 98 per cent of all unpaid family members, 25 per cent of all regular employees, and 61 per cent of all temporary and day-labour employees (Table 3.3).

Table 3.3 Summary of distribution of people engaged, establishments with fewer than 10 regular employees, private sector, excluding agriculture, 1981

Item	Number (000)	% of total of item
Establishments	5,600	89.8
People engaged	19,000	41.7
Individual proprietors	4,000	21.2
Unpaid family members	2,900	98.0
Salaried managers and directors	2,000	64.5
Employees	10,000	28.2
Of whom:		
Regular	8,000	25.0 of all regulars
Temporary and day labour	2,000	61.0 of all temporary and day labour

Source: Compiled from *Establishment Census 1981*, Prime Minister's Office, Tokyo, 1982.

AGRO-INDUSTRIAL WORKERS AND INDUSTRIAL HOMEWORKERS

An examination of two additional categories of non-regular workers reveals features that accord with these trends in the peripheral workforce. The first consists of workers referred to in this book as agro-industrial workers. These workers are associated with the rural workforce and work in industry as a primary or secondary job. The second category consists of industrial homeworkers, who, working at home, are classified as self-employed. Almost all industrial homeworkers (hereafter referred to as homeworkers) provide contract labour for small and very small firms, particularly sub-contractors. Industrial homeworkers should not be confused with cottage-industry workers who are engaged in traditional arts and crafts.[3]

Workers in both groups are involved in the ongoing rationalization of industry, but, as will be pointed out, neither group is in a position to negotiate terms concerning changing conditions of work or rewards for labour. Workers such as these have little potential to build a power base compatible with the concept of a pluralist society. In the case of agro-industrial workers, there is the likelihood of the conservatism and the values of the rural community being brought into the industrial environment, thus militating against the relatively radical step of unionization. The situation of homeworkers, many of whom are also agro-industrial workers, is relevant for additional reasons. Since they are not employees but nominally self-employed, they are denied normal channels of labour organization and the regulations covering employees. Nevertheless, homeworkers are a source of labour which contributes to a total production process. Their relationship with management is a one-to-one arrangement, and is only regulated by a special protective law if the fact of their employment is officially known. The examination of these two categories of non-regular workers in Japan raises some of the points brought out in Paci (1981) in his analysis of the peripheral workforce and peripheral firms in Italy.

Agro-industrial workers

Agro-industrial workers are not unique to Japan. Nor is it a new phenomenon for agricultural workers to spend part of their working life in industry. In the Japanese experience, one type of agro-industrial worker is the seasonal worker, or *dekasegi*.[4] Unable to farm in Japan's winter months, seasonal workers have long been recruited and brought from home, particularly from the northern prefectures of Honshu and from the northern island of Hokkaido, to work for wages for part of the year. They frequently work in the construction industry as navvies or maintenance workers and in similar unskilled jobs. Since Japan's high-growth period, numbers of *dekasegi* have been declining and the type of work they usually do has been changing. According to the Ministry of Agriculture, Forestry and Fisheries (1982: 10–11, 32–3), the number of households with members hired as *dekasegi* has declined noticeably in recent years, from 75,000 households in 1976 to 50,000 in 1981. Over the same period, numbers of male workers in this category have declined from 197,000 to 118,000 and females from 18,000 to 12,000.

A change in Japan's industrial structure is partly responsible for this decline. As already noted (Chapter 2), large manufacturing enterprises have tended to establish their plants in rural and semi-rural areas and, in so doing, have absorbed workers from the local labour market. There are cases where this has taken place on a major scale. For example, Hitachi has created a metropolis in Hitachi City, now a large and growing industrial area. The effect of this movement on Japan's *dekasegi* is that some seasonal workers are moving into new categories of employment. Some seasonal work can take the form of part-time work (contracted for part of the year) in nearby plants or sub-contract firms. There is less need to travel away from home or to stay in the dormitories of industries in the metropolitan areas for half the year. Wages for seasonal workers in these circumstances tend to be higher than those for navvies moving from construction site to construction site in the cities. Skills can be developed while working in locally based industries with the result that trained agro-industrial workers can return each year to the same plant as known and experienced employees — if work is available. In this way *dekasegi* numbers decline but the practice persists, with casual/seasonal workers coming under other classifications.

While there have been changes in the situation for *dekasegi*, there have also been changes for other types of agro-industrial workers (Ministry of Agriculture, Forestry and Fisheries 1982). First, between 1976 and 1981 the numbers of agro-industrial workers operating their own side business have declined. Second, numbers working as day labourers have increased. A third and most noticeable change is the increase in the numbers, particularly females, who are 'mainly engaged in constant work', although still involved in farming households. Examples of this third trend were found in case studies of workers in factories in rural Nagano Prefecture (Chapter 5). The workforce in each of three case studies was involved in farming. They worked on a nominally full-time arrangement, but one that allowed them to share their time between the factory and farm. At times, production demands affected the need for these Nagano workers to work overtime. At other times, harvesting, planting and other farm responsibilities required them to leave the factory for hours, days, or weeks, in their case, not the full period of the winter months.

This is another aspect of labour-market segmentation within the agricultural-industrial dichotomy. According to the agricultural ministry (1982: 5, 8–9), the total number of farm households has decreased. In 1976 there were around 4.9 million, in 1981 there were 4.6 million (12.8 per cent of all households). In that period the farming population also decreased both in absolute numbers and as a percentage of Japan's total population (from 20.2 per cent in 1976 to 18.3 per cent in 1981). Side by side with this change, increasing numbers of farmers and their families have become partially involved in industrial wage labour. It is significant that 87.4 per cent of the total number of farming households (4.3 million in 1981) are part-time farming households. This means that in the overwhelming majority, at least one household member is engaged in work other than farming. It is even more significant that 79.4 per cent of these part-time farming households (3.2 million) have one member or more whose main income comes from work other than farming although they remain within the farming community. Distribution of households by full-time and part-time is shown in Table 3.4.

The decline in the agricultural population is clear, nevertheless the division between agricultural and industrial workers is not discrete. Change is not merely demographic but involves dynamic social movement. This movement suggests a complex process within the industrial workforce. A report on trends in agriculture for fiscal 1981 (Ministry of Agriculture, in Foreign Press Centre, 1982b) draws attention to some relevant trends in

Table 3.4 Farm households, classified by full-time and part-time, source of earned income, and type of side job, 1981

Item	Number	%
Total farm households	4,614,450	100.0
Full-time farm households	579,940	12.6
Part-time farm households	4,034,300	89.4
Part-time:		
(a) Main income from farming:		
total	829,360	100.0
Head of household engaged in:		
full-time farming	600,610	72.4
mainly farming	60,460	7.3
mainly other jobs	87,110	10.5
others	81,200	9.8
(b) Main income from other jobs:		
total	3,205,150	100.0
Head of household engaged in:		
full-time farming	317,180	10.0
mainly farming	73,240	2.3
constant work	1,474,700	46.0
dekasegi	47,570	1.5
temporary and day labour	444,530	13.9
only other jobs	491,050	15.3
others	345,890	10.8

Source: The 57th Statistical Yearbook 1980–1981, Ministry of Agriculture, Forestry and Fisheries, Tokyo, 1982.

this process. First, the growth of decentralized employment opportunities in recent years has led not only to a rapid decline in the movement of the rural population to urban areas but to a reverse drift of people to rural areas. Second, there has been an increase in the number of non-farm households in farm villages in addition to an increase of part-time farm households. This has stimulated the gradual spread of a more sophisticated lifestyle to some rural communities. As a result, the percentage of communities where farm households are in a majority fell from 78 per cent in 1970 to 65 per cent in 1980. The percentage of farm households in a rural community fell from 46 per cent of the total in 1970 to 23 per cent in 1980. The report commented that:

With the spread of the mixed lifestyle, the ratio of rural

villages which perform co-operative functions such as the management of farm roads, irrigation, and drainage waterways has declined, indicating the decline of the village as a unit.

(Ministry of Agriculture, Forestry and Fishing,
in Foreign Press Centre, 1982b: 28)

Part-time farming is now stabilized according to the agricultural report. In this context, the report makes the following points. The majority of farm households have members who are hired by others. An accompanying trend is for the farm population to age at a rate considerably higher than for Japan as a whole. The rate of population ageing is even higher in the full-time farming population than in the part-time. According to the report, this suggests that many aged people have no other choice but to work on farms in order to earn their living. With regard to types of side jobs of part-time farming, these include *dekasegi*, full-time work for an employer, temporary and part-time work, day labour, or the operation of a side business. The report notes that part-time farmers frequently derive their income from working in a number of jobs. The reason, according to the ministry, is that their earnings from work other than farming are still low compared with the earnings of other employed workers. In this context, it should be recalled that 46 per cent of part-time farm households where income is mainly derived from non-farm work have the household head engaged 'in constant work', that is, in full-time or permanent part-time employment (Table 3.4 above). Despite permanent part-time work, earnings for such agro-industrial workers are deemed by the ministry analysts to be in the relatively low wage bracket.

While some agro-industrial workers are on part-time or full-time wages, others are part-time entrepreneurs and, according to Ikeda (1979), part-time factory owners. Research in Japan's electronic industry in the Kami-ina region of Nagano Prefecture (Ikeda 1979, 1982) found that the number of manufacturing businesses has increased dramatically since 1965. The majority of these firms are sub-contractors, many are very small, employing fewer than 20 workers, with contract pieceworkers at the bottom of the sub-contract network. Ikeda argues that:

These sub-contractors sold milking cows and cattle to buy lathes and pressing machinery, and renovated/converted cowsheds into factories. Their business was initiated as [a] side business of farm households. At these part-time factories owned by farmers the majority of the employees are middle-aged or older part-time farmers.

(1979: 52–3)

These part-time factory owners employ permanent part-time farmers or put out work to other part-time farmers. They are the region's industrial workers who own a piece of land and not — as officially perceived — farmers doing a side job in industry (Ikeda, interview, 25 January 1983). Ikeda sums up the farming entrepreneurs in the precision machinery industries as follows:

the starting fund of no more than ¥0.5 million could suffice to open a small factory equipped with a small benchtop lathe. In starting a new factory, the most expensive [costs] were land and construction. . . .

The farm households that also engaged in side-jobs had an advantage over their part-time factories. Even when they decided to construct a small factory, they would minimize expenses by switching some of the part-time vegetable fields into a factory site. This is the main reason that when the economy made progress at [an] all-time high pace during the . . . 1960s and 1970s, the farm households could so easily come to own minute scale sub-contracted factories.

(Ikeda 1979: 49, 57, 60)

The agro-industrial workforce then is complex. *Dekasegi* leave and return to the village community for part of each year. These and other casual workers are frequently a source of day labour in the major industrial centres, particularly in the construction industry.[5] Some work in small businesses they have set up in a corner of their fields. Others walk across the fields to work for part of a day or part of a week in a neighbour's small firm. Still others have permanent part-time work in the larger enterprises around which the small sub-contractors and ancillary firms cluster. Agro-industrial workers in small firms come within the lower income range of workers. At the same time their employment is erratic. This is due in part to their agricultural responsibilities; however, their jobs are also unstable in that small and medium firms in the rural and semi-rural areas, as has been pointed out, are particularly sensitive to economic fluctuations, are the first to feel the effects of a downturn, the last to recover.

Despite the increasing sophistication of the rural environment and the interweaving of farm and factory, the factory is strongly linked to the local community and its values and attitudes. This raises a point made earlier concerning the rural factor; it is extremely difficult to separate the community from the business, to separate labour relations from social relations. This tends to maintain the acceptance of informal forms of control over labour and conservative attitudes towards unionization. The foregoing analysis of agro-industrial workers raises a question not addressed in this book, but one worthy of further research — whether the increasing incursion of industry into the village communities may ultimately break down entrenched conservatism with regard to management and labour relations.

Industrial homeworkers

In turning to industrial homeworkers, it is first relevant to look at some of the features of self-employment, which is the employment status that covers this category of non-regular workers. According to the 1979 survey of employment status (PMO 1980), of 54.7 million persons with a job, 9.5 million are self-employed. An overwhelming majority, 99.8 per cent, have jobs in non-agricultural industries and 77 per cent of these have jobs in the manufacturing industry. Two million self-employed persons employ one or more paid workers, but 6.5 million have no employees except unpaid family members. It should be noted that among the self-employed there are 900,000 'home handicraft workers', 97 per cent of whom are females. Self-employed workers engaged in cottage or traditional crafts are not officially classed as industrial homeworkers.[6] Self-employed persons such as office workers, typists, translators, interpreters, hostesses, and guides are also not officially classed as industrial homeworkers. Nevertheless, these self-employed white-collar workers, as housewives with a side job (*naishu*), tend to work under conditions similar to those experienced by industrial home-workers (Fujii, MOL, interview, 8 January 1983).

Industrial homeworkers, a particular category of workers, are engaged in manual work in industry. An industrial homeworker, as defined by the Industrial Homework Law (1970), is one to whom goods are supplied or entrusted for use in manufacture, using the supplied goods as parts, fittings, or raw materials, or the processing, transformation, repair, cleaning, sorting, packaging, or dismantling of the supplied goods. In other words, they are blue-collar workers who work at home instead of in the factory. In addition, although homeworkers normally work alone, they may have assistants who are relatives living with them.

Information concerning homeworkers and their assistants is supplied to the labour ministry through record books provided for under the law (Fujii 1982: 44−52). These record books, kept by both orderers and homeworkers, are intended to show work to be done, payment rates, dates of delivery and collection, and so on. They must be made available for labour standards inspectors located in approximately 350 inspection offices throughout the prefectures. (There are approximately 10,000 labour standard inspectors who have the authority of police officers and who report to local police stations, Fujii, MOL, interview, 8 January 1983). The law, with obligations resting mainly with the orderer, also makes provision for minimum wages and sets out standards of safety and health.

Homeworkers are usually paid on a piecework basis and payment is referred to as wages. This is paid in two ways. First, payment is for the processing done by the worker, that is, the quantity of piecework completed with materials supplied. Second, materials are sold to the homeworker and the finished work purchased by the orderer. In this case, payment is the difference in the price paid by the homeworker and the buy-back price paid by the orderer. Fujii (interview, MOL, 8 January 1983) explained that piecework rates are determined by units of production, for example, by the number of buttons attached to a shirt in an hour, the number of automobile accessories, insert boards or camera parts processed. A central Industrial Homeworkers Council, a small committee within the MOL, determines minimum wages. As of July 1981, minimum wages had been determined for 183 cases covering 30 per cent of known homeworkers (Fujii 1982: 48). There are five representatives from national trade-union centres on this council but the union centres are not necessarily connected with industries or enterprises that use homeworkers. There are similar councils located in each prefecture. In these local councils there is seldom a direct representative of homeworkers but sometimes there is one from the trade unions.

With regard to numbers of industrial homeworkers, it is difficult to obtain a clear picture. According to MOL estimates (Fujii 1982: 44–52), in 1981 there were approximately 1.4 million, 92 per cent of whom were females (Table 3.5).

Table 3.5 Number (estimated) and composition of industrial homeworkers, by sex and working pattern, at 1 October 1981

	Industrial homeworkers Total A + B		Industrial homeworkers A	Assistants B
Total	1,388,100	(100.0%)	1,289,700	98,400
Sex				
Male	108,500	(7.8%)	99,600	8,900
Female	1,279,600	(92.2%)	1,190,100	89,500
Working pattern				
Full-time	135,400	(9.8%)	97,800	37,600
Part-time	1,226,100	(88.3%)	1,168,300	57,800
Second job	26,600	(1.9%)	23,600	3,000

Source: Seminar for Public Administration Officers in Women's Problems, 1982 Fiscal Year: Outline of Lectures, Government of Japan, Tokyo, 1982.

Notes: 'Full-time' industrial homeworkers here refers to those engaged on a full-time basis and breadwinners of their households, working alone or with family members.

'Part-time' refers to those engaged on a part-time basis, predominantly housewives or older people, working to supplement their family income in addition to the main occupation of the breadwinners of the household.

'Second job' refers to those industrial homeworkers who perform their work at home as their second job in spare moments from their main line of work, working alone or with family members.

Since estimates are based on inspectors' reports and the homeworker's record books, it is acknowledged that there are significant numbers of hidden homeworkers. As noted previously, the numbers of inspectors are believed to be inadequate and many orderers and homeworkers are in default of the homework record book requirement. The ministry is continually giving 'administrative guidance' to stimulate their wider use. As at 1982–3, 60 to 70 per cent of orderers did not record or report on the homeworkers they had on contract, and record books were being used by only about 70 per cent of known homeworkers. At the same time, 50 per cent of record books sighted were only partially completed in line with MOL requirements and only about 20 per cent satisfactorily so (Fujii, MOL, interview, 8 January 1983). The estimate of 1.4 million homeworkers can be assumed, therefore, to be vastly understated.

Several features of homework employment emerge. First, rates of pay are very low, particularly for females who constitute the majority. Second, like *dekasegi*, the number of homeworkers is decreasing. Third, also like *dekasegi*, the type of work they do is changing. As shown by figures in Table 3.5, of the estimated 1.4 million homeworkers, 1.9 per cent were engaged in industrial homework as a second job, 9.8 per cent were doing homework full-time but the majority, 88.3 per cent, were doing homework part-time.

Ninety-two per cent of the known homeworkers were women and most were housewives. Among the relatively few male homeworkers, the majority were working full-time, had high skill levels and worked with good machinery and production facilities. It is not surprising that other differences between the working conditions of male and female homeworkers emerged from these MOL data. Male homeworkers averaged 9.6 hours per day, 23.6 days per month. Female workers averaged 5.9 hours per day, 20.5 days per month.

It is with regard to average hourly rates of earnings (income less necessary expenses divided by hours worked) that differences between male and female workers' conditions were most marked (Fujii 1982). The hourly rate for male homeworkers was ¥833, while for females it was ¥309. These average wages do not reveal wages for homeworkers' assistants who, according to Fujii (MOL, interview, 8 January 1983), are mainly the old parents and children of the homeworkers. Information as to their wages is not available but the rate can be assumed to be less.

Using MOL wage survey statistics for 1981 (MOL 1983) as a reference point, an index of the female wage rates is as follows: full-time regular female workers, 100; female part-timers, 76; female homeworkers, 51. However, it will be recalled that average wages for regular female workers are about 50 per cent of the male full-time regular rate (see Chapter 2). A report from Lester P. Slezak, US Labour Counsellor in Tokyo (US Report 1982) states that there were 1,210,000 female homeworkers (1981) and the femal hourly rate of pay was ¥ ($US1.36 at the then current rate of exchange). A 1982 MOL White Paper on female labour reported that 90,000 firms are officially known to be employing homeworkers (almost all these firms are sub-contractors). Press commentaries on the White Paper (*Asahi Evening News*, 15 December 1982; *Japan Times*, 25 October 1982) noted that only 36 per cent of these firms adhere to the legal minimum-wage rates, and 17 per cent owe their survival to the low rates paid to their female homeworkers.

Pressure to lift the working conditions and wages of industrial homeworkers began to have some effect in 1959 (Fujii 1982: 46). Homeworkers themselves had no direct power base to push for reforms — the pressure came from popular protest and through political lobbying. In 1959, the enactment of the Minimum Wages Law provided for a mechanism to determine minimum industrial homework wages. At that time also, the problem of occupational health and safety was highlighted by the frequent occurrence of fatal cases of benzene poisoning among home-workers engaged in the manufacture of vinyl sandals. In 1968, consultative councils set up by MOL recommended legislation that was designed to cover what were seen to be the most basic and urgent problems and in 1970 the Industrial Homework Law was passed.[7] Redress for alleged abuses is available to home-workers through provisions of the Industrial Homework Law and the Labour Standards Law (Fujii, MOL, interview, 8 January 1983). If a complaint is investigated and if it is found to be justified, the labour ministry asks the orderer to correct the situation. If the orderer fails to comply with MOL recommenda-tions, he is dealt with in one of two main ways. First, he can be fined, though as Fujii pointed out, the fine is very low. Second, the ministry can report the case to organizations the orderer belongs to, such as employers' associations or chambers of commerce — there are such organizations all over Japan. There are also Women's Employment Assistance Centres in the prefec-tures to which female homeworkers can go for help.

However, it is not surprising that complaints are few. Accord-ing to Fujii (interview, 8 January 1983), homeworkers who com-plain and whose problems are followed up usually cease getting orders, thus losing their jobs. They have no unemployment insurance. Homeworkers who lose their jobs are not included in unemployment statistics because, as will be pointed out later in this chapter, they have not been 'employed'.

As to the decline in numbers of homeworkers and changes in

types of employment, Fujii's view is that there is a tendency, particularly among female homeworkers, to move to temporary and part-time status (interview, 8 January 1983). She argues that there are several reasons for this movement. First, in order to earn an income, part-time or casual work has become an option because new household aids allow greater freedom from housework. There is less need to do piecework at home in between household chores or at night. A second and related reason is that, even though the income from temporary and part-time work is low, it is an improvement on the income attached to homework, which is among the lowest and most unpredictable experienced by any category of worker. Income from industrial homework is also highly unstable. The Labour Ministry White Paper on which this background is based, points out that industrial homework is extremely susceptible to the impact of economic change. For example, during Japan's period of high economic growth, the number of homeworkers increased from 840,000 (1965) to more than 1.8 million (1973). Numbers then began to decrease following the oil crisis (1973) and the subsequent business recession. Other factors affect the amount of homework being done.

Despite a turn to economic recovery from 1976, changes in industrial structures and production methods began to contribute to a decline in numbers of homeworkers. The decline was in part due to the drift of female workers to part-time work. There was also a significant decline in some industries where homeworkers were concentrated, notably in textiles. More importantly, the introduction of labour-saving technology since the mid-1970s generally throughout the manufacturing industry has tended to make the work of many homeworkers redundant.

The garment and textile industries still absorb the majority of homeworkers. Official figures show that 30 per cent work in the hosiery and garment industry, 20 per cent in textiles, 15 per cent in general manufacturing (dolls, artificial flowers, match boxes, fireworks), 14 per cent in electrical manufacturing and assembly (mainly coil wiring, welding, Christmas tree lamps), and the remainder work in rubber, paper, and leather goods, machinery, and tools (Fujii 1982: 49–52).

Very small firms are orderers for many of Japan's unrecorded and unknown homeworkers. First, these firms are less likely to be subject to the official inspection that would reveal the use of homeworkers. Second, very small firms, already employing a high proportion of Japan's temporaries and day labour and family members, tend to be informal and unregulated organizations and likely to be unaware of or ignore administrative guidance regarding the keeping of record books. Such an interpretation is supported, at least in the electronics industry, by research referred to earlier (Ikeda 1979, 1982). Fujii (interview, 8 January 1983) believes this is the likely situation, although official estimates, which refer to known homeworkers, show that more than 50 per cent of homeworkers do piecework for firms with between 30 and 300 regulars on staff.

Other forces are in progress in industries such as electronics where rationalization of industrial structures and the increased use of high technology affect the practice of using homeworkers. First, numbers of homeworkers tend to decline when outside contracts for low-cost piecework is incorporated into the technology of small businesses or into the firms of prime contractors/orderers. Second, homework that used to require dexterity in manual skills now calls for dexterity in technological skills. In the latter case, the work performed by homeworkers is tending to become more highly skilled and subject to high standards of quality and precision within a total production process.

Irrespective of these changes, the orderer-contract labour relationship between management and homeworkers is personal and individual. This also applies, of course, to most other relationships involving contract labour. Whereas some contract labour is performed within the firm (see Chapter 4), homeworkers work in their own homes isolated from the firm's other workers. This means that the possibility of their being in a workers' organization in the firm of the orderer is even more remote than is the case with contract labour working on the job site. If a union exists in an enterprise using homeworkers, they would not be members because they are not regular employees of the enterprise concerned. Although this feature of non-regular employment will be examined later (see Chapter 6), it should be noted at this point that unionization rates in the private sector vary from approximately 1 per cent to 12 per cent (MOL 1981a) in firms with fewer than 300 regular employees, that is in firms in which known homeworkers are frequently engaged.

There are no general unions for homeworkers, although Fujii (MOL, interview, 8 January 1983) noted one exception. In

Asakusa (Tokyo), the Federation of Industrial Homeworkers' Union (Kanai Rodo Soren) has an estimated membership of 4,000. Members of this union, mostly males, are involved in shoes and leather goods industries.[8] Apart from this exception, there are cases where individual leaders emerge from the ranks of homeworkers. These leaders attempt to negotiate informally with orderers regarding allocation and payment for work but this phenomenon occurs only infrequently (Fujii, MOL, interview, 8 January 1983).

There is one further point to be raised concerning homeworkers and organization. It was pointed out earlier (Chapter 2) that in the rural and semi-rural areas workers and management are in close social contact. Close links are clearly more likely in village communities than in urban areas, despite the increasing urbanization that may be encroaching on community ties. In this context, it could be enlightening to explore relationships between management and the clusters of homeworkers around particular industries in urban districts. For example, in the Asakusa area of Tokyo there are concentrations of non-organized female homeworkers in the shoe and leather goods branch of manufacturing and also in textiles and doll-making. The unanswered question is whether propinquity gives rise to any links between such workers that are comparable to social links in a village community. Although the question will not be pursued in this book, it is clear that industrial structures and techniques that incorporate outside unit production into the final assembled product do not bring homeworkers within the purview of the union movement. Industrial homeworkers may be given orders through an intermediary such as a labour recruiter (body-hire agent) or production foreman, or directly by management, nevertheless their relationship with management is as individuals. They are highly unlikely, in these circumstances, to be able to negotiate their wage rates, working conditions, and continuity of employment.

UNEMPLOYMENT AND THE PERIPHERAL WORKFORCE

Lack of job security is a feature of working in the small and medium environment or on a non-regular basis. From the perspective of Japan's peripheral workers, this is the reality of flexibility. The question of unemployment is particularly relevant to

Japan's non-regular workers in the peripheral workforce. The possibility of their becoming totally unemployed produces pressures to conform in their work behaviour, to be 'good' and 'loyal workers'. On the one hand, there is the possibility of non-regular employees becoming totally and completely unemployed, and on the other, there is the stronger possibility that non-regular workers will become and remain under-employed. Nor are there any guarantees for those non-regular workers who are employed in large enterprises — their job security is still tenuous because they are part of the flexible labour force in these enterprises. Even for regular employees, job security in the small and medium sector tends to be unstable, but it is at greater risk for those who work under fixed-term contracts or informal arrangements for piecework. In the large-enterprise sector, powerful unions are in a position to negotiate with management concerning continuity of employment for regular workers, but minor unions in small and medium unionized enterprises are relatively powerless to negotiate such protection. The relative power of core and peripheral unions to effectively protect their members will be examined later (Chapter 6), but it is appropriate to raise some points about job security *per se* at this juncture.

An important feature of unemployment in Japan is that the rate is low compared with that in other advanced industrial societies. It is also a feature of unemployment in Japan, as elsewhere, that official statistics serve to understate the position. It is likely that understatement is relatively higher in Japan. For example, an official of the semi-governmental agency, the Japan Institute of Labour, believes that if the criteria used in the United States were applied, the rate would be doubled (Kuwahara Yasuo, interview, 12 October 1982). According to the London *Observer*, Japan's jobless rate would be only 3 per cent if British criteria were used (cited in *Asahi Evening News*, 14 December 1982: 6). The official estimate (1982) was 2.2 per cent and unofficial estimates were as high as 6 per cent. These unofficial estimates, however, are still low by international standards in that year: Britain 12 per cent, Canada 10.9 per cent, United States 9.7 per cent, West Germany 7.5 per cent (*Japan Times*, 2 February 1983: 2).

There are no official estimates of Japan's rate of partial employment. The criteria used in estimating total unemployment, nevertheless, have implications for the problem of partial employment. The Japanese unemployment rate is based on the numbers of people who can show they have been actively seeking work. This excludes those who are alienated to the point of giving up or who avoid the indignity of surviving under official protection. More importantly, the rate is based only on those people who have been employed previously. This excludes the many housewives wishing to enter the workforce and school leavers who have never had a job. It also excludes the self-employed such as homeworkers. As has been noted, such people may be jobless, but they are not officially unemployed. More-over, unemployment must be total — people who may otherwise meet the criteria but have worked one hour a week in the survey period are not regarded as unemployed. Some or all of these criteria may be the norm in other industrialized countries. Given the particular configuration of Japan's labour-market segmentation and its large, flexible workforce, it is likely that its official rates of unemployment are particularly misleading.

Workers who meet the totally unemployed criteria are eligible for unemployment benefits but there are qualifications, more-over, these benefits are unevenly distributed. An unemployed worker under 30 years of age is entitled to 90 days' (maximum) unemployment benefits. The entitlement period is extended for older-age cohorts, until it reaches 300 days (maximum) for those over 55. The limited period of entitlement is a strong argument to dissuade younger workers from quitting and seeking other work. In this way, the prospect of unemployment imposes a control on job mobility. In addition, the prospect of becoming unemployed is a control on work behaviour. The incentive for young workers to try to avoid dismissal is high because there is a relative scarcity of 'good' job opportunities. For older workers, the incentive to avoid dismissal lies in the trend for mid-career hiring in another job to follow a downward movement. Re-employment is likely to be in jobs of a lower status and/or in smaller firms with lower wages and more arduous conditions. More so than in other countries, it is among Japan's older members of the workforce, not the young, that unemployment poses the more serious problem. A final aspect of unemploy-ment that materially affects the peripheral sector is that relevant regulations reinforce inequalities. The amount of unemploy-ment benefit is calculated on the basis of the earnings received by the totally unemployed worker on his or her last job. The implications of this are clear: the lower the income before becoming eligible for benefits, the lower the amount of benefit.

Notwithstanding these disincentives to mobility and the implied controls over work behaviour, changing jobs or quitting is not uncommon, as noted in the previous chapter.

Changing jobs or leaving the firm is frequently the result of management initiatives. These initiatives tend to be euphemistically described as relocation of staff, transfer of staff to affiliates or subsidiaries, restrictions on employment (cuts in overtime), suspension of employment other than new graduates, rationalization, and employment adjustment. Firing or dismissing workers is seldom referred to in direct terms.

It is not easy to fire standard workers (regulars hired immediately after graduation) because of a strong commitment and expectation that theirs is a full career appointment. In addition, there are provisions under the Labour Standards Law which restrain management from firing any regular employees (employees without a fixed-term contract) unless 'just cause' can be shown. Regular employees in older-age cohorts who are redundant can be 'given the tap on the shoulder', which, in idiomatic translation, means they can be encouraged to resign with a 'golden handshake'. Younger redundant workers can be loaned temporarily to an associated firm. Employment adjustment can also be achieved by 'promotion upstairs' to consultant positions, frequently on part-time status, or 'promotion sideways' to alternative occupations such as salesmen.

Outside these options, terminating full-time employment requires more indirect strategies on the part of management in order to avoid litigation under such provisions as 'unfair labour practices' (see Chapter 7). A regular worker can be made to feel sufficiently alienated to quit. By contrast, terminating non-regular workers' association with the firm is simply a matter of allowing their term of employment to expire in the case of employees (temporary and day labour) or cancelling orders in the case of workers on contract (outside pieceworkers or contract labour). Alternatively, contracts can be renegotiated for shortened periods and orders to contract labour reduced in order to minimize hours of labour expended. In smaller firms, as noted previously (Tables 2.12, 2.13 above), awareness of the instability of a company is sufficient to stimulate some workers to look for other employment. In addition, adjustment of a firm's source of labour is easily 'managed' by having a smaller ratio of regular to non-regular employees.

The advantages to management of a largely unregulated

supplementary workforce are obvious, and there are abundant anecdotes of serious abuse. One revealing perspective on management attitudes is evident in the advice given by Thomas Nevins, an executive member of the American Chamber of Commerce (Japan).[9] Nevins has written widely for foreign managers on such matters as Japan's employment practices and its labour laws, how to discharge an employee, how to manage employees by using 'strategically phrased work rules', how to reduce staff and control labour costs and, under the title 'There's no need to be stuck with a lemon forever', how to manage poor performers out of the company. Although Nevins is primarily concerned with managing the workforce in small companies, the implications of his advice to managers are clear.[10]

One focus of Nevins's advice concerns ways to discharge workers using 'strategically phrased work rules'. (Work rules are dealt with in some depth in Chapter 6.) Nevins recommends that work rules include clear-cut reasons for discharge. The inclusion of such clauses as part of a package that defines workers' expectations can protect management from court action on the grounds of unfair dismissal under the Labour Standards Law.

Nevins also advises non-Japanese management to follow the example of Japanese managers by hiring non-regular employees as temporaries on contract. (In the US, workers without a contract are considered to be 'at-will' employees. In Japan, by contrast, it is the employee with no contract that is the most protected.) He also recommends separate work rules for regular and non-regular employees. The courts have on occasion ruled to the effect that the work rules applying to regular employees (*seishain*) must be extended to cover temporary workers if those rules do not specifically exclude non-regular workers. A final point made by Nevins concerns the advantage to management in hiring relatively short-term contract labour; workers on contracts of less than one year are not only expendable, but severance pay is not obligatory. Nor is it necessary to pay bonuses. Meanwhile, to reinforce the expectations of non-regular status, if a bonus is paid it should be less than the bonus paid to a regular employee.

The foregoing illustrates some aspects of the relative insecurity of employment for non-regular workers. While a major aim of work rules is to specify employment practices (see Chapter 6), within each firm there is a range of conditions under which cause for dismissal can be stipulated. At the same time, no reason is required for the termination of contracts or the intermittent use of contract labour.

In this respect, Japan's labour laws have little or no relevance for many workers. While they ensure a degree of security for regulars, these same laws implicitly institutionalize unstable employment for non-regulars. A brief examination of the relevance of Japan's labour laws to non-regular status of employment is germane at this point.

LABOUR LAWS: REGULATED AND UNREGULATED LABOUR

The basis on which management hires a worker has clear implications within the firm with regard to first, regulation, and second, organization. Peripheral workers are largely non-unionized not only because they tend to be concentrated in the smaller-firm environment where unionization is negligible but because their non-regular employment status is a barrier to their joining any union that might exist. This has important consequences for their potential to engage in organized industrial activity such as collective bargaining and the determination of work rules. It enhances the probability of their relationships with management being personal and informal and for their conditions to be decided arbitrarily by management. It is in this context that Japan's labour laws become relevant.

The Labour Standards Law, Articles 9 and 10, defines workers and management in the following terms: the worker, irrespective of occupation, is one who is employed in enterprises or offices (hereafter enterprises) and receives wages therefrom; the employer is the owner or manager of the enterprise or any other person who acts on behalf of the owner in matters concerning the workers of the enterprise. Employer and worker can and do change legal status. For example, a worker promoted to the administration staff and a union official brought on to the board of directors[11]cease to be employees. Under the Trade Union Law, both types of promotion mean that the persons concerned must leave the firm's union. As one respondent commented (Slezak, interview, 4 March 1983), leading members of enterprise unions join their companies' boards of directors with surprising frequency. A 1981 survey of over 6,000 board members (Japan Federation of Employers' Associations 1982: 6)

101

showed that 74 per cent of the firms involved had board members with union leadership backgrounds (see Appendix 3).

Under the provisions of the Labour Standards Law (Articles 89 and 90), work rules are a crucial mechanism in the management of labour. Work rules are more than just one or two shop-soiled pages of words pinned to a firm's notice board. They are the formalized on-site committal to expectations of working conditions and work behaviour. Work rules must be agreed upon between management and employees and the opinion of the two parties documented. They have no legal force unless they are attested to by management and workers, submitted together with the documented opinion of workers' representatives and registered with the Labour Ministry. Workers are represented by a union if there is one. If there is more than one union, only the union covering the majority of workers is consulted. If there is no union, the second party conferring with management is a representative of the majority of workers in the firm to whom the rules are to apply.

In this way, work rules institutionalize working conditions at each job site. They must cover start and 'knock off' times, breaks, rest days and holidays, shift work arrangements, wage payment methods, stipulations related to wage increases, and items relevant to retirement. Clauses on non-obligatory matters must also be clearly stipulated to be enforceable. Such non-obligatory items could cover bonuses and minimum wages, training, compensation, safety and health, provisions for commendation and sanctions, and workers' responsibility for costs such as food and equipment. According to Hanami (interview, 22 December 1982), the requirements of the Labour Standards Law with respect to work rules certainly provide some basic guarantees on working conditions. Nevertheless, providing the substance of the rules conforms to the legal standards, they legitimize differentials that exist between firms by size and industry and between workers by age, sex, education, and employment status.

The Labour Standards Law (Article 89) requires only employers who continuously employ ten or more workers to draw up work rules (Rules of Employment). Thus management and workers in small firms with fewer than ten employees — about 42 per cent of the private sector workforce (see Table 2.1 above) — are exempted from a legal obligation to formalize terms of employment. In practice, some very small firms have work rules while some larger firms ignore the law. MOL officials, union members, and key officials from Japan's major union federations, interviewed during research for this study, claimed that *de facto* work rules with the power of custom are adopted in many small firms, while in some larger firms, the requirement for *de jure* work rules is ignored. Of five case studies included in the research for this book (Chapter 5), each had more than ten workers continuously employed and therefore was legally obliged to have work rules. There were unions in two firms and both had work rules. In each of the remaining three, there was no union and no work rules. In the words of the manager of one of these firms (with over forty workers), it was a case of 'everyone knows the arrangements' (Mochizuki, interview, 1 February 1983).

As noted previously, Sano (1983) makes the significant point that the Labour Standards Law offers little protection for non-full-time and non-regular workers. She argues that the law does not properly regulate working hours and other working conditions for part-timers or temporary workers. More importantly, she points out that the law sets out to control conditions only for people who are already employed — it does not concern hiring, screening, or recruiting, particularly when it comes to discrimination in these areas.

Unfortunately, statistics on the extent of use and abuse of the law with respect to work rules were not available at the time of the research for this book, but actors who were interviewed claim that abuse is common. They argue that the number of inspectors is quite inadequate for any effective monitoring of this and other provisions in the Labour Standards Law or, indeed, with respect to matters covered by other labour laws: Trade Union Law, Security of Wage Payment Law, Minimum Wages Law, Industrial Homework Law, and so on. These additional labour laws are applicable to even the smallest of firms and theoretically should be under the scrutiny of Labour Standards Inspectors.

Respondents from Sohyo (General Council of Trade Unions of Japan) pointed out that management in many small firms does not even pay minimum wages:

When we have investigated complaints, the manager says 'the firm will go bankrupt if I have to pay minimum wages'. So what can we do? The workers don't want us to take any action

103

such as reporting the case to the labour standards office — they would all lose their jobs if management was forced to raise their wages.

(Sano and Ogawa, interview, 16 November 1982)

Aspects of work rules and collective bargaining relevant to the peripheral workforce are dealt with later (Chapter 6), but at this point it should be noted that management in firms with a medium-to-large workforce favour unionization because the union takes over some problems of work organization and can maximize effective management. This, of course, is highly likely to involve management in collective agreement bargaining, which is a rigid constraint on both management and workers in the enterprise, compared with the flexibility of work rules. Work rules are the softer option and it is not difficult to adjust their terms at any time, and to do so arbitrarily in the case of informal rules in small firms.

Data on the frequency with which firms formalize work rules are not available, however, they begin to be operative in terms of the relevant law in firms with more than ten regular workers. They are most likely to exist in unionized firms, but as noted earlier, unionization rates are negligible in the small-firm sector: 0.8 per cent in firms that employ fewer than 30 regulars and virtually non-existent in smaller firms (see Chapter 6).

If work rules exist in very small and non-unionized firms it is not because work rules are a right or an obligation but rather because it is expedient (for efficient organization) or a concession (bestowed in response to custom and practice). Clearly, work rules can be a simple mechanism of control by legitimizing management prerogative. More importantly, they can serve to offset any perceived need to form a union. This applies particularly to firms where a small core of regular labour is supplemented by a flexible force of non-regular workers. In this context, it is important to note that each firm has complete autonomy with respect to the terms of work rules (or, of course, the decision to form a workers' association or a union). One significant anomaly that flows from the firm-by-firm autonomy is that in large contracting firms where several sub-contractors operate, different work rules can apply in each sub-contract firm as to conditions for its workers of various employment status (see Chapter 4). In this way, differentials in rewards and expectations 'under the one roof' are formalized, encouraging the internalization of stratification.

Firm-by-firm autonomy with respect to working conditions overlaps other features associated with the peripheral environment to entrench divisions in the workforce. The probability of the dominance of informal and unregulated job environments under arbitrary management, whether benevolent or not, is more likely to affect the peripheral segment of the workforce. This is particularly so in each of the firms in the private sector that employ fewer than ten workers — 89 per cent of all private sector firms. In this context, it is important to bear in mind that workers who tend to have less advantaged and secure employment are concentrated in these firms.

CONCLUSION: THE PERIPHERAL WORKFORCE

This chapter has offered a profile of Japan's non-regular employees and workers. As firms employ fewer numbers of workers along the peripheral continuum, non-regular workers increase in absolute numbers, and within each firm, the ratio of non-regular to regular workers increases. Non-regular workers tend to work outside institutionalized systems of rules and regulations and receive little protection from Japan's labour laws by reason of limitations in the laws' applicability and enforcement.

The profiles drawn in this and the previous chapter point to some of the significant ways in which industrial structures and employment practices in Japan affect relationships between management and peripheral workers. Relationships in the peripheral segment of the workforce reflect a quasi-unitarist approach to industrial relations whereby management exercises arbitrary control over its workers. Relationships involving the peripheral workforce tend to be informal, particularly in very small firms (almost half of Japan's privately owned establishments), where management, family members, and temporaries/ day labourers comprise the firm's workforce.

Personal and informal relationships are almost inevitable when the labour involved is a family member or a neighbouring farmer, a casual itinerant or a worker operating at home for the firm. With regard to organization, as has been pointed out, it becomes increasingly difficult to establish a union as the numbers of workers in each firm decreases. In addition, membership of an enterprise union, if one exists, is not an option for non-regular workers, primarily because of their status but also because of the mobility that non-regular status implies.[12] Workers' associations become a more frequent phenomenon as firm size decreases (see Chapter 6), but there are strong indications that these associations rarely include non-regular workers.

Conflict in the large-enterprise sector may be minimized because conditions likely to elicit protest are more prevalent in the peripheral environment. Conflict in the peripheral sector may also be minimized because in this environment, workers' expectations are lower, their means of articulation restricted, and the organization of labour weak and dispersed. This raises again the question of the extent to which relations in the elite segment of the workforce are affected by segmentation among industrial workers and the increasing powerlessness of workers along the peripheral continuum.

Insights into this broader question emerge in the following examination of some processes in industry. The main focus will be the practice of sub-contracting and changes in production techniques associated with the introduction of micro-electronics and related techniques. The central issue to be addressed will be the way these industrial processes and changes in production techniques affect the distribution of power in relations between management and peripheral labour.

NOTES

1. It should be noted that workers who were not employed at the time of the census (July) are excluded from the data. July is mid-summer, by which time people who work in industry only during the winter months as casuals and day labourers have returned to the farms and orchards. Although such workers are relatively few in number, their exclusion can affect calculations regarding ratios of regular to temporary and day-labour employees.

Other definitions related to the workforce can be misleading but in a different way. For example, calculations concerning Japan's unemployed are underestimated due to the fact that only employees can be *un*employed. Entrepreneurs, working family members, the nominally self-employed, and contract labour are included in the numbers of people with a job but to be jobless is not necessarily to be unemployed. Bankruptcies or failure to get orders, hence loss of source of income, does not mean their entry into the unemployed category. This point will be discussed further.

2. According to the editor of a national magazine of the steel fabrication industry (interview, 1 February 1983), it is standard practice for workers' associations to exclude non-regular workers, although they may include permanent on-site contract labour. The situation in one workers' association is reported below in a case study of a steel fabrication (construction) factory in Chiba Prefecture (Chapter 5). Temporaries were excluded from this association.

3. The following discussion on agro-industrial workers and industrial homeworkers is based on interviews and material gathered during meetings with officials in the Ministry of Agriculture and the Industrial Homeworkers Section of the Labour Ministry. Further material was obtained during case studies (see Chapter 5), and interviews with respondents, particularly Ikeda (25 January 1983), Eguchi (16 February 1983).

4. *Dekasegi*: those who are employed for one to twelve months, living far from home. Defined in the *57th Statistical Yearbook 1980–81*, Ministry of Agriculture, Forestry and Fisheries, Tokyo, 1982.

5. The way in which *dekasegi* are recruited is one of their few contacts with organized labour. The role of the main union concerned, Zen'ichijiro, of the *yakuza*, and of official employment centres will be dealt with in Chapter 6.

6. Craft/cottage workers are steadily decreasing in numbers. According to Fujii Kiyoko, Director, Industrial Homeworkers Division, MOL, the manufacture of *geta*, kimono and abacus, for example, has continued to decline and there are fewer people wanting to follow their father's and mother's craft occupations (interview, 8 January 1983).

7. Since 1970, six types of dangerous homework have been covered under a special section of the Workers' Compensation Act. Examples are press work and work using toxic materials such as organic solvents and lead compounds. The Labour Ministry has also been giving administrative guidance to extend workers' compensation to cover other specified types of industrial homework (Fujii, MOL, 1982: 49).

8. The union was once a Sohyo affiliate, now it is independent (see Chapter 6). In the limited time of the research for this book, it was not possible to enquire further.

9. Nevins is managing director of Technology/Management Transfer Inc. In the early 1970s Nevins worked as a researcher with the Japan Institute of Labour. This outline of advice to management is based on his articles in *Tradepia International* (1982, 12: 8–11) and a series of articles in *Japan Times* (1981).

10. Nevins's firm, according to its publications, is primarily concerned with 'the writing and strategic tightening up of work rules, formation and restructuring of compensation packages to minimize costs and maximize benefits, allowing for salary and bonus payment by permitting management to identify, document, and weed out poor performance'. The firm also 'assists clients in maintaining a union-free environment through interview and employee attitude tools' (Program, *Seminar on Management of Labour in Japan*, 26 November 1982).

11. The following case illustrates the upward movement of union officials to management. Under the headline 'Top Unionist Director of

Matsushita', *Yomiuri*, one of Japan's four major daily newspapers, reported the appointment of Takahata Keiichi as a director of the company, a first time for Matsushita. Takahata had been chairman of the union for 19 years and was a prominent figure in the labour union movement. According to the report, 'by taking this executive position at Matsushita Electric Industrial Co. Ltd, Takahata will live up to his view that a labour union of a company should take part in the company's operations' (*Yomiuri*, 20 January 1983).

12. One small union for full-time industrial homeworkers has been noted. As will be seen later, there are some unions not confined to any one enterprise, and in many of these general unions, membership criteria are more flexible.

4

Japan's sub-contract workers and contract labour

Sub-contract workers, whose working conditions and relationships with management are already affected by their employment status, the type of industry, and size of the firm for which they work, and the firm's rural or urban location, are also subject to the influence of an inherent dichotomy within the sub-contracting process: it unites the labour effort of workers in both patron and sub-contract firms while separating and isolating the teams of workers who are involved. Individual contract labour is similarly affected. This dichotomy has specific implications for sub-contract and contract labour in the peripheral workforce. It adds a further dimension to the question of control over their capacity to organize and their relationships with management. Moreover, sub-contracting is so widely used that in the aggregate its impact is felt in the wider industrial community.

Sub-contracting is, of course, not exclusive to Japan. The Japanese and the European or American experiences differ in that the practice is more extensive in Japan where large-scale enterprises are responsible for only a small part of the total process, primarily assembling unit parts and sub-assembly/processing put out to sub-contractors and contract labour (MITI 1980, in Ikeda 1982).[1] In automobile manufacture, for example, 75 per cent of car parts and 70 per cent to 80 per cent of colour television parts are made outside the major companies. This is a very high proportion compared with rates of 50 per cent in the US and 60 per cent in Britain (Ikeda 1979, 1982; see also Appendix 4: 'Comparison of automobile manufacture, Japan–US').

The jobs of most of Japan's peripheral workers are associated with sub-contracting. The general picture shows that more than 99 per cent of Japan's small and medium businesses in the private sector are involved in sub-contracting relationships and they employ more than 80 per cent of the workforce (*Japan Times*, 9 January 1983: 10). It is also important to note that the majority of sub-contract transactions in Japan are not based on tendering but are made in the form of verbal agreements (MITI, White Paper, 1981: 3).

Japan's minute and small establishments dominate the sub-contract field. Fifty per cent of these firms employ one to three people and 80 per cent employ fewer than ten, according to surveys of sub-contracting practice by MITI's Small and Medium Enterprise Agency (hereafter SMEA, Survey, 1978 and SMEA, Survey, 1979). Looking at the manufacturing and construction industries, 60 per cent and almost 100 per cent of firms respectively are sub-contractors (SMEA, Survey, 1979). These two industries (in 1979) account for 39 per cent of the total workforce and 43 per cent of its regular, temporary, and day-labour employees (PMO 1982). The largest segment of the peripheral workforce thus tends to be affected by the demands and expectations of the practice.

In the Japanese sub-contracting experience, controls over the workforce are reflected in three related processes. First, management in sub-contracting firms tend to operate as *de facto* foremen who intercede between the patron management and tiers of work teams. Although sub-contractors are responsible to the contractor, they are responsible for work and work behaviour on the job. In this way, their workers are completely separated from the management of the prime company for whom they are in effect working. They are also separated from workers directly employed by patron firms and from workers in other firms in a sub-contract network. In this context, it will be recalled that unionization is negligible in the small-firm sector, that is, in the environment where the majority operate. Should a council of unions or an umbrella labour union operate within the network to which a unionized sub-contractor belongs, such a union is self-contained and must negotiate directly with the immediate management. Thus management relations with a union are confined to each individual job site. In non-unionized, very small firms, labour relations tend to be a matter of unitary authority (see Chapter 7).

A second control within the sub-contracting relationship

concerns parent company pressure on sub-contract management. The sub-contract firm's structure, the composition of the workforce on the job and the job environment, including wages and conditions, must be geared to meet the expectations and pre-requisites of the patron enterprise. Such pressure weakens the autonomy of the sub-contractor. Theoretically, the affairs of each sub-contract firm are administered by its management; however, sub-contract workers are structurally controlled by the patron. The patron sets the pace and standard of work to be carried out by intermediary management along a sub-contracting chain of command throughout the network.

Finally, the sub-contracting relationship influences styles of worker organization and management-labour relations in sub-contract firms. As will be discussed further in this chapter, patron firms place a high priority on a policy of 'stable' labour relations within their sub-contract firms; co-operation between workers and management is expected, unionization discouraged, and militancy unacceptable. In a highly competitive arena, sub-contracting management and sub-contract workers are under pressure to respond to the controls expressed through the patron firm's policy.

Some sub-contracting firms are very stable and efficient and acknowledged for their innovative approach, dynamism, flexibility, and resilience. Such firms are frequently medium in scale with relatively high levels of automation and productivity. The larger of such firms are likely to be unionized, their core workers relatively privileged and with their job security assured. Despite the more independent status of these firms and the more privileged position of their workers, however, the expectation and the requirements of the patron company remain paramount.

Degrees of control by the patron company are modified, strengthened or filtered by a variety of factors present in the relationship, three of which will be discussed here. The first factor is the relationship between the parent and the sub-contractor — the balance of dependency between the parties to the arrangement. ('Dependency' here is used as the measure of the percentage of shipments ordered by contractors or supplied by sub-contractors or sub-sub-contractors.) The second factor is structural: whether the patron uses external or intra-firm sub-contracting and whether the sub-contractor supplies labour only, labour and materials or labour, materials, and equipment. The third and increasingly significant factor concerns production techniques: the extent to which changes in technology and production techniques in the patron firm lead to a rationalization of sub-contractors and a redeployment of labour throughout a network.

DEPENDENCY AND CONTROL

Sub-contract management autonomy over site conditions and the disposition of the firm's workers is conditioned by the degree of dependence existing in the relationship. A large enterprise may depend heavily on the sub-contracting practice as such, but it is of little concern to the patron which of a plethora of competitive firms receive contracts. This raises the point made by Friedman (1977) concerning the relative expendability of peripheral firms and of those who work in such an environment (see Chapter 1). A sub-contract relationship seldom involves a balance in intra-firm dependency. Of course, a particular firm may fill a specialized and indispensable role in a relationship, in which case the balance of interdependency approaches some parity and the expendability of the firm decreases. Otherwise, although a task, a product, or a service may be essential to an orderer, the existence of an array of suppliers and aspiring suppliers gives the patron firm a powerful advantage. MITI analysts (SMEA, Survey, 1979), argue that the relationship rests on the prime orderer's strong negotiating position and its non-negotiable requirements regarding quality, price, and speed of delivery. This places sub-contracting firms in an inferior position. They can easily be replaced if they fail to comply with the prime company's terms and to respond to its requirements.

In the sub-contracting industry, it is a buyer's market for labour effort and the process of 'buying' and 'selling' is highly stratified. Patron firms engage firms who in their turn engage more firms in a pyramid formation that commonly extends to a fourth tier — often considerably further (SMEA, Survey, 1979). At the base, the pyramid rests on minute firms or individual workers such as homeworkers and independent proprietors. Sub-contract structures also vary between industries and between branches of each industry. For example, in the manufacturing industry, the higher the degree of processing, the higher the percentage of enterprises involved in the practice (MITI, White Paper, 1982: 53). Figures in Table 4.1 indicate that more than 60 per cent of manufacturing companies place orders with sub-contractors. The percentage varies considerably between different branches of manufacturing, rising to over 80 per cent of firms in machinery and textile and clothing manufacture and over 86 per cent in the automobile branch of manufacturing (SMEA, Survey, 1979).

Table 4.1 Sub-contracting in Japan, manufacturing industry, 1976

Industry	Total number companies	Companies doing sub-contract work in industry	Number of parent companies per sub-contractor
		%	
Total	615,220	60.7	3
Foodstuffs	74,353	14.5	2
Textile industry	103,531	84.5	2
Apparel/personal effects	34,258	83.9	2
Lumber/wooden products	41,324	42.9	5
Furniture	35,728	41.2	4
Pulp and paper	15,170	44.8	5
Publishing/printing	31,488	50.8	6
Chemical industry	4,690	37.1	3
Oil and coal	241	27.0	6
Rubber industry	5,567	61.1	3
Leather	9,961	62.5	2
Ceramics	25,513	29.4	3
Iron and steel	7,663	70.4	6
Non-ferrous metals	4,769	68.4	6
Metal products	68,075	74.8	5
General machinery	51,967	82.7	4
Electrical machines	23,718	82.3	3
Transportation machines	17,501	86.2	3
Precision machines	9,149	72.4	3
Others	50,554	56.5	3

Source: '5th Basic Survey Report on State of Industry', Small and Medium Enterprise Agency, Ministry of International Trade and Industry, 1976, in 'Survey of the sub-contracting industry', Small and Medium Enterprise Agency, Ministry of International Trade and Industry, 1979.

Large contractors use an average of 67 sub-contractors but in the precision machinery segment, the average is 132 (SMEA, Survey, 1979). The Toyota Motor Corporation uses 36,400 sub-contractors (*Japan Times*, 9 January 1983: 10) and 73,000 of

Nippon Steel Corporation's 140,000 workers (1977) are sub-contract labour (data supplied by Kato, interview, 13 January 1983). Figures in Table 4.2 indicate that the smaller the sub-contractor, the greater the tendency to depend on fewer patrons. Approximately half of the firms in the survey have only one and two patrons and firms that employ fewer than 20 people are likely to have the least number of patrons. There is a trend among firms with more than one patron to diversify their outlets among three or more patrons; nevertheless they still retain a dependency on one prime orderer, that is, one main sales outlet (Ikeda 1982: 8).

The economic position of sub-contractors is poor compared with that of other small and medium enterprises. This situation, as reported by MITI's SMEA, stems from weaknesses that are common to sub-contractors and from advantages the system has for orderers. From the sub-contractors' perspective: first, they are vulnerable to business fluctuations; second, they are dependent on orders which, in turn, reduces their capacity to produce a rational manufacturing plan; third, they are frequently forced to accept non-negotiable terms from the contractors such as low prices; fourth, they have poor capital accumulation because they are predominantly small in scale; and finally, they are inhibited by low-level techniques, equipment, and technical staff (SMEA, Survey, 1979).

From the patron companies' perspective, the advantages lie in their ability to use a sub-contractor's equipment and make use of its capital, they can depend on a sub-contractor's low production costs, they can use sub-contractors as a buffer against business fluctuations and, finally, patron companies are relieved of the responsibility of labour problems involving workers in their sub-contracting firm (SMEA, Survey, 1979). In addition to these general advantages, patron companies tend to exploit their advantages by holding down the contract unit price paid to small and medium sub-contractors, while some avoid giving estimates of orders at the time of making a sub-contract arrangement (SMEA, Survey, 1979). Official references to these abuses are worded cautiously and in positive terms by noting an improvement in the percentage of sub-contractors who do receive estimates (64 per cent) and a 'strong sentiment' to discourage patrons' price control over their sub-contractors (SMEA, Survey, 1979).

The SMEA assessment above, which lists disadvantages that

Table 4.2 Number of related client enterprises, by enterprise size and industry, 1976 (%)

Enterprise size and industry	Enterprises with one patron	Enterprises with two patrons	Enterprises with three or more patrons
By enterprise size (number of employees)			
1–20	35.5	20.6	43.8
21–50	30.1	19.0	50.9
51–100	36.2	13.3	50.5
101–300	36.5	13.1	50.4
300 or more	45.2	8.9	46.0
Total	34.9	16.1	49.0
By industry			
Heavy electrical equipment	39.2	18.3	42.5
Home electrical appliances	43.5	16.3	40.2
Automobiles	25.8	14.9	59.3
Ships	44.5	18.7	36.8
Precision machines	34.8	11.6	53.6
Steel/non-ferrous metals	32.3	6.8	60.9
Metal products	26.1	10.5	63.4
Total	38.7	18.8	42.5

Source: 'Current situation in sub-contracting industry', Shoko Chukin Bank, 1977, in Ikeda Masayoshi, 1982, 'Special characteristics of and actual conditions in Japan's smaller enterprises', Tokyo, Chuo University, unpublished.

Note: The survey was conducted on 4,320 enterprises at the end of June, 1976. Replies were received from 2,179 enterprises.

are common to sub-contractors and advantages that are common to patrons, may be an over-simplification — one that fails to take account of some of the constraints at work among sub-contract firms. In some cases, fierce competition between major firms tends to restrain what could otherwise be unfettered exploitation of sub-contracted workers. Patron firms must offer attractive inducements to those sub-contractors on whom they depend for expertise in order to keep them within their network. Similarly, in order to attract and retain a skilled workforce, sub-contract firms must attempt to provide wages, benefits, site conditions, and degrees of job security that approach the standards enjoyed by regular workers in the larger patron firms.[2] Such inducements are possible if the sub-contractor is well established, productivity levels are high, and the firm performs a relatively indispensable role in the production network. The sub-contractor in these circumstances has a greater degree of independence in the sub-contract relationship. Regular employees involved in such firms work within an arrangement that is likely to be stable and relatively privileged.

Other sub-contracting firms, primarily the smaller establishments, survive precariously on a graduated scale of expendability *vis-à-vis* their patron firms. They exist in a highly competitive milieu where the patrons' pressures for cost reduction are constant, requests for delivery on an hourly basis are increasing, and the demand for improved quality has the highest priority. For example, the fraction defective in electronic parts processing has reached the amazing level where parts per million are quoted (Ikeda 1982: 15, 18). Workers in these firms, whether they are management, regular workers, or non-regular workers, participate in an unstable and inequitable relationship.[3]

Simple or unitary forms of control that tend to operate generally in small firms are rendered more complex in small sub-contract firms because of the effects of dependence. As argued by Friedman (1977), workers in such firms are peripheral on two counts. First, they work in a segment of the workforce that is expendable, particularly if they are engaged indirectly through contract work or on a non-regular basis. Second, they work in firms that are expendable. More importantly, the style of relationship between management and labour in small sub-contract firms is subject to the patron's structural, technical, and policy requirements in addition to the instability associated with the open labour market. The patron firm's control extends to the outer limits of its network, progressively involving smaller firms, increasing numbers of firms, and increasing numbers of temporary and day-labour workers relative to regular employees (see Chapter 3). Individual proprietors, family workers, and self-employed homeworkers are also involved in the patron's sphere of influence. Although they may be at the outer perimeter of the sub-contract network, they are ultimately tied to the patron firm's requirements and policies and must meet these demands or risk their continuity of contract work. In a similar way, the limited sales outlets of the smaller firms (their greater degree of dependency) accentuates their sensitivity to patron control. The way which patron enterprises structure their sub-contracted production then becomes a significant factor.

STRUCTURAL CONTROL

The constraints on sub-contract workers that stem from their firm's unequal and dependent relationship with the patron firm are reinforced or varied according to the ways in which orderers structure their sub-contract work. Sub-contract planning, co-ordination, and execution vary to some extent according to inbuilt features of a particular type of industry, the nature of the product or level of processing with which the prime orderer is concerned. These variations in sub-contract structures tend to control degrees of independence of the patron's so-called co-operating firms. Some examples illustrate this phenomenon.

Surveys of the sub-contracting practice (SMEA, Survey, 1978, 1979), show that very small firms tend to gather in highly dependent teams around larger contractors, which are themselves frequently sub-contractors to larger firms. The very small firms are often no more than self-employed workers or individual proprietors who in turn may engage casuals or day labourers. In the textile branch of the manufacturing industry, sub-contractors cluster around a wholesaler and the use of homeworkers is common (see Chapter 3). In automobile manufacturing, very small firms are highly dependent on giant enterprises and frequently use unpaid family workers. In the home appliance branch of manufacturing, small firms make and sub-assemble parts and components. In this industry more than others, there are sub-contractors with special expertise and, as noted in the surveys, with a higher level of interdependence in the sub-contract relationship.

In some industries, mainly in branches of manufacturing, service, wholesale/retail, and construction, sub-contractors are merely hiring agents to recruit casual and day labour.[4] Some sub-contract agents (*tehaishi*) receive a lump sum payment from which they pay casual workers. Others collect a commission from an orderer for providing the required labour to small offices, shops, factories, or construction sites. Another type of sub-contractor, or labour agent, is paid to recruit homeworkers, then to deliver kits for sub-assembly. This would include kits for making components for insert boards, sewing buttons or pockets on garments, or making parts of shoes or handbags. At times sub-contractors or their agents sell kits to homeworkers for the latter to make items for later repurchase, such as the materials needed to make artificial flowers or wigs, period costumes, head dresses, and bodies that will be made into festival dolls. The practice itself is not new. Casual workers in pre-industrial Japan were recruited by *oyakata* (labour bosses) and elements of the *yakuza* (organized crime). As is the case today, such workers were primarily manual, semi-skilled, and unskilled workers.

Unskilled labour remains the main target of casual recruitment but in recent years there has been a growth of a new variety of body hire firms. According to a recent report (*Japan Labor Bulletin*, February 1985: 5–8), agencies in the new 'temporary help service industry' now supply office workers, computer operators, maintenance workers, and other white-collar workers, many with high technical skills. The new industry is a response to management's strategic aim to minimize its labour force of core, regular workers. The industry's rate of growth is expected to accelerate, according to the report; estimates by those in the industry show that only about 50,000 females are working as a result of the activities of almost 100 agencies (1985) but the estimated number of persons registered on waiting lists is twice that number. MOL officials are currently (1985) drafting legislation to regulate working conditions, which are not covered under existing laws.

Within industry-related patterns of sub-contracting, there are three main strategic approaches to sub-contract labour: first, as suppliers of labour effort; second, as suppliers of labour and machinery; and third, as suppliers of labour, machinery, and materials. Patron firms structure each or all of these methods into their total production system either within the enterprise (intra-firm sub-contracting) or externally (outside or ordinary sub-contracting). External sub-contracting is commonly found in electronic machinery and automobile manufacture and the intra-firm method in steel, ship-building, and chemical and construction industries.[5]

The first method of structuring sub-contract labour is through sub-contract contractors that supply labour only and is frequently associated with intra-firm sub-contracting. 'Labour only' firms are highly dependent. Workers in these firms form a work team that operates side by side with regular and non-regular workers of the patron company and also beside work teams of other intra-firm sub-contractors. Each intra-firm sub-contractor may have a fluctuating workforce of casual and day labourers in addition to its core of regular workers. Each may also sub-sub-contract smaller firms which work under them on the site. Each intra-firm sub-contractor may engage individual contract labour or homeworkers on piece rates as adjuncts to their basic workforce.

Regular workers employed by intra-firm sub-contractors cannot join the patron company's union in the event that one exists. In theory they can form their own autonomous unit union and, under an umbrella labour union, may join with other internal unions and the union of the patron firm. Thus the structural connection between patrons and sub-contractors is not reflected in like patterns of connections between organizations of labour. By appearances, the only difference between all such workers on the site is that some wear different helmets or *hachimachi* (head bands) (Sano and Ogawa, Sohyo, interview, 16 November 1983).

Two examples of pyramid sub-contracting from the iron and steel industry (Kato 1980) illustrate intra-firm structures. The first looks at the Kimitsu Works of Nippon Steel Corporation. Within the enterprise there are 30 sub-contractors with between 10 and 1,200 employees. In the structure of one of these (500 employees), there are 7 sub-contractors with between 6 and 20 employees. One of these 7 has 4 sub-sub-sub-contractors with between 2 and 7 employees.

A second example is Nippon Kokan Steel Corporation. This enterprise has 11 intra-firm sub-contractors. One of these (1,200 employees) has 19 sub-sub-contractors, one of which (500 employees) has 4 sub-sub-sub-contractors. These 4 intra-firm sub-sub-sub-contractors employ between 2 and 10 workers and 1 (with 6 employees) has 4 contract workers. (The case studies examined in Chapter 5 further illustrate patterns of internal and external sub-contracting.) Though the workers of all the firms involved, including those of the patron firm, are operating more or less under the same roof, their working conditions, wage rates and work rules (if any) vary from firm to firm. Relations between management and labour are specific to each; for example, collective bargaining and work rules must be negotiated firm by firm.

A second method of sub-contracting is for a patron firm to place orders with firms that supply labour and machinery. This frequently occurs with external (ordinary) sub-contracting. Sub-contractors that have equipment on site to offer have a capacity to diversify their sales outlets, and therefore to operate with relatively more independence than if they were supplying labour effort only. As with all types of sub-contractors who in turn put out work, they also have a protective buffer; they can engage or dispense with their non-regular labour or reduce their sub-sub-contract orders as demand requires. Workers in external sub-contract firms, like those in intra-firm structures, relate to their own management independently on a firm-by-firm basis.

Finally, the supply of labour, machinery, and materials tends to be associated with external sub-contractors. Frequently such firms fill a specialist role. With their capacity to complete a whole component or stage of processing, they are relatively independent. They are likely to have available their own networks of smaller sub-sub-contractors inside or outside the firm.

Whether a patron firm sub-contracts labour only, labour and machinery, or labour, machinery, and materials, and whether sub-contract work is performed within or outside the prime firm, are matters of considerable importance to both management and workers. It is clear that the choices can mean greater or less efficiency and economy in total production. It is also clear that, from the perspective of sub-contract workers, the choices can represent greater or less independence of the firm for which they work, with significant outcomes for their situation. The unequal bargaining position of the sub-contract firm affects its management's ability to secure a planned production schedule and to bargain over unit prices. These factors then affect continuity of employment, levels of wages, benefits, and conditions — in management terms, sub-contract labour costs. The question of sub-contract unit price and sub-contract labour costs is central to the patron in the course of planning sub-contract strategy; but the results of negotiations, largely to the advantage of the patron, materially affect sub-contract workers' security, income, and benefits on the job. This is the bottom line of the sub-contract relationship.

For both management and labour, the labour cost question, considered in terms of outlays on wages and benefits, raises the question of differentials. It will be recalled from earlier discussion (Chapters 2 and 3) that there are many who assert a causal relationship between levels of productivity and differentials in wages and conditions. In that earlier discussion, it was pointed out that the smaller the firm, the lower the productivity, the greater the wage differentials and the greater the ratio of low wage earners to more privileged regular-status workers. The above discussion of sub-contract dependency and sub-contract strategies lends support to the second and different interpretation then proposed: that it is the less productive, less profitable work that is either channelled to the small and medium firms and their workers or put out to sub-contract firms and sub-contract labour in a 'weight off management' strategy.

Aspects of the current restructuring of Japanese industry are relevant to both interpretations, and tend to fortify the 'weight off management' interpretation. An important change associated with sub-contract strategies and restructuring is the trend for large-scale orderers to complete a whole process within the enterprise (MITI, White Paper, 1982: 56–8). This trend takes two forms. First, increasing numbers of large firms are extending their use of numerically controlled machinery. One outcome of this change is that some of the labour-intensive work previously done by less productive sub-contract labour is performed by workers in the prime company and incorporated into its internal processing. (The impact of micro-electronics and associated restructuring of the workforce is dealt with later in this chapter.) This means that the jobs of outside workers are in jeopardy. Their jobs are being performed by patron company workers so that low-priced, low-productivity labour is replaced by high-priced, high-productivity labour.

In a second trend, large firms are tending to increase their use of intra-firm sub-contracting at the expense of outside ordering (MITI, White Paper, 1982: 56–8). The prime company's increasingly sophisticated machinery can be used within the enterprises by sub-contract workers and, together with the tighter and more efficient co-ordination of work that follows, sub-contract workers' productivity improves. In this case, low-priced, low-productivity labour is replaced by low-priced, high-productivity labour.

In both situations, wage and other differentials between regular workers in the patron company and sub-contract workers outside are still maintained, including the greater expendability of the latter. In the context of the productivity versus the weight-off-management arguments, these trends in restructuring accelerate the transfer of residual and lower productivity production and services to the lower-labour-cost and labour-intensive sector. At the same time, these trends serve to retain lower-wage peripheral labour (internal sub-contract

121

labour) in the capital-intensive sector.

This suggests, particularly in the case of sub-contract labour, that differentials are associated with the rationale of industrial structures and processes rather than with the productivity of sub-contract workers. Orders placed throughout the sub-contract structure under this industrial logic usually consist of sub-assembly and sub-sub-assembly, or manufacture of a part or component for a whole process or job. Frequently orders are for large-variety small-scale tasks or job lots or for labour-intensive work. In short, orders tend to be tasks that are outside the capacity of the orderer or that are not economically viable in terms of the patron's labour costs. In this way, privately owned sub-contracting firms fill the role of managed assembly lines and are generally restricted to that role.

Sub-contractors are also likely to remain within the small-scale assembly line roles. This is particularly so for the small and minute firms on the periphery. They are primarily labour-intensive and highly dependent for survival on sub-contractual relationships. Among these firms, 'smallness', and characteristics associated with it, are endemic. Low capitalization and poor access to finance mean that they have little, if any, scope to finance the generation of higher productivity or embark on research and development (SMEA, Survey, 1979). The exceptions, of course, are sub-contractors who are financed through loans from their patrons.[6] In this case, these firms can add economic dependence to their situation. In short, there is little potential for expansion or increased independence or for improvement in their workers' conditions or employment status. As a result, there are few opportunities for upward mobility of peripheral workers, among them the many older workers for whom downward mobility by size of firm, status, and working conditions outweighs recorded upward trends. The ways in which sub-contracting is structured and rationalized are significant factors in controlling firm size and scale of operation. More importantly, structure and rationalization strategies are crucial factors in determining degrees of control over sub-contract workers' and managements' autonomy. In this way, sub-contracting strategies interact with and compound the restraints that emanate from the dependency aspects of the sub-contract practice.

It is arguable that management in the smaller sector, particularly management of sub-contracting firms, may come within the peripheral category of workers. 'Small' management is subject to control by patron management. To paraphrase Edwards (1979: 17), the patron firm has a capacity to obtain desired work behaviour from sub-contract management, conditioned by their relative strength in the sub-contract relationship. Management of the peripheral firm, while subject to the control of a patron company, nevertheless in turn exerts control over sub-contract and contract labour through the authority of managerial prerogative. This being said, a distinction between primary and peripheral management is as important in the context of a power-relations analysis as a distinction between primary and secondary regular workers. The distinction is highlighted in the following discussion of the *kanban* production process and developments in micro-electronic technology.

CONTROL BY TECHNIQUES AND TECHNOLOGY

Changes in technology within a prime company clearly affect outside suppliers. Parts and sub-let work must be compatible with increasingly sophisticated machinery introduced into the prime company. Work that is done external to the patron company must also conform to new production techniques that are designed to optimize the efficiency of technological change. The effects of changes in technology and production techniques extend to parts suppliers and sub-contractors, even to the most remote of firms and outside contract labour at the perimeter of a sub-contracting network. One widely used technique, a corollary to the introduction of micro-electronics, is Japan's *kanban* (just-in-time) system.[7] The effects of this technique on peripheral workers will be examined before addressing other problems associated with the micro-electronic revolution.

The *kanban* production technique

Kanban is basically a production technique that is incorporated into a prime company in order to control quality, cost, and efficiency. It has direct effects on parts suppliers and sub-contractors and has significant implications for their workers. Not only does the technique affect the job environment, but workers become the objects of labour-inventory control. The

123

kanban technique, initially called the Toyota production system, rationalizes labour effort — the system not only takes inventories of units of productions but takes inventories of labour. According to the report on which the following brief history and outline are based, the technique 'is widely acclaimed as a philosophy which surpasses the Taylor system (scientific management) and the Ford system (mass assembly line concept)' (*Japan Economic Journal*, 30 March 1982: 12).

The *kanban* technique was developed by Ōno Taiichi of Toyota and grew from his perception of the need to manufacture many different kinds of cars from the same assembly line. He also believed there was a need to eliminate a number of identifiable wastes from the production process: the waste of making too many units, of waiting time at the machine, of transporting units, of some processing techniques, of inventory, of motion, and of defective units. Ōno built the system on two pillars: first, the pillar of 'just-in-time', and second, the pillar of 'autonomation'. Just-in-time called for only the necessary components to arrive at the next process and for them to arrive at the right time. 'Autonomation' called for the installation of a signboard at every stage of production to warn a worker if a cut-off mechanism had halted the process because it had detected faulty production. The just-in-time aspect shortened lead time, reduced work other than processing, reduced stock inventories, provided better balance between different processes, and readily identified problem areas. Autonomation released the worker from watching the machines. One worker could attend to many machines, only having to take action when the sign indicated a problem. This vastly increased the worker's productivity. By 1962, after 10 years' trial, Ōno's technique was adopted in all Toyota plants. He then began to extend the idea to the sub-contractors, who initially visited the plants to observe the method. Ōno later sent out engineers as advisers. Now Toyota has virtually no warehouses. When sub-contracted manufacture, processing, and sub-assembly of units are complete, components are taken directly from delivery trucks to the required point in the process of final assembly. The system then calls for:

> the greatly expanded responsibilities and mutiple skills of workers as they must handle many different machines at a time. This presupposes the existence of a co-operative technique at the plant between labour and management. It

also calls for close ties and constant co-operation between Toyota and its sub-contractors.

(*Japan Economic Journal*, 30 March 1982: 12)

The system is not confined to Toyota and its several thousand sub-contractors. Variations or adaptations of the technique, illustrated in Figure 4.1, are used in other firms and in other industries. The system is also being copied and adapted outside Japan. In the Japanese experience, sub-contractors and sub-sub-contractors, already subject to the ebb and flow of orders that accompany business fluctuations, are now called upon to cope with a new imperative. Under newly introduced techniques, sub-contractors must conform to the integrated timing that is basic to *kanban* and *kanban*-style techniques. Clearly, completion of orders for components and sub-assembled units and their subsequent delivery must neatly co-ordinate with the schedules of the orderer. The *necessary* number of *necessary* units must arrive at the *necessary* time.

Co-ordination of the *kanban* production process requires predictable production or work schedules. As noted earlier, forward ordering has tended to improve and by 1979, 64 per cent of sub-contracting firms were receiving estimates at the time of making sub-contracting transactions (SMEA, Survey, 1979). The SMEA report of this trend also notes, however, that orders previously placed on a monthly delivery basis, then weekly, were now called for on daily, even hourly, estimates from the orderer. With regard to sub-contractors in the automobile and home appliance branches of manufacturing, MITI (White Paper, 1982: 56) notes that forward planning from patron firms is as high as 95 per cent. At the same time, 70 per cent or more of patron companies designate delivery periods by days, while 10 per cent require deliveries on an hourly basis. The speed-up is most noticeable among patron companies which have introduced mechatronic equipment:

The rise and fall of inventory levels of the sub-contracting small and medium enterprises along with the introduction of mechatronic equipment and the observance of delivery periods may therefore be thought of as governed principally by the degree to which patron companies plan their orders and by the degree to which the sub-contractors manage their inventories accordingly.

(MITI, White Paper, 1982: 56)

Figure 4.1 *Kanban* implementation path

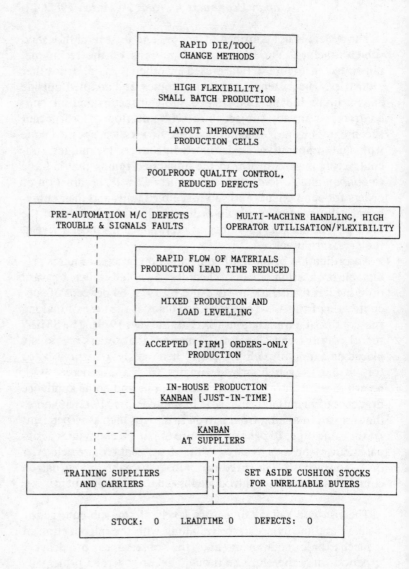

RAPID DIE/TOOL
CHANGE METHODS

HIGH FLEXIBILITY,
SMALL BATCH PRODUCTION

LAYOUT IMPROVEMENT
PRODUCTION CELLS

FOOLPROOF QUALITY CONTROL,
REDUCED DEFECTS

PRE-AUTOMATION M/C DEFECTS
TROUBLE & SIGNALS FAULTS

MULTI-MACHINE HANDLING, HIGH
OPERATOR UTILISATION/FLEXIBILITY

RAPID FLOW OF MATERIALS
PRODUCTION LEAD TIME REDUCED

MIXED PRODUCTION AND
LOAD LEVELLING

ACCEPTED [FIRM] ORDERS-ONLY
PRODUCTION

IN-HOUSE PRODUCTION
KANBAN [JUST-IN-TIME]

KANBAN
AT SUPPLIERS

TRAINING SUPPLIERS
AND CARRIERS

SET ASIDE CUSHION STOCKS
FOR UNRELIABLE BUYERS

STOCK: 0   LEADTIME 0   DEFECTS: 0

Source: Australian Financial Review, 7 March 1984.

The Toyota Motor Company, for example, under what is known as the good-will system, requires its sub-contractors to have on hand the basic minimum quantities of their specialty parts for their patron firm, so that, 'even under conditions of highly diversified parts and many different models of cars . . . the master company can get hold of necessary parts virtually at a moment's notice without having to carry any inventories of [its] own' (Kato 1982: 15).

In these circumstances, sub-contractors are obliged to carry inventories in anticipation of orders and to have an 'inventory' of labour effort — a fluctuating workforce — to meet changes in demand. The economic viability of carrying inventories on behalf of the orderer decreases as sub-contractors become smaller in scale or closer to the perimeter of a network. It is then likely that they must resort more frequently to the use of available and dispensable labour to speed up the pace of work, slow down or suspend operations as an alternative to carrying stock inventories.

Non-regular workers, their position basically destabilized as a result of their vulnerability to fluctuations in the economy, find their employment more insecure under the new Toyota version of Taylorism. Even core workers are at times under heavy pressure of work and long hours and at other times are laid off or work for reduced hours. Their monthly wages are frequently calculated on daily or even hourly rates to allow for irregular employment, though they may not be classified as casuals or day labourers. The stronger negotiating position of the orderer with regard to the unit price tends to preclude any upward adjustments of rewards to sub-contract workers that would be commensurate with harder work, added diligence, or enforced redundancy — either temporary or permanent. In addition, the prime company's dominance in the relationship with its suppliers places it in a position where it can insist on new skills that are needed to ensure quality and precision — the compatibility of units with the end product. More importantly, the patron company is also in a position to reorganize its sub-contracted work teams in keeping with its own restructuring policies without recourse to discussion beyond its immediate jurisdiction.

It is not clear to what extent *kanban* or similar technology-related techniques are currently being used or planned throughout Japanese industry. Nor is it yet clear to what extent such techniques affect Japan's workers. It *is* clear that parts suppliers and sub-contractors are a major and basic segment of Japanese industry and that technological innovation is increasing rapidly. Thus it is highly likely that techniques such as *kanban* are common practices and are likely to become more widespread. It can be expected that sub-contract workers in the peripheral workforce are among the most profoundly affected if their jobs are connected with industries moving towards extensive and increasing use of micro-electronic and numerically controlled machinery. This expectation is reinforced in the light of an examination of some of the effects of the micro-electronic revolution.

The micro-electronic revolution

By 1983 more than 14,000 programmable robots, about 60 per cent of the world's total, were in use in Japan, more than 20 per cent of small and medium size firms had introduced them and 54 per cent were hoping to do so (Tokyo Chamber of Commerce, cited in *Japan Times*, 9 January 1983: 10). The rapid spread of numerically controlled machines and micro-electronics since 1977 has been a catalyst for extensive rationalization in industry. Between 1977 and 1982, approximately 14 per cent of Japan's patron companies had restructured their sub-contract networks — 19 per cent of those who had introduced micro-electronics and 10 per cent of those who had not (MITI, White Paper, 1982: 56–7).

During this same period, sub-contractors who improved their level of technology gained greater stability in the relationship with their patron as a result of their increased capacity to ensure uniform quality, shorter lead time, faster delivery, and reduced labour costs (MITI, 1982: 56–7). At the same time, some major firms moved towards the manufacture of whole products within the enterprise and others began competing with sub-contractors for orders for processing, sub-assembly, and the production of components (*Japan Times*, 9 January 1983: 10). Research into technological innovation in the engineering industry found that:

> selection of sub-contractors is being carried out depending on a sub-contractor's capability to adapt to [the] parent

company's request for new products and/or production technologies. . . . When the current sub-contractor is incapable of
responding to their requests, parent companies pursue
changes in sub-contract ordering by development of new sub-
contractors and promotion of self-supply. This, eventually,
results in quite drastic reorganization of sub-contractors.

(*Engineering Industries of Japan*, Economic Research
Institute (KSK), no. 22, 1982: 1–21)

Under the impact of high technology, a polarization among
sub-contractors is occurring based on the degree to which they
can adapt to the change. Stricter criteria for selection of sub-
contractors have stimulated the process (SMEA, Survey, 1979).
This development is documented in surveys conducted by KSK
(1982), a MITI-sponsored economic research institute in the
engineering industry. The KSK report found that parent companies give the highest priority to strict selection of sub-
contractors but 74 per cent of those surveyed planned even
tighter selection standards (KSK, 1982).[8] Changes in the priorities that parent companies and sub-contractors perceive to be
important in the sub-contracting relationship (Table 4.3) reflect
these tighter criteria. The major criteria in selecting sub-
contractors are now: a positive approach to the development of
new processing skills, efficient management, and sufficient
technical personnel. These requirements replace, in ranked
order, the following: a sub-contractor's 'reliability supported by
long business relationship', special processing 'know-how', and
the skills of its workers.

Figures in Table 4.3 also indicate some differences between
patron and sub-contract perceptions. From the perspective of
sub-contractors, while they show an awareness of the increasing
advantage that new processing skills would bring to their
relationships with patrons, they remain insensitive to patron
firms' keener search for managerial ability. Perhaps more significantly, sub-contractors retain a belief that long-standing
business association is the primary factor holding the patron/
sub-contractor relationship together.

The priority that sub-contractors give to old loyalties is surprising in view of their own more pragmatic approach to their
sub-sub-contractors. Data elsewhere in the KSK report highlight
this dual-role standard. Thirty per cent of sub-contractors felt
that 'long-business relationships' were important in their past

Table 4.3 Reasons for sub-contract utilization by parent companies: changes in perceptions of parent companies and sub-contractors (%)

Area	Item	Parent companies		Sub-contractors	
		Past	Future	Past	Future
Technical	Special processing skills and know-how	58	51	32	28
	Positive attitude to development of new processing skills	33	69	18	30
Facility	Possession of high-performance equipment	26	45	15	13
Labour	High skills of workers	45	30	20	12
	Sufficient number of technical staff	20	55	11	16
	Stable management-labour relationship	42	50	21	17
Management	High managerial ability	30	61	5	8
	Powerful and stable financial/personal connections	22	26	16	14
	Reliability supported by long business relationship	67	45	60	33

Source: 'Progress of technological innovation in the Japanese machine industry', in *Engineering Industries in Japan*, Economic Research Institute (KSK), Japan Society for the Promotion of Machine Industry, no. 22, 1982, pp. 1–21.

relationship with their sub-sub-contractors, but only 9 per cent gave old loyalties a high priority in the future. Pragmatism was in this way accelerating down the pyramid sub-contracting structure.

According to the KSK analysis of the survey results, automation and labour-saving have become a necessity and the speed of this change in requirements has accelerated. In this context, the report argues, it is extremely difficult for small-scale rank-and-file sub-contractors to cope with this new imperative, bearing in mind their inadequate funds and technology. In addition, car manufacturers' policies for the four to five years preceding the survey had been to press for cost reduction, and now their future plans include 'requests' to their parts manufacturers and sub-contractors for a 10 per cent to 15 per cent 'cost-down' or for a lower 'break-even point'. The KSK report then points out that small enterprises situated at the bottom of the industry — actually under pressure to 'cost-down' since the oil crisis — had already taken steps such as using more part-timers or sub-sub-contractors. Irrespective of these steps, they are now being asked to reduce costs still further. An unsatisfactory response from one of the manufacturer's group means the selection of a non-group factory and non-group sub-contractors, the report concluded.

The improvement of techniques and technology has 'catch 22' aspects. MITI's argument is that because of the severity of the competitive environment, the introduction of mechatronic equipment by a sub-contractor has not necessarily led to its having a stronger position in unit price negotiations with patron companies (MITI, White Paper, 1982: 56). Ikehata (1982: 3) points out that management of a firm which introduces micro-electronics will find the parent company 'clamouring' to have the cost saving per unit passed on. Takahiro Taguchi, head of the Japan Robot Leasing Company (cited in Ikehata 1982: 6) predicts that smaller businesses that do *not* bring their technology into line will find that their products are not competitive in the prevailing market. Unpublished data covering the period 1973 to 1982 (supplied by MITI's SMEA, interview, 7 February 1983), show that prices for sub-contracted units have dropped since 1977; as at 1982, they were the lowest since the partial recovery that followed each of the oil crises of 1974 to 1975 and 1978 to 1979. These data also show that orders placed with sub-contractors have fluctuated more than unit prices after a record low late in 1973 (recession and first oil shock); as at 1982, they were at their lowest since the recession of 1977 to 1978 when the rising cost of the yen curtailed stock purchases/exports.[9] While trends in numbers of orders and unit prices (with time-lag responses) reflect the sensitivity of sub-contractors to economic conditions, overall declines in orders and unit prices reflect the intense competition among sub-contractors. Their absolute numbers have not declined over this period and their viability depends individually on their ability to conform to patron criteria.

Patron companies' criteria also demand readjustments to the workforce to conform with rationalization of the workforce as a corollary of the micro-electronic revolution. Rationalization is high on enterprise management and union agendas and has been widely researched by government ministries, employer organizations, union federations, and tripartite organizations such as the Japan Productivity Centre. According to these research reports, the micro-electronic revolution has had little effect on the size of the workforce but a considerable effect on its disposition. For example, new job categories are created and, where possible, employees who would otherwise be redundant are retained and re-educated to acquire new skills that are now needed. Other workers are kept on the payroll through job-sharing arrangements — a euphemism for temporary lay-offs — and still others are transferred to different occupations or to affiliates of the enterprise. In addition, these studies point out that the reduced intake of new employees, natural attrition and the 'tap on the shoulder' serve to ease some of the employment problems associated with the transition to higher technology.[10]

There is little doubt that these analyses are mainly applicable to Japan's large and well-established medium-size firms. In these firms, the numerous reports also agree that rationalization of the workforce has not triggered major labour unrest. In such firms, the higher frequency of unions begins to have some significance. There has been little resistance to the introduction of robots from unions within an enterprise provided the company does not reduce its workforce or guarantees job security through transfers (Ikehata 1982). With such guarantees, unions or councils of unions within an enterprise's sphere of operation are able to arrive at consensus with management. Outside that sphere, their jurisdiction ends. Through a weight-off-union mechanism, enterprise unions are relieved of responsibility to negotiate on the effects of rationalization and the micro-electronics revolution on workers in smaller sub-contract or parts firms or contract workers in the enterprise network. There are very few reports that look at the impact of technology on workers in firms with fewer than 30 regulars.

In evaluations of the impact of high technology on the work-force, claims that there has been no significant reduction in any one firm's workforce can be misleading for the following reasons. First, 'attrition' acquires a new meaning. Indirect attrition occurs with the closure of sub-contract firms, reduction of orders or cessation of contract or other non-regular labour. The core workforce of large firms remains relatively intact. Second, there comes a halt along a network in the capacity of smaller management to adopt strategies available to larger companies. It can be assumed that for small firms, including sub-contractors, it is hardly an option for management to transfer workers to another occupation. It is also highly unlikely that small firms have a plant or auxiliary, which would make transfers of personnel a possibility. In these circumstances and in response to a decreasing need for labour-intensive operations, job-sharing, temporary stand-downs, or lending and borrowing regular workers are the remaining options. As discussed earlier (Chapter 2), management in smaller firms with a low ratio of regular workers can allow short-term employment contracts merely to expire. Short of closing the business, self-employed workers on contract can be dispensed with through management prerogatives. In other words, they can be given smaller and less frequent orders (a higher degree of under-employment) or none at all.

The Japan Productivity Centre (JPC) argues that close contact at the workshop level is particularly important as an avenue to minimize the negative aspects of the micro-electronic revolution (JPC 1982a: 11). The Centre lays even greater stress on the positive role of management consultation and co-operation with unions in the enterprise. Such avenues of consultation have little relevance for sub-contracted workers in firms which are in effect the outside 'workshops' of a patron firm, and in which management and labour relations are virtually union-free (see Chapter 7). Their workers are unconnected with the patron insofar as labour problems are concerned. Despite the flow-on effect of technology-related restructuring and rationalization throughout a sub-contract network, sub-contract workers are cut off from any communication or consultation with the management of the patron enterprise or its union. They have no voice in an orderer's policy decisions that ultimately control the sub-contract world of work: to restructure production or business techniques; to install new technological equipment; to change their criteria for selecting their sub-contractors; and to rationalize their sub-contract network. If a union in a sub-contract firm exists, some upward communication is possible, but any negotiations on problems caused by restructuring by the patron company must be resolved within the patron's guidelines such as increased productivity, zero defect, speedy delivery, reduced labour costs, and lower unit prices.

In addition to such demands, industrial peace and stability have a very high priority as elements in a patron's total production system. As noted above (Table 4.3), patron companies surveyed by KSK see stable industrial relationships in sub-contracting firms as a significant and growing consideration. By contrast, figures in this data indicated that sub-contractors do not rate this factor very highly, and moreover, they expect the issue to become less important in the future. Reasons for the discrepancy are obscure, but under the manifest constraints under which sub-contracting firms operate, it is possible that smaller sub-contractors are determined to ensure stable labour-management relations and are prepared to express their confidence that they can do so. It is also possible that deeper concern expressed by patron firms indicates their determination to ensure that, under threat of discrimination, the confidence of sub-contracting management is not misplaced. In any event, the message from patron to sub-contractor is clear: keep your industrial relations in order.[11]

It is not surprising that there is little evidence of organized resistance to rationalization. Shirai argues that employers in smaller enterprises tend to have the most negative attitude to unions and the most anti-union policies:

the management of most of the firms in this sector is not separate from the ownership, as it is in the large stock corporations. Rather, in a typical case, a one-man owner-operator, or his family or relatives, maintain tight control over all company operations. Most of them take a conservative view in their industrial relations because they firmly believe that they cannot afford to do anything else, considering the environmental constraints under which they must operate: an excessively competitive market; heavy dependency on a parent company, client companies, or financial institutions; the relatively low productivity of their employees; their low profits; and the high ratio of their [labour] costs to total costs.

(Shirai 1983: 377–9)

By way of qualification, Shirai points out that management philosophies in some small enterprises are extremely democratic, more so than the attitudes of management in some larger corporations. Nevertheless he argues (confirming the KSK survey analysis) that Japanese management generally rate a non-unionized company higher than one where a union exists. Like employers in other countries, Japanese managers would like to avoid the checks to their unilateral decision-making that accompany unionization and collective bargaining:

> The employers in small and medium-sized companies are the ones who are particularly disconcerted by unions in their establishments, and they often resort to rather extreme measures in their attempts to drive them out.
>
> (Shirai 1983: 377–9)

CONCLUSION

The philosophies and policies of management in the peripheral workforce are no doubt powerful factors in determining on-site styles of industrial relations. Irrespective of whether these relations are formal or informal, the relative strength of labour in negotiation is decisively influenced by characteristics of the peripheral environment. The widespread practice of sub-contracting adds to the formidable constraints on labour organization already present in this environment. Sub-contracting segregates workers who supply the labour used in a total production strategy yet denies them a direct relationship with the orderer. It also impinges on the autonomy of a sub-contract firm's management in direct proportion to levels of the firm's dependence on its patron or patrons. Such lack of autonomy influences the sub-contractor's employment and production strategies in that they must be geared to the patron's requirements.

Sub-contract management is thus caught in an even deeper dilemma than management in independent small and medium firms. In the face of fierce competition, sub-contract firms must attempt to attract and retain a skilled workforce and, at the same time, respond to pressure from patron firms to cost-down. The necessity for a component to be compatible with the total product in quality and precision and for delivery of the right quantity just-in-time, have resulted in quite drastic restructuring of sub-contract networks. Workers involved are subject to weekly, daily or even hourly delivery demands. Patron

135

companies place a high priority on stable labour relations in their selection criteria, thereby overtly, if indirectly, managing sub-contract labour behaviour and making control of labour more stringent.

Unionization, communication, and conflict in industrial relations will be addressed in concluding chapters of this book, but by way of an introduction to these issues, the following case studies are useful. They will serve to illustrate aspects of work in the peripheral environment: working and earning in small and medium firms; ways in which non-regular workers are engaged in industry; and some of the effects on workers of the sub-contracting process and technological change. Although each case study has particular characteristics, observation and cross-reference to research material suggest that they are not exceptional.

NOTES

1. The term 'sub-contractor' will apply to sub-contractors and sub-sub-contractors throughout this book unless it is necessary to make a distinction between levels of sub-contracting.

2. It is not always the case that the prime orderer is the larger-scale firm. For example, Sord (established by three 'drop outs' from large establishments), is almost completely devoted to research and development (R&D), and 'employs' Mitsubishi as a major sub-contractor. (Charles Smith, Far East Editor, *London Financial Times*, interview, 9 February 1983.)

3. An example occurs in the case of homeworkers who are used almost exclusively by sub-contractors. As noted earlier, of 90,000 firms officially known to be employing homeworkers, 36 per cent adhere to the minimum rates laid down under provisions of the Labour Standards Law; 17 per cent owe their survival to the low rates paid to their female homeworkers (MOL surveys reported in *Asahi Evening News*, 15 May 1982 and *Japan Times*, 25 October 1982.)

4. This aspect of hiring contract labour was discussed in interviews with respondents. The practice is widespread in the Japanese experience, particularly in the construction industry (interviews: Fujii, MOL, Homeworkers' Division, 8 January 1983; Sano and Ogawa, Sohyo, 16 January 1982; Kato, Day Labourers' and Unemployed Workers' Union, 22 December 1982, 11 March 1983; Ikeda, Chuo University, 25 January 1983).

A similar form of labour hiring exists in Australia, where it is known as 'body hire', but is not so widely practised as in Japan. Overtly, it exists in centres that supply relief office staff, for example. Such workers usually receive award conditions and pay the hiring agency a commission. This form of body hire is generally accepted as a legitimate form of securing labour. Covertly, the practice is concentrated in the unskilled and semi-skilled labour force, particularly in industries such as building and construction.

Australian employers who pick up labour in this way and the workers thus employed avoid paying an intermediary, but the workers receive less than the standards laid down in industrial awards. This often involves a cash-in-hand payment thus avoiding tax but also denying workers access to other entitlements. In this latter respect, the Australian situation resembles that in Japan.

5. The following analysis of sub-contract strategy is based on the case studies researched for this book (February, 1983), discussions with respondents (Eguchi, 16 February 1983; Kato, 13 January 1983; Sano and Ogawa, Sohyo, 16 November 1983) and relevant material supplied during interviews.

6. It should be noted that many major enterprises own part or all of the capital of their parts suppliers, affiliates or subsidiaries. It is likely that groups of sub-contracting networks are in this way linked to one another and to the primary enterprise, either directly or indirectly. These links could have relevance for the plethora of work teams being co-ordinated through intra-industry economic connections in the context of the organization of work. Economic links, however, and the implications of patron investment in sub-contract firms, are matters beyond the scope of this book.

7. For a description of the *kanban* system, see Ōno Taiichi, *Toyota Production System*, Diamond Company, Tokyo, 1978. The *Australian Financial Review* (7 March 1984) reports that the Japanese technique is credited with the ability to double or treble productivity and reduce turnover time by half.

According to *Australian National Times* (21–7 October 1983: 38, 40), Bill Dix, head of the Ford Motor Company in Australia, has introduced the *kanban* system into the company. This is in line with his strategies for rationalization, streamlining, and corporate efficiency. The yards around Ford headquarters at Broadmeadows, Victoria, once full of cars, are now empty. In the words of one of his associates in the company:

[Dix] brought back from Tokyo what the Japanese call the *kanban* system. . . . Instead of building up stocks, your components are delivered straight to the production line. Of course, you need a well-oiled system for it to work.

(*Australian National Times*, 21–7 October 1983: 38, 40)

8. The surveys covered 750 establishments: 152 parent companies and 598 sub-contractors. The term 'selectivity' used in the survey referred primarily to the emphasis given by respondents to unitization of parts ordered (over 50 per cent), centralization of ordering (40 per cent), and promotion of self-supply (almost 40 per cent) (KSK 1982).

9. Data on peaks and lows were supplied to SMEA, MITI, by the Economic Planning Agency's Statistical Survey of Business Conditions.

10. Such steps do not absorb the full shock of redundancy. The increase in unemployment (in 1982 the level was the highest in 28 years) is generally attributed to the lingering recession and the effect of the technological revolution. One-third of 3,400 manufacturing, wholesale, and retail firms employing more than 30 workers indicated that they intended to cut hours and personnel because of reduced production, increased labour costs, and the implementation of labour-saving and rationalization policies (MOL, reported in *Japan Times*, 7 March 1984). The intended cutbacks were notably higher in large manufacturing firms than in wholesale and retail. So-called 'adjustment' plans included reduced overtime and the suspension of new hiring and, with regard to excess workers, their reassignment or loan to other firms.

11. The pressure to conform to an orderer's criteria is reminiscent of aspects of the Australia/Japan trade relationship. Japanese steel mills, backed by the Japanese government, argue for diversification of supply sources for their coal imports, that Australia's industrial relations performance is less than satisfactory. For their part, Australian mining companies, backed by the Australian government, call for Australian union moderation, otherwise Japan may reduce its Australian quota with a consequent loss of Australian jobs (Chalmers 1980).

There is a point at which the analogy falls short. The number of coal exporting countries is small and their prices relatively high, therefore Australia, as an established and cheaper supplier, has some strength in negotiations. In Japan, the number of potential 'suppliers' — subcontractors — is legion and each is extremely vulnerable to criteria control such as 'stable industrial relations'.

5

Case studies

The first part of this chapter consists of five case studies in the manufacturing and construction industries.[1] Two firms are near Tokyo, in the industrial areas of Chiba and Saitama Prefectures; and three are in rural areas, in Nagano Prefecture. Four of the case studies are medium and small firms. The fifth is a large enterprise — the patron of one of the small rural firms. The second section of this chapter will consider the outcomes of the industrial structures and processes operating in these five firms with regard to on-site management and labour relations, labour organization and the dichotomy of core and peripheral industrial relations.

CASE 1: MOCHIZUKI STEEL FABRICATION LIMITED[2]

Mochizuki Steel is a medium-size construction enterprise in Chiba Prefecture. Its work yard is situated not far from Narita airport and the now famous Japanese Disneyland. Less well known is that one of Japan's scattered colonies of wild monkeys lives in the south of the prefecture. Chiba's wild monkeys still raid the small farms in the fertile valleys and plains and attract visitors such as 'monkey watchers', wild-life protectionists, researchers, and national park rangers. These visitors must be prepared to clamber up steep and often muddy mountain trails, thrash through thick forests, rest in abandoned and isolated farmhouses, or shelter from the rain in the disused caves of the charcoal burners of pre-industrial Japan. In sharp contrast to the mountains and farms, large areas of Chiba Prefecture are heavily industrialized, and host numerous small and medium firms, many in the steel fabrication branch of the construction industry.

Steel fabrication is a comparatively new industry. It developed from timber construction with its long pre-war history in areas such as bridge building. The growth of industries such as iron and steel, ship building, automobile, and electronic equipment gave impetus to its development. The industry is co-ordinated by three national federations. One caters for large companies and has 70 to 80 enterprises as members and 3,200 medium-scale firms belong to the second. Ninety per cent of fabrication firms are small or very small, and the third national federation serves these firms. Turnover of members of the three federations is frequent, mainly among the smaller firms. For example, in 1983, bankruptcies exceeded new entries, with a 2 per cent reduction in the number of member firms since 1980 to 1981.

The company

Mochizuki Steel Fabrications Limited, which assembles and erects steel girders, was established on its present site 20 years ago. It is both a sub-contracting firm and a contractor, and its structure follows Japan's pyramid sub-contracting pattern. As a sub-contracting firm, Mochizuki Steel usually receives orders from a client or a master builder and is in the second or third layer of their networks.[3] Mochizuki Steel does sub-contract work for about 60 clients each year, about 40 of whom place repeat orders. Although this suggests a high level of diversification, 70 per cent of the firm's output flows to only 7 or 8 major regular clients.

The company's independence *vis-à-vis* its patrons varies. For much of its output, the company has several advantages. It generally supplies materials for a job, sub-assembly is done at the firm's work yards, and assembly is completed on the construction site. This tends to give the firm control of the job through to the final stage. However, the company is at a disadvantage when a job order comes from one of its large-scale clients. In this case, Mochizuki usually supplies only equipment and the manpower of its own personnel, its intra-firm sub-contract workers and, at times, its outside sub-contract labour. This decreases the company's independence. Management at

Mochizuki acknowledges its weaker position in its relationship with large orderers. According to the president, Mochizuki's major orderers used to demand 5 per cent reduction in quotes on big jobs prior to the recession of the early 1980s, but 'now they are demanding between 10 and 15 per cent reduction and they have the strength to enforce these demands'.

As a contractor, Mochizuki Steel has a sub-sub-contract network. Intra-firm sub-contract firms are constantly used in this structure but there are also links with outside firms.[4] Each of the company's 5 or 6 external sub-contractors is very small, employing 3 to 4 people. They function as reserves to be called on in the event of a very large order from one of the major master builders or clients or in excessively busy periods. These outside sub-sub-contract firms have other orderers and exist only partly on Mochizuki's intermittent orders. In this way, the autonomy of the external sub-contract workforce is likely to be greater than that of the company's regular intra-firm sub-contract labour, who can expect permanent work but are entirely dependent on the company.

Mochizuki's intra-firm network consists of 12 small sub-sub-contractors. The structure is complex, although at first sight the on-site organization of the workforce appears to be simple. A copy of the firm's 1982 statistical return (to MOL) shows that the company declared itself as medium in size, with 7 people in administration and 37 regular employees. More precisely, however, the total complement of 44 people have jobs with the 13 firms on the site, made up of Mochizuki Steel itself (the patron) and 12 independently owned firms. The 44 people on the workforce are distributed among these firms (Table 5.1). The patron company is responsible for planning and administration, while the small on-site firms and their employees undertake the manual execution of orders from Mochizuki's clients. At the time of this case study, 1983, 2 of these firms were employing a total of 5 temporary workers. These temporaries were not included in the regular workforce total of 44, nor are any of the casual workers who occasionally go on to the payrolls. When needed, casuals are often borrowed from other firms nearby under a loose reciprocal basis whereby excess temporary workers can be exchanged. On rare occasions, for example if business is particularly slack, some of the proprietors of the 12 internal sub-contract firms look for outside work. Notwithstanding such occasional fluctuations in the basic workforce, the 12 firms

Table 5.1 Mochizuki Steel Fabrications Limited, distribution of workforce

Firm	People with a job	Number of people with a job	Total
Mochizuki Steel	owner, consultant, management	7	
	engineering, office staff	13	
	total of patron workforce		20
Internal sub-contractors			
Cutting	proprietor	1	
	employees	2	3
Sub-assembly	proprietor	1	
	employees	5	6
Assembly	proprietor	1	
	employees	5	6
Parts	proprietors	3	3
Painting	proprietors	2	2
Welding	proprietors	2	2
Load/deliver	proprietors	2	2
	total of sub-contract workforce		24
Total workforce			44

Source: Case Study, Mochizuki Steel Fabrications Limited, 1 February 1983.

attached to Mochizuki Steel have a permanent relationship with their patron company.

With regard to wages and conditions, each section proprietor negotiates the price for the job to be done with Mochizuki management, usually the president. Occasionally there is disagreement as to terms, in which case negotiations may be prolonged. The final agreed price becomes the quote for the job, which is then executed under a centrally planned flow chart. Top management, again usually the president, determines conditions of work such as hours, holidays, bonus levels, and any increase in the rates on which quotes are based. Bonuses for all proprietors and employees are distributed by the patron company. In this sense, the people on the site work for Mochizuki Steel. Under this umbrella-management of labour, proprietors of the sections that themselves employ labour (cutting, sub-assembly, and assembly sections) are responsible for the control of their own workers: hiring and firing, training, organizing workloads, and paying wages from the price of the job. Similarly, the section proprietors (often in the welding and loading and delivery sections) are responsible for their own casuals and temporaries in the Mochizuki yard.

Wage rates for employees in sub-contract firms are based on technical skills, though older workers tend to be on higher wages. The workforce is generally in the older age bracket, with the majority being between 40 and 50 years. Employees' monthly wages at the time of the case study varied between ¥200,000 and ¥250,000. This wage was similar to the national average of earnings (including bonuses) for the construction industry (all sizes of establishments) but was considerably more than the average, ¥170,000, earned by workers in construction firms of a similar size, that is, employing between 1 and 4 regulars (PMO 1982b). Over and above this income, all workers at Mochizuki, whether directly or indirectly employed, receive bi-annual bonuses. These are based on workers' remuneration, be it income or wage, and normally equal to 1.5 months' income according to the previous year's average. The workers' expectations regarding bonuses and the strong pressure these expectations had for management were explained by the proprietor of the firm's assembly section:

'The amount of bonuses, as with wage increases, depends on our President, but if business is poor, even in the red, the enterprise must pay this bonus. The President needs the confidence of the workers. He is well aware of this discipline.'

Japan's spring labour offensive, *shunto*, has an indirect effect on wage increases within the company. In January each year, the president determines the rate of increase, which he set at 7 per cent in 1982. This was higher than the rate granted to many small to medium firms and close to the national average. In 1982–3, as a result of the somewhat depressed state of the industry, the president had to reconsider the situation:

'I decided that there would be no increase for management and senior workers. But I am concerned about the situation of younger workers and lower-income earners — there will be a small increase for them.'

With regard to other conditions in the yard, workers do an eight-hour day, a six-day week. They do not have days off on festival public holidays. These practices, said respondents, are common in the construction industry. The president outlined the firm's practice of giving the men eight days' paid annual leave plus one day for each year of service. 'This leave,' he said, 'is made up of five days for New Year [31 December to 4 January], but I leave the decision to them whether they take the other three days, which are due in the summer break'. Some do not take this summer leave.

The employment and training of apprentices at Mochizuki Steel is worth noting. Mostly high-school graduates, they are engaged by the sub-contracting firm proprietors. They work and train on the job to learn particular skills (normally for three years). At the end of their apprenticeships they are cutters or welders, and so on, according to which firm apprentices them. In Mochizuki Steel, as elsewhere in Japan, demarcation is not an issue although trade skills are specific.

Labour turnover in the firm reflects a general characteristic of the construction industry. Workers are constantly changing jobs, nevertheless a few have remained with this firm for many years. In the assembly section the average length of service is seven to eight years, somewhat longer than the national average for construction firms. Retirement is customarily at age 60, but given the risks attached to some aspects of the work (such as assembling girders on high-rise construction sites), older workers are unsuitable for some tasks. Such workers are transferred to other work or retired at an earlier age.

There are no official work rules at Mochizuki Steel.[5] As the firm's president explained, 'work rules are not needed because all the workers are fully aware of the customary routine'. This statement implicitly expresses three features of management's relations with the workers in the company: first, management's unquestioned prerogative over working conditions; second, management's assumption that the internal sub-contractors and their workers belong to the company; and third, management's expectation that workers on the site tacitly accept the work practices. In this environment, there has never been a routine or requested inspection by the Labour Standards Bureau. Bearing in mind that working conditions are not regulated, the company has a long history of industrial peace, and respondents were agreed that management and labour relations were excellent.

Mochizuki Limited Workers' Association[6]

Although there has never been a union at Mochizuki Steel, there is an organization among the contract workers through which liaison with management is maintained. The *koyukai*, Mochizuki Limited Workers' Association, covers all 24 blue-collar workers, the body of men that includes the proprietors of the small sub-contracting firms and the men they regularly employ. Because some are on wages and others on income from job contracts, membership fees (of 1 per cent) are calculated on the amount of 'remuneration'. Membership of the association is not open to any of Mochizuki Steel's white-collar staff (management, engineers, draftsmen, and office workers). Nor is it open to casuals or temporaries who are engaged from time to time by the internal sub-contractors. The organization and operation of the company's workers' association is usual for firms of this size and in this industry, according to Mochizuki respondents, and confirmed by questions put to a non-member of the firm — the editor of the steel fabrication industry journal.

Members of the *koyukai* negotiate with management through the association chairman, the owner/proprietor of the assembly section. He explained the association's rules, aims, and activities, which are, as set out in the handbook: to improve the welfare of members, co-operate with the company, promote technological education, hold study meetings, take part in study trips to similar steel fabrication firms, organize outings and social functions, and 'develop comradeship'. The handbook gives no indication that Mochizuki's workers' association has any external connection or communication with other workers' associations or organizations such as unions. The workers' association is only involved with Mochizuki Steel.

Mochizuki Steel's affiliations

In contrast to the isolation of the workers' association, management is actively associated with owner and management groups. The firm is affiliated with the prefectural branches of Japan's Employers' Federation and Chamber of Commerce and an organization of the steel fabrication industry noted previously — the National Federation of Medium-Sized Steel Fabrication Enterprises. In this industry federation, Mochizuki Limited is treated as a medium-size enterprise.

Affiliations such as these are to be expected. The activities of senior management, however, are less conventional. Mochizuki Steel's owner/president and senior managers play leading and active roles in the National Association of Managers of Small and Medium Enterprises.[7] The association is overtly political. Its philosophy holds that management prerogative is inviolable but at the same time it vigorously encourages management of small and medium firms to accept responsibility for raising the standards under which their employees work. The association advocates the promotion of 'worker participation and democracy' and on-site *esprit de corps*. Its main aims are not only to improve workers' conditions on the job but to alleviate the serious situation its members believe to be facing small and medium sector firms. It is constantly engaged in campaigning and lobbying to check the domination of the small and medium sector by large contractors. The national body covers all branches of industry, including manufacturing, in which firms in the following four cases operate.

CASE 2: DAITOKOGYO MANUFACTURING COMPANY

The Daitokogyo Company factory, Saitama Prefecture, is not far from Oji railway station on Tokyo's busy central line but far enough to warrant a ride in the city's last remaining tram service, a relic of the district's pre-war industrial development. The company produces gear pumps which attract a significant level of capital investment by the chemical industry. The high-precision pumps are designed for particular needs, primarily for chemical liquids of high viscosity pumped at high pressure.

The company[8]

Daitokogyo Company Limited is a medium-size enterprise. It was established in 1935 and today consists of two sections. The main workshop is located in Oji and there is a small section about one hour's travel away in Omiya. The company directly employs about 80 people at the Oji workshop and a further 20 at the Omiya section. In addition to the designers, tradesmen, and sales staff, there are 2 or 3 students working part-time (*arubaito*),

7 female office clerks and 1 casual worker — an elderly woman — in the paint shop. There is little staff turnover (average length of service is about 15 years) but mobility is very high in a small percentage of the workforce. The smaller shop in Omiya makes standard gear pumps while orders to specifications for small lots and for large pumps (70 per cent of orders) are manufactured in the main Oji factory. As a result of its small-lot and large-variety operation, mass production is limited. There are some multi-purpose lathes on the shop floor and production is predominantly labour-intensive, based on one man, one lathe.

Daitokogyo Company's specialized technology and high levels of accuracy have two outcomes. First, there is no serious competition from large companies that do not want to produce small lots and who need the company's expertise. Second, the company is at a disadvantage in that production is so specialized it cannot diversify or become capital-intensive. According to Mr Inoue, junior owner and president of Daitokogyo:

'This firm is highly labour-intensive. Wage costs are high, productivity per man is not so good. We need many "indirect" employees such as draftsmen and inspectors (each new pump must be individually inspected). About a quarter of our staff are people not directly working on the pumps themselves, including 17 salesmen. We also need many people on deliveries. We have a lot of sub-contractors making parts.'

Daitokogyo is the patron firm of a network of almost 50 sub-contractors. Many of the relationships with these firms go back to 1935 when the patron company was established by Inoue's father. Inoue has now organized a co-operative group of about 30 of these firms, *Kyoryoku kaisha*, but there is a permanent work relationship with almost all of the remaining sub-contractors. The numbers of workers in each varies. Some are very small with only 5 people, others employ up to 50. Most of these sub-contractors have other clients. The highest rate at which any sub-contractor depends on Daitokogyo Company is about 50 per cent and in some firms the percentage is very small. In the president's experience, sub-contractors' dependency on the main company is generally not high in Tokyo. He approves of this situation:

'In our company, we don't want our sub-contractors to

concentrate all their business into one channel because if we go bankrupt we don't want to take others with us. Unfortunately, small businesses fluctuate and their fortunes are tied up with ours.'

The president is clearly aware of patron responsibility but his further comments suggest that his firm's approach to long-standing sub-contract relationships is also pragmatic:[9]

Q *Your 50 sub-contractors . . . do they see your company as the 'parent company'?*

A Yes. We have a friendly intimate relationship, but we are not so close economically. They are diversified with respect to numbers of clients — about 50/50. For example, we may have a long association with a sub-contractor, but quality and reliable delivery are important.

Q *If quality and delivery standards were in question, would you change your sub-contractor?*

A I maintain economic discipline, but I ask a sub-contractor with whom we have a close relationship to please improve. If there is no improvement, then we would go to a cheaper sub-contractor . . . provided the quality is the same. Of two companies with equal standards in quality and price, we would choose a firm with an old association — we would give an old friend a chance to reduce his price if the other made a competitive offer. We have to survive.

The company-union relationship

Management's pragmatic approach to the company's sub-contractors is also evident in management and labour relations in the Daitokogyo firm. There is a union in the enterprise and although the relationship between management and union is co-operative, there is no loss of management and union role identification. Survival of the company emerged as a key theme in President Inoue's perception of this relationship. The Daitokogyo Company Employees' Union, established in 1957, is the only union in the enterprise. (According to Inoue, a one-union situation is usual in firms of a similar size.) His records show that of the total regular workforce of 100, 75 are members of the union. The 25 people not in the union are top and middle management and some workers who do not want to join.

Between 1957 and 1972 to 1973 there had been a great deal of management and labour conflict, and in 1972 to 1973 the level was particularly high.[10] It was at this stage that management and labour attitudes underwent a change and since 1973 there has been no serious industrial trouble such as strikes in the company. Inoue argued there were two main reasons for this dramatic change in his firm's industrial relations. The first arose out of the poor economic conditions that followed the first oil shock. This affected management and workers generally, according to the company president:

'If we have industrial conflict, the company may fail, so workers don't want conflict. In some small companies such as ours, almost all the workers can see their firm's prospects, can predict the outcome of disputes . . . they don't make irresponsible demands if the enterprise is small.'

A second and more basic reason for the improvement in management and labour relations at Daitokogyo was the change in the president's policies and attitudes to the company's workers. President Inoue explained how, a decade ago, this change occurred.

'I wanted good relations with our workers and I believed I needed their confidence, not their enmity. I opened the company's books, disclosed our accounts. Our workers began to have more confidence and trust. During the previous period of conflict and strikes, from 1957 until then, the early 1970s, the people from Nikkeiren [National Federation of Employers] told me workers are the enemy. But I doubted this. I thought: workers want work and want to work hard, so they are not the enemy. If we want prosperity, president and workers must work together — united. Management must co-operate with workers.

The senior owner, my father, agreed to a proposed change in the wage structure. Until 1972 to 1973, our workers were paid on a daily rate — many other small enterprises still pay day rates — but here, since about 1973, they are on a monthly salary. My father also agreed to the idea of consultation. I requested top management to give me the responsibility for industrial relations. They were only too happy to pass on the problem! My father needed some persuasion before he could trust me to try a different approach to labour — older people's ideas of labour problems are quite different from those of the younger generation. Now we regularly disclose our situation, we have conferences — consultation every month. I cannot lie to the workers — they know the firm's affairs, see the state of the business for themselves. There is trust. Now relationships are much smoother, work goes better.'

The workers responded to these changes and, according to Inoue, where there had previously been opposition there was now co-operation. Inoue then outlined the usual methods of dealing with Daitokogyo workers' problems. Within the company's union, decisions are made after *shunto* regarding demands on levels of bonuses and wage increases. Then these demands, and other problems such as working conditions, safety, and terms of employment, are talked over at meetings and monthly consultations. From the perspective of the union in the enterprise, survival of the Daitokogyo Company also emerges as a major concern. There are three participants at these meetings: the president representing top management, representatives from middle management, and the union.

Union of Daitokogyo Company Employees[11]

The union president, Mr Sato, was formerly a tradesman with the Daitokogyo Company and is now one of its 17 salesmen. He works full-time and can only engage in union activities outside working hours. If he has some union responsibility to attend a meeting away from the Oji factory in working hours, he may do so without loss of pay. However, there are limits on the time he is allowed to spend away from his job and if he exceeds these limits he loses wages. Sato told his history with the company and the union in remarkably few words:

'I work full-time for this company. I've been here for 19 years. Since 1982, I've been president of the Daitokogyo Company Employees' Union — I was secretary for 10 years before that. There was an election last year when the former president stepped down after 20 years. There were nearly 20 candidates for the union presidency.'

This small autonomous union is a unit union of the national Metal Industries Union (Zen'kin) and is affiliated to Sohyo, the national union federation. (Unit unions and the roles of national unions and union federations are dealt with in Chapters 6 and 7.) The union of Daitokogyo employees meets on the initiative of the union executive or as required by members, always in the lunch hour or after work. Meetings occur more frequently, three or four times a week, in the period leading up to and immediately following *shunto* to consider the debates between Japan's major union and employer federations, and the implications of the national manoeuvres for the situation in the Daitokogyo works. One of Sato's jobs as union president is to see that members are kept informed of Sohyo research and activities, particular campaigns and rallies, or demonstrations such as the joint struggles leading up to *shunto*. After the decisions on base-up wage increases have been reached at national level, the Daitokogyo union's domestic demands will be determined and put to management. Wages, bonuses, and working conditions at the enterprise's two workshops are naturally of concern to members of the Daitokogyo Company Union. These are the principal matters that will be raised in consultation meetings with top and middle management, although social and political matters are sometimes raised.

Sato's special problem was a personal matter, but one with implications for his union activities. Like many other Daitokogyo workers, he lived far from the factory. Up to one and a half hours morning and night were spent commuting. This caused difficulties for him in coping with his work, his after-hours union responsibilities, and his home life. Of more general concern to the union were staffing levels in the firm. According to Sato, 'when a worker retires, management does not want to fill the vacancy with new staff, and as a result, the work load for regular staff becomes heavier'. Union members were discussing this issue and trying to negotiate on the problem.

A further and major worry for all Daitokogyo Company workers was related to their prospects at the enterprise. In the early 1980s, Japan was experiencing a prolonged business recession but, more importantly, extensive rationalization was taking place in industry generally. The effect on the Daitokogyo company was of immediate concern to the workers. The union president, Sato, posed the problem as follows.

'There are not many job opportunities here, less than before, and they are decreasing. The number of plants needing our product is decreasing because oil and chemical plants using gear pumps are moving overseas, for example to Korea. Customers are getting fewer. Sumitomo has closed down a big plant in Shikoku on the grounds that costs are too high.'

Given these pressing problems, Sato nevertheless believes that the employment structure in his enterprise has improved since he started work there 19 years ago. Occupations are now more flexible, so that a worker can change his job. In Sato's view, 'this is a good thing, because workers in small firms need wide skills'. He confirmed the company president's view of relations between his union and management. During the term of office of the union's previous president, good relations were established and now the responsibilities attached to being a union president were less difficult:

'Now there are no secrets — everything in the company is open. Also, workers can decide their own goals and they work spontaneously. Workers think they should have some responsibility for the firm, and management has met this difficulty. Now workers want the business to succeed.'

The Daitokogyo union news bulletin

The social, political, and industrial role of the union is reflected in its weekly news bulletin. This roneoed publication, liberally decorated with comic line sketches, is circulated throughout the company's two workshops. A selection of items in two issues (published in the two weeks prior to the interview with Sato) is summarized below:

- Sohyo's progress regarding forthcoming *shunto* demands
- A schedule of study for union members: 'How to struggle'
- A progress report from Daitokogyo Company Research Centre
- Article: 'It has been one year since the last dispute . . . keep struggling against exploitation of workers' [referring to the previous year's base-up negotiations]

- List of demands: proposals for submission to Daitokogyo management
- Announcements: bowls competition details and meeting of volleyball group
- Article: 'Despite US and USSR confrontation and the dangers of nuclear war, let's protect workers' living standards'
- Two game plays: *go* and *shogi*

Two other articles in the union newsletter are particularly interesting. The first gives comprehensive details about a new intake at Daitokogyo Company. The report gives his age, birthplace, address, when his parents died, his education standard (junior high school), hobby (fishing), his last job (Hitachi for 8 years, then at Towa Company for 5 years), and a résumé of his wages, hours, and working conditions on his most recent job. Such a detailed report about a new employee in the workshop, together with other items about social activities and sport in the firm, suggests a high level of communication among the company's workforce. The new intake was quoted:

'I've never smoked, but I can drink as much as anyone, particularly *sake*. . . . Compared with my last job, this company is much more go-ahead. I came here because I wanted to get on. I want to learn my job and work hard.'

The second article concerns news of the establishment of a small union that had recently been formed by workers in a timber company. The new union came into being as a result of the firm's serious economic difficulties, and its members had started negotiations with the company regarding continuity of the company and guaranteed employment for its workers. This report is one of the more political items in the union newsletters. There are intimations of workers' control in the new union's initiative to keep the enterprise viable and ensure job stability. It is also a pointer to one of the ways in which small unions come into being through an immediate and localized problem, in this case a business and jobs under threat. The inclusion of this item in the newsletter shows an interest in other workers' problems. It also indicates a line of communication with small unions beyond the immediate boundaries of Daitokogyo, and in addition to national union links already noted.

153

Despite the militancy of terms used in many of the items in the union news bulletins, their content does not show a conflictual relationship within Daitokogyo. The union attitude is consistent with a style of industrial relations apparently acceptable to both the company management and its workers. It is probable that Daitokogyo management's sympathetic and liberal attitude and initiatives are major factors in the firm's recent industrial relations accord. For management, relative industrial peace has gone far in sustaining the success of the business. From the perspective of the Daitokogyo workers, a perceived need to retain their jobs may also be a major ingredient in this accord and accommodation.

CASE 3: INA SANKYO COMPANY LIMITED[12]

Moving from the industrial areas of Chiba and Saitama, the following three case studies look at industrial workshops in Japan's Ina Valley, Nagano Prefecture. Ina Valley is about 200 kilometres north-west of Tokyo in the Central Alps. It is a centre for tourism and ski sports and the area is renowned for its production of rice, apples, pears, and vegetables. Industry is not new to the area. Once a centre of Japan's sericulture, factories were set up during the Pacific War to make communication equipment for the Japanese army and, by 1983, the Ina Valley area was one of Japan's major centres for the production of electronic and precision machinery. More than 1,500 large electronic and electrical appliance plants operate in the prefecture and each is surrounded by constellations of small sub-contract firms that supply parts or work on sub-assembly for larger firms and by small and minute firms that supply ancillary services (Eguchi, interview, 16 February 1983; Ikeda, 1979; Ikeda, interview, 25 January 1983).

The company

Ina Sankyo is part of a large national and transnational enterprise. It comes within the Sankyo group and is a subsidiary of Sankyo Seiki. Ina Sankyo is a distributor and supplier to Sony, Hitachi, JVC, Mitsubishi, and Sanyo. It also has links with IBM from whom it leases robots. Ninety-five per cent of the products manufactured and distributed by Ina Sankyo are made by its five affiliates. Two of these, like Ina Sankyo, are located in the

Nagano Prefecture and one in the north of Honshu in Akita. Of the remaining two, one is in Taiwan and the other in Singapore. Ina Sankyo's main focus is on research and development (R&D). It designs and makes machinery for its affiliates but also manufactures micro-motors and precision instruments.

Located in the town of Komagane, Ina Sankyo is an industrial enclave within the rural community. The Ina Sankyo plant is housed in extensive modern premises (completed in 1981) which are air-conditioned, earthquake-proof, dust-proof, and sound-insulated.[13] The buildings are set on spacious landscaped grounds and are surrounded by lawns and cherry trees. The new buildings, according to the company brochure, have 'developed harmony with the environment attractive to local people as well as employees'. There are many facilities for the employees such as dining rooms (leased to a small local firm), gymnasium, and sports grounds (hockey, tennis, baseball, and volleyball). The company sponsors its own sports festival for the staff and also a cultural festival at which employees' handicrafts are exhibited (wood carving, ikebana, photography, and oil painting).

Ina Sankyo draws its workforce primarily from the local labour market. There are 561 people in the workforce, 336 male and 225 female. Five hundred of the firm's employees are engaged full-time. All of the part-timers and temporaries are female workers. Almost 100 per cent of the firm's large workforce are farmers or children of farmers, whose families have lived in Komagane for generations. Others have 'migrated' from agricultural areas in less economically advantaged areas such as Kyushu, Tohoku, and Hokkaido. Seventy per cent own their own house, 30 per cent live in company houses or bachelor dormitories. Of the 561 workers employed, about 450 own cars, the balance live close to the plant and walk to work or travel by motorbike or local bus.

There have been changes in recent years in types of labour used in some sections of the plant. New machinery is sometimes leased but is constantly being developed by the R&D section for work that was previously labour-intensive. For example, intra-firm sub-contract firms once worked in the core section (case pressing, high-speed rotor cores, rotors, and assembly). Now these jobs are automated, because, according to the respondent, 'in-plant machinery saves labour, and makes the quality and delivery time more reliable'. The wiring section is also automated. Each shift now processes 8,000 items where previously two shifts produced 3,500 items by hand. In another section, where parts are assembled, there is a process involving three machines. They are looked after by one employee and assembly takes five minutes. Previously, work done in this assembly was put out to farmers' wives in their homes. At the time of the research (1983), the plant was completing 3 million micro-motors each month. Overtime was running at between 70 and 80 hours per month (overtime rates were 30 per cent of wages and 60 per cent for the midnight shift — after 10 pm). There are 80 Quality Control circles (QCs) in the plant.

With regard to management and labour relations at the plant, the respondent advised that there is a union in the enterprise.[14] The Union of Ina Sankyo Employees is independent (not affiliated with national federations or confederations, see Chapter 6), but has links with the Metal Trades Federation (IMF-JC). There has never been a labour inspector on the premises and industrial disputes have been rare. The most recent strike was in the mid-1970s during the peak of industrial disputation after the oil shock and was linked to national action at the time of *shunto*.

The company's extended labour resources

In addition to the workers who are directly employed by the enterprise, Ina Sankyo's local labour resources include workers in its 5 sub-contract firms nearby. The pattern of pyramid manufacturing used by Ina Sankyo also applies to its 2 affiliated companies in the Ina Valley area. Each affiliate uses between 20 and 30 sub-contractors at the second level of their networks. These in turn have sub-sub-contractors, which vary considerably in size, employing as few as 5 and as many as 80 workers and an unknown number of homeworkers. (Information regarding the sub-contracting structure of other affiliates in Akita, Taiwan, and Singapore was not available.)

Ina Sankyo has fewer sub-contractors than its affiliates because of its concentration on R&D rather than production. The company nevertheless has 5 local sub-contractors. Four of these are very small (5 to 6 workers) and the fifth — Ōshima Seisakusho — employs 36 people. In a structure similar to that of its affiliated companies, each of Ina Sankyo's sub-contractors has sub-sub-contractors and homeworkers — farmers' wives working at home. The largest of Ina Sankyo's sub-contractors,

Ōshima Seisakusho, directly and also indirectly through its 5 sub-sub-contractors, puts out work to about 120 agro-industrial homeworkers. This sub-contractor, Ōshima Seisakusho, is the subject of the following case study.

CASE 4: ŌSHIMA SEISAKUSHO[15]

The company

Ōshima Seisakusho depends on Ina Sankyo for 98 per cent of its shipments, mainly the processing of parts for micro-motors. The kits of materials for processing are supplied by the parent company, Ina Sankyo, and Ōshima Seisakusho supplies machinery and labour only. Processes suitable for simple assembly line production are done on the premises or by Ōshima Seisakusho's own 5 sub-sub-contract firms, which are very small firms employing only 5 or 6 workers. The balance of the work is distributed by the owner/manager, Mr Ōshima, to farming housewives nearby. One of Ōshima's sub-sub-contractors has 5 such homeworkers and another has 20. Sub-assembled components are then collected by Ōshima for further processing and sub-assembly in his workshop ready for delivery to Ina Sankyo or its 2 affiliates in the area. The processing allocated to the Ōshima Seisakusho workers is not suitable for automation, mainly because job lots are small and of a large variety. Usually there are about 80 types of units. Of these, the largest job lot is between 70,000 and 80,000 and the smallest 500. Ōshima Seisakusho's contract rate with Ina Sankyo is negotiated directly with the prime company's management. At the time of the research (1983), the rate was ¥15 per minute.

There are many problems related to Ōshima Seisakusho's sub-contract relationship with Ina Sankyo. For example, the kits to be processed often arrive from the patron company short of one or more items. The onus is on Mr Ōshima to go to the patron company for the missing parts and he is still expected to deliver orders in time. A greater problem is that the parent company, Ina Sankyo, has introduced an adaptation of the *kanban*, just-in-time system. This means that the parent company holds few inventories, its orders are unpredictable and irregular, and delivery times are becoming increasingly short. Ōshima sometimes takes work out and collects finished work from his sub-contractors and homeworkers twice a day:

> 'We are now asked to deliver completed work to Ina Sankyo in six days. In that time, materials have to be part-processed here, sorted, and delivered to our outside assembly lines [Ōshima's sub-sub-contractors] and homeworkers. Then the outside work has to be picked up, processed again, sub-assembled, checked repeatedly for quality, and delivered on time.'

The company and the community

The firm's small workshop occupies a shed on one corner of a paddy field, and it is an integral part of the local community from whom it draws its entire workforce. The assistant manager is the eldest son of a farmer and owns a small piece of land. He told how he is hoping to become a junior partner in the firm. As assistant manager, he wants to upgrade the firm's technology, believing that higher levels of technology would not affect the company's employees or homeworkers because the firm's orders would increase. Before joining Ōshima Seisakusho, he worked as a senior technical adviser at the patron firm until, under rationalization, the company insisted on his transfer to its Akita affiliate. He strongly opposed this transfer:

> 'I've always lived in this area and I didn't want to go. The union did nothing to help me, so I resigned. I tried full-time farming but couldn't earn a living. Fortunately, Mr Ōshima was eager to have me use my skills here.'

Now, as assistant manager, he is keen to introduce a multi-purpose machine into the factory. He has loaned his personal computer to the business and this saves office work and helps with inventory control. 'It cost me ¥1.5 million,' he said.

The owner/manager, Mr Ōshima, was also once a full-time farmer. He then worked as a part-time farmer, part-time sub-contractor until his factory opened in 1974. He believes the operation of the firm has one important advantage in that 'business overhead is low because it is a small enterprise', but he is concerned about serious problems facing the firm. It depends on Ina Sankyo for 98 per cent of its orders, and the patron's pressure to cost-down is of particular concern:

'Our problems would be less if we had more parent companies. We are in a poor negotiating position. In the current recession, Ina Sankyo has insisted our sub-contract rate be reduced from ¥15 to ¥12 per minute.'

The village environment further complicates Ōshima's problems. He is involved in many of the village committees and community activities, and it can be very late at night before he is free from meetings concerned with a village festival or ceremonies such as a wedding or funeral. On these occasions, 'sometimes it is 2 o'clock in the morning when I collect the day's finished work and drop materials for the next day's work'. He makes arrangements with his homeworkers to leave their work in some secure place at the farmhouse — in a tool shed or in some farm machinery. Ōshima's homeworkers are paid on piece rates which were calculated at a rate of ¥4 to ¥6 per minute. At ¥240 to ¥360 per hour, this is higher than average female homeworkers' income as quoted by MOL Industrial Homeworkers' Division (see Chapter 3). The quantity of orders varies. Some of Ōshima homeworkers work only 2 hours a day, others work up to 10 hours.

There are between 36 and 40 people regularly working at the factory. All are from farming households nearby and, with the exception of the owner/manager and assistant manager, all are women. Of 32 women working in the factory at the time of this study, 5 discussed their jobs while Ōshima left to make some deliveries. Their wages are paid monthly but calculated on an hourly rate. This method of calculating their income means that they can take time off whenever necessary for planting or harvesting or for necessary care of the farm. The base rate of pay increases with length of service. According to the women, management is generous with pay and bonuses. While a bonus of 2 to 3 months' wages calculated on their previous year's earnings is usual, it is sometimes as much as 3 to 5 months' wages. Paid annual leave is also generous. They are given 6 days' leave after 2 years of service, increasing by 1 day with each further year. The firm is frequently busy and workers are asked to volunteer to do overtime, working a 10-hour day up to four times a week.

Five women took part in an informal talk about their work at

Ōshima Seisakusho. Each had worked in industry before being employed at this factory and wanted to continue working — although one said she may have to leave to look after her ageing father and mother-in-law. Some of their comments are given in tabular form for clarity (Table 5.2).

Table 5.2 Interview with female workers, Ōshima Seisakusho, Ina Valley, Nagano Prefecture, 1983

Respondent	Length of service (years)	Size of previous workplace (number of employees)	Leisure activity	Reason for working
1	10	100	koto ikebana	quiet at home on small field, it's good to be here, likes to keep busy
2	7	80	volleyball, ikebana	supplementing income as farmer's wife, and to have own cash
3	7	50	traditional dancing	husband is a farmer, this work supports his income
4	10	30	traditional dancing, ikebana	widow, main income earner in the home, supports mother-in-law, children
5	8	70	traditional dancing, ikebana, badminton	sending son to high school

Source: Case Study, Ōshima Seisakusho, 25 February 1983.

Several interesting points emerge from these responses. First, working at Ōshima was not a first job for the respondents, and, with the exception of one of the foundation staff members in the group, these women had worked previously in larger firms. As the workers were all middle-aged (the average age in the total workforce was 45), this may reflect the trend for female workers to re-enter the workforce after earlier employment in larger firms followed by a period devoted to marriage and child rearing. However, this and alternative possibilities were not pursued. The second point concerns the respondents' leisure activities. On closer questioning, it was found that not only the five respondents but all the female staff belonged to or had an interest in one or another local sport and traditional art and dancing clubs, reflecting the close-knit nature of working and living in a village environment.

The third point of interest to emerge from discussion with these workers is that they had been with the firm for a relatively long period (two joined the firm when it was established). This may not be representative — it is possible only senior staff were chosen or volunteered to join the discussions. However, there were incentives for low levels of mobility at the Ōshima factory. The business is well established and has an assured (if unequal) relationship with its patron, and the generosity of management is acknowledged. Aspects of the rural environment are also important considerations. The factory is conveniently close to home, and, moreover, industrial and agricultural work and leisure occur in a close social and economic environment. In the light of the rural factor, it would not be surprising if further research found a significant difference in mobility in the urban and rural labour markets.

The final point of interest in the workers' responses concerns their reasons for working. It is clear that their wages were a welcome addition to other household income. For one worker, it was the only source, for another the extra cash meant greater independence, and for yet another, the means to educate her son. In addition, in one woman's words: 'We all enjoy being together, besides, we are all used to hard work and now we are paid to do it. And we need the extra money.' She then added that, on her first pay-day, her husband came to collect her wages and to thank Mr Ōshima.

There is, of course, a generally accepted belief that Japanese housewives are the home business managers of their husbands' incomes. Perhaps this practice is less widespread in the Ina Valley working/farming community, and the male household-head may have more input into the administration of the household income.

CASE 5: TAKAMORI TSUSHIN[16]

The Takamori Company is located in a small village, also in the

Ina Valley and not far from the Ōshima Seisakusho factory. According to the president of the company, there are between 100 and 150 villages in the area that are centres for similar sub-assembly firms. As an indication of the firm's prestige and also as a welcome to the first foreign researcher to visit the area, the village's leading elder attended, and, with considerable respect, was introduced as the owner of almost two acres of land — the largest farm in the district. Now retired, he was formerly a member of the Village Assembly and is still consulted on many local questions concerning business, farming, and villagers' personal problems. His daughter works in the Takamori company factory and one daughter-in-law, as well as helping him on his farm, is an industrial homeworker.

The company

The village where the Takamori factory is situated has a strong farmers' co-operative and, like most communities, has its local festival committee. Takamori Tsushin is affiliated to the local *shokukai* (Chamber of Commerce). The factory is a two-storey wooden construction fronting the main street — a narrow bitumen road running parallel with the local rail link to the major Nagano city of Sowa. The main part of the workshop is on the second floor — one above street level. It is reached from a landing — with the usual cupboard to leave outdoor shoes and collect slippers — up a steep flight of steps and through a small partitioned reception and office area.

Takamori manufactures audio volume controls and switches for television sets and radios, which are produced under a sub-contract relationship with Teikoku Tsushin Kogyo Company Limited (Teitsu). The patron, Teitsu, is a large establishment with more than 1,000 employees, which is situated in the Komagane area (also the site of the large enterprise Ina Sankyo, Case study 3, above). While Teitsu is the patron company for the small Takamori firm, it is itself a parts supplier (mainly to RCA and GE but also to other major enterprises such as Sharp and Mitsubishi), and orders completed by Takamori Tsushin are despatched direct to its patron's customers. Each day 30,000 Takamori switches and volume controls are sent to RCA and GE from the total production of 35,000 to 40,000 units. Approximately 100,000 per month are for RCA and 40,000 for GE. At the time of this interview, four types of switch were being pro-cessed at a cost to the patron of between ¥500 and ¥1,000 (Aust. $2.5 and Aust. $5.0 per item at the then rate of exchange of ¥200 to the Aust. $).

The company is totally dependent on Teitsu, its patron, for sales of its products. The president, who is also owner and manager, has tried unsuccessfully to reduce this dependency by selling some of his products direct to customers, including over-seas buyers such as Canadian and German manufacturers. He approached MITI for help in this regard but found their advice was of no practical use: 'I tried to make contacts for direct export. All MITI did was to give me a sample letter and some addresses. I have had no success.'

Other problems hold back the president's initiative for expansion. For example, there are patents on some of the switches he has developed but his parent company's customers keep changing their product and this in turn affects specifica-tions.

The floor at street level houses a company delivery truck and, displayed with great enthusiasm, a newly installed automatic machine. With this equipment 3 operators would soon be able to do work currently being done by 8 workers. The 5 displaced workers are to stay on the assembly lines in the workshop above. These lines consist of short conveyor belts at which 4 or 5 women work. There was a QC circle for each of the 4 types of switch or control knob currently in production.

There are 40 local people on the workforce: the president, 3 male workers and 36 females. The average age of 45 is the same as at the Oshima factory. Rates of pay were only slightly affected by overtime, which is not frequent in this company. At the time this case study was conducted (1983), the average daily wage was ¥3,700. For an 8-hour day, this represents ¥462.5 per hour. As with Oshima workers, workforce turnover is low. With regard to the 40 people in the factory itself (including the president), 12 had worked with Takamori for 17 years, having joined the company when it was established. The company also engages 5 part-timers, and there are 20 homeworkers attached to the firm. Some homeworkers had been with the firm for 10 or more years, and it is not unusual for them to work for 6 to 7 hours a day. The rate of pay for homeworkers was ¥400 per hour, which was considerably higher than the national average of ¥309 per hour for female homeworkers noted earlier. The

163

Takamori Tsushin rate for homeworkers was higher than the ¥360 rate paid by Ōshima Seisakusho nearby, suggesting that there was no 'going rate' for homeworkers engaged by these two firms in the same local area. In addition to this workforce, Takamori Tsushin has 4 very small sub-sub-contractors nearby, each with 4 or 5 workers. One of them uses 8 homeworkers. None has any technology.

The company and the community

All the workers connected with Takamori Tsushin and its small network live locally, the furthest, 4 kilometres away. They all belong to the village's social committees, sporting clubs (volleyball is very popular), and recreation clubs such as traditional dancing and music and ikebana. Most of the workers also have part-time farming responsibilities. As was the case with Ōshima Seisakusho agro-industrial workers, wages are calculated on a daily rate. The president explained:

> 'No work, no pay. This is a feature of the employment of local workers from farm households. But the wages we pay are relatively high. If we don't pay well, our workers will not stay with our firm. Their income from farming is low, so they have to stay in the locality and work — there is no alternative — although they think if they could go to the city, work would be less boring.'

Two of the female workers from the workshops who joined the interview had widely different work experience. The elder was the factory forewoman. She had been with the firm since it was established and had prior factory experience. She was now working to supplement the income her husband made as a farmer. The younger woman had never worked before. She had been with the company for five years: 'I work because my children are older and now I have nothing much to do. I want to be with the girls working here, and besides, I have a son in primary school.'

As with other small and non-unionized firms in these case studies, everyone at the Takamori factory knew the routine — the unwritten work rules. In the president's words: '. . . a union! . . . What would we want a union for?' Decisions regarding work practices, wages, benefits and conditions, irrespective of their generosity or otherwise, were the sole prerogative of management. However, this is not to say that such decisions were free of constraints.

There are, of course, a variety of checks and balances that intervene in the conditioning of decision making and management and labour relations in each of the firms discussed in this chapter. The following discussion will assess some of these processes.

DISCUSSION

The five businesses looked at in this chapter do not depart to any significant degree from the general trends outlined in earlier analyses of the peripheral environment. In most respects, the case-study environments described above also conform closely to research and analyses cited previously, such as the MITI and SMEA reports on the small and medium sector and the KSK report of sub-contracting strategies. Each case study provided examples of working and earning in the peripheral environment, and at the same time threw some light on aspects of the broader issues that have been dealt with, particularly the issues of industrial and social mechanisms of control. However, several points that emerged warrant further discussion.

Employment practices

In the four smaller firms, the overwhelming majority of workers were blue-collar workers, and there was a tendency for these workers to be women, in a middle- to older-age cohort, and for them to be engaged on a non-regular basis. The entire blue-collar workforce in the two small Ina Valley sub-contract firms were women.

The production and employment structures operating in each of the four medium/small firms resulted in different outcomes as to the ways in which white- and blue-collar workers were disaggregated. In the Ina Valley sub-contract firms, blue-collar owner-managers worked alongside other employees. This intimacy tended to reinforce informal and familial relationships between management and labour that flowed from features of these firms' agricultural/industrial structuring. Nevertheless, intimate relationships did not obscure the management and the managed dichotomy within the firm. (Implications of blue-collar management are dealt with in Chapter 7.) The separation of white- from blue-collar workers was very clear in the structure of the urban construction firm, Mochizuki Steel, and its intra-firm sub-contractors. The prime firm consisted entirely of white-collar workers and workers in the intra-firm sub-contract sections were all blue-collar tradesmen, including the section proprietors who, like the owner-managers of the rural sub-contract firms, were blue-collar management. The line between management and labour was well defined in the Daitokogyo gear pump factory, and both white- and blue-collar workers were all covered by the firm's union. The union's president was a white-collar worker (salesman), consistent with Cole's finding (1971) that there is a clear trend in mixed white- and blue-collar unions for leadership positions to be held by white-collar employees.

Dependency relationships

Owners of the Ōshima Seisakusho and Takamori Tsushin factories were anxious to reduce their dependency — both firms were almost entirely dependent on their patron firms. This dependency on limited sales outlets increased the uncertainty about the firms' stability and threatened their workers' employment security. This fear was particularly clear at the gear pump factory, Daitokogyo; the company's large client firms were turning to overseas sources with lower labour costs in the process of rationalization. While this strategy was affecting Daitokogyo Company's workers, in turn it would have flow-on effects on the prospects of the firm's sub-contractors and their workers. For the internal sub-contract workers at Mochizuki Steel, employment was more secure. This firm's strong R&D focus was contributing to its viability and its dependence on major clients was more diversified.

Management and labour relations

Styles of relationships between workers and management in the rural industrial firms, sensitive to a conjuncture of factory and farming community influences, were informal, and conformed to paternalistic, unitarist approaches to labour relations. This sensitivity appeared to be substantially reduced in the large patron firm, Ina Sankyo, despite the large number of workers recruited from the local labour market. In this case, other factors intervened: the plant is part of a national enterprise structure; administrators and R&D technocrats tended to be metropolitan; some members of the workforce came from outside the area and others from outside the prefecture; in-house social activities would tend to break down close and co-operative life-styles in the community; this plant was unionized.

There were no industrial organizations of workers in either of the small rural sub-contract firms. Management and labour relations were socialized rather than formalized or institutionalized. Home, farm, and work tended to be integrated for owner-managers, employees, sub-contract labour, and homeworkers alike. As a result, management prerogative and authority, though paramount, were subject to a degree of social pressure. Terms and conditions of workers' employment, details of each firm's day-to-day operations, and managements' handling of rewards or sanctions were open to village judgement. Working owners of the small firms would be aware of their exposure to social approbation or censure. Management prerogative and authority were also paramount in relationships in the urban firms, Mochizuki Steel and the Daitokogyo Company. In these urban workshops, management and labour relationships were more formalized. Relations with management at Mochizuki were conducted through the workers' association and at Daitokogyo through a union of employees — a formalized workers' organization and an institutionalized labour union respectively.

As to other forms of organization, there was no suggestion in the rural firms that the workers were involved in joint consultations (other than at QC production level) or any factory based workers' organization. At the unionized pump factory, Daitokogyo workers had an institutionalized avenue through which to negotiate with management. It was significant that they were to some extent privy to the business affairs of the company through this mechanism. There is little doubt that concern for survival of the firm — a 'shared goal' perspective — was a strong factor in the relationship, tending to keep the union on a short leash. At the construction job, the workers' association had exclusive blue-collar membership and excluded temporary workers. The association was confined to social and welfare activities (including the welfare of the firm).

Because this book focuses on the largely non-unionized peripheral sector, the structure and function of the workers' association at Mochizuki Steel is particularly interesting. The chairman of the workers' association acted as the representative of the workers at the site, although these workers were not in fact direct 'employees' of the company and some were working proprietors. The liaison role of the chairman could resemble that of the union president at the Daitokogyo Company, but any similarity between the Mochizuki association and the Daitokogyo union ends there. The association could not become a union given the employment status of its members and its welfare and social objectives (see Chapter 6). The association therefore could not exercise the usual options available to a union under Japan's labour laws.

Weight-off management

Firms in the case studies illustrate the weight-off management process by which larger firms, while retaining production control, relegate work that is labour-intensive to smaller firms. In the smaller firms, labour costs were minimized, and putting out work to sub-sub-sub-contractors and contract labour was extensively practised. Daitokogyo had a significant external sub-contract network, and Mochizuki's tradesmen worked within an intra-firm sub-contract structure. Both small electrical appliance firms in the Ina Valley used more external homeworkers than intra-firm staff.

The situation in these two rural firms supports arguments referred to earlier (Chapter 3), that the practice of falling back on the labour of homeworkers is more widespread than official estimates indicate. Considered together, Ōshima and Takamori engaged a total of almost 150 homeworkers, some indirectly through their sub-sub-contractors. This means that, in two firms situated in adjacent villages in one small area of the Ina Valley, homeworkers outnumbered the intra-firm permanent workers by roughly 2 to 1.

With regard to parts suppliers and sub-contract labour, Ina Sankyo, as a transnational enterprise, kept a tight control over total production through a plethora of highly competitive, dependent, and vulnerable peripheral firms. Although the domestic firms, Daitokogyo and Mochizuki, were in a patronage position relative to their networks, the relationships between these small/medium firms and their sub-contractors were considerably more equitable. The pressures that are inherent in these strategies contribute to a complex control process. Where a highly competitive and diversified supply system operated, the control functions of the core enterprises were clear, as is the highly unequal distribution of power in the core-peripheral relationship. This was exemplified in the cost, quality, and delivery demands made on Takamori Tsushin by its patron, the large enterprise Teitsu, and similar pressures on Ōshima Seisakusho by its patron, Ina Sankyo. The owner-managers had no recourse but to conform with production controls and to transmit these controls to their external homeworkers and sub-contractors — their 'outside assembly lines'. The extended control process was particularly evident in the Ōshima case, where the patron firm had introduced a *kanban* production technique. The pressures associated with this technique were being transmitted in a downward progression to the sub-contractor's sub-sub-contractors and homeworkers.

In an important sense, weight-off management means 'problem dumping'. Problems such as lower wages, inferior working conditions, and unstable employment, which are not endemic in Japan's large-enterprise sector, were features of the smaller-firm environments. In this way, the core enterprise's production control was extended to encompass control over industrial behaviour in the smaller firms. The process, as observed in the case studies and shown in the macro-data, was not simply confined to a large and small firm dichotomy. Rather, the process is one that moves from small firm to smaller firm, from smaller firm to even smaller and from minute firm to self-employed contract labour.

It is reasonable to assume that a major priority of the management of both sub-contractors, Ōshima Seisakusho and Takamori Tsushin, was to ensure that no labour 'problems' interrupted processing and production schedules in their plants or among workers in their smaller sub-sub-contract firms. Such an assumption is derived not only from the case study analyses but the macro-analysis of sub-contracting in a highly competitive environment (Chapter 4). At the same time, any isolated

169

eruption of dissent is not likely to affect major firms or hold them to ransom because networks of part suppliers and sub-contractors are so widely cast and competitors are in such abundance.

As will be discussed in the following chapters of this book, problem dumping is a process that may contribute to the maximization of co-operative industrial relations at the larger-firm level. The process is not only one of weight-off large-enterprise management but one involving weight-off large-enterprise unions. As Clegg (1975) argued, powerful interest groups are heard at the expense of the unheard segment of the workforce. Areas of potential conflict are externalized, and in this way, problems of peripheral labour are left to managers and workers in segregated sites that are non-unionized and relatively non-regulated. Progressively, problems become greater as the power of unions becomes weaker, eventually reaching the non-unionized or non-organized milieu.

Case studies and the industrial relations literature

It is clear that the case studies raise many issues concerning industrial relations on which there is scant empirical evidence. Insights into these issues cannot be drawn from the industrial relations literature generally or concerning Japan in particular. As pointed out in the opening chapter of this book, Japan-related research almost completely bypasses the peripheral sector. It was also pointed out that a major outcome of this neglect has been the creation and maintenance of stereotypical models of industrial relations in Japan and an over-emphasis on 'traditional' values. The analyses of these case studies indicate a considerable departure from the popular models, and they modify the emphasis placed on tradition. In several ways, these case studies highlight the vulnerability of peripheral workers to the much-vaunted 'flexible' status and bring into relief the importance of industrial, economic, legal, political, and social processes in controlling Japan's industrial relations.

Furthermore, the analyses of dependency, expectations, and power relations in this and previous chapters reveal an inter-action between core and peripheral relationships, into which there has been little sustained or systematic research. This inter-action is pursued in the following and final chapters, which discuss labour organization, then turn to communication and conflict in management and labour relations.

NOTES

1. Types of firms and branches of industry were selected according to criteria outlined in the introduction to this book. Note that steel fabrication comes under Japan's industrial classification of 'construction'. Arrangements to meet with management and workers in these five firms were made by Professor Ikeda Masayoshi, who also acted as interpreter.

2. Information, records, and data concerning steel fabrication in general and Mochizuki Steel Fabrications Limited in particular were obtained during interviews at the work yard (1 February 1983). Comments reported or quoted in this study are taken from interview records. Taking part were: the owner/manager (president of the company), the chief consulting engineer, administrative staff, and the proprietor of one of the small firms working on the site who is also chairman of Mochizuki Steel Workers' Association. The editor of a national magazine of the steel fabrication industry (tri-monthly circulation 8,000) also participated.

3. According to respondents, Mochizuki's sub-contracting relationships with its clients and master builders as orderers is typical of pyramid sub-contracting in the construction industry.

4. The editor of the national magazine of the industry interjected to remark that Mochizuki Steel's structure of permanent intra-firm sub-contracting is standard. He noted that, in one respect, Mochizuki Steel was different. The ratio of company white-collar staff (excluding management) to sub-contracted labour is higher than usual, mainly as a result of this company's special efforts with respect to R&D. The ratio at Mochizuki Steel is 13 administration to 24 manual workers, whereas it is more common in other steel fabrication firms to find a ratio of 5 to 25.

5. As pointed out earlier, the Labour Standards Law specifies that work rules are required in firms with more than 10 people regularly employed. None of the internal sub-contracting firms has sufficient numbers of workers (the largest has 5 employees) to make such rules obligatory. It is possible that work rules could be obligatory if management treats its 37 contract workers as regular employees.

6. One of the respondents taking part in the interviews at Mochizuki Steel was the proprietor of the assembly section, who is also chairman of the workers' association. He supplied the following information and a copy of the association's handbook.

7. This review of the work and aims of the small and medium management association is based on discussions with members of the national board and official material published by the organization, following interviews with senior management of Mochizuki Steel Fabrications. An historical reference to this organization appears in Chapter 1.

8. The junior owner/president of the Daitokogyo Company supplied the material for this study of his company's operations (interview, 1 February 1983). One of the president's main responsibilities on the board of directors is to look after labour problems and personnel affairs. He is also an executive member of the Labour Problems Committee of the Association of Management of Small and Medium Enterprises, which was referred to in the Mochizuki Steel case study.

9. Extracts from the transcription have been edited for clarity without changing the substance.

10. This was the period when the impact of the first oil shock was at its highest. Inflation was running high, and as a result of labour unrest and organized union pressure, the agreed base-up wage increase was over 30 per cent.

11. From the transcription of discussion with the president of the Union of Employees of Daitokogyo Company Limited, 1 February 1983. Interviews with management and union were conducted separately.

12. This case study involved a visit to the Ina Sankyo plant and an interview with a senior executive/member of the board of management, 24 February 1983.

13. Soundproofing separates high level noise operations in the processing sections in the plant. In some assembly sections visited during the case study, the noise level drowned discussion. Workers had no protective gear and some wore cottonwool earplugs. It could be observed that some processing was robotized or automated but that some workers were operating with basic tools on labour-intensive line assembly.

14. Because of shortage of time, it was not possible to interview officials of the union. This brief reference to relations with the union is therefore from the management perspective.

15. Interviews at Ōshima Seisakusho (25 February 1983) included discussions with the owner/manager, the assistant manager, and 5 of the 32 female workers regularly employed in the factory.

16. This study of the Takamori Tsushin workshop took place on 25 February 1983. A former leading member of the village assembly attended the discussions, and Takamori's president/ owner/manager and two of three male staff participated. Later, two women from the production lines, one of whom was forewoman, joined the group.

6

Japan's peripheral workers: unionization and organization

Management and labour relations in the peripheral segment of Japan's workforce have been discussed to this point through two grids: the division and deployment of workers (Chapters 2 and 3); the stratification of workers' labour effort under subcontracting and rationalization (Chapter 4). The experiences of workers in five plants offered illustrations of industrial relations through both grids (Chapter 5). This chapter will look at management and labour relations in the peripheral segment through a third grid, labour organization and its segmentation. The main focus will be on Japan's enterprise union system and the right of workers to organize. There is a large body of literature on this subject; however, the following discussion pursues a specific aspect: the capacity of peripheral workers to exercise this right to organize and bargain collectively. This discussion will conclude with an assessment of the exclusiveness of enterprise unionism and the implications of the system for those workers it excludes.

ENTERPRISE UNIONISM

The right to organize

The right of workers to organize and to bargain and act collectively is guaranteed under Article 28 of Japan's 1949 Constitution.[1] Unionization within an enterprise is the dominant form of organization under which this right is exercised. This institutional aspect of industrial relations has been well documented.[2]

Briefly, the characteristics of unions in Japan, as institutionalized in its labour laws, qualify the right to organize. They lay down the status of a union according to whether it operates in privately owned enterprises or public corporations, national or local public enterprises, or covers national or local public servants. Seventy-two per cent of Japan's 12.5 million union members belong to unions in the private sector (MOL 1981).

Private sector unions are covered by the Trade Union Law (1949). The purpose of this law is:

> to elevate the status of workers by promoting that they shall be on equal standing with their employer in their bargaining with the employer; to protect the exercise by workers of autonomous self-organization and association in trade unions so that they may carry out collective action including the designation of representatives of their own choosing to negotiate the terms and conditions of work; and to encourage the practice and procedure of collective bargaining resulting in collective agreements governing relations between employers and workers.
>
> (Preamble, Trade Union Law, 1949)

Characteristics of enterprise unions

Enterprise unions in the private sector have the following characteristics. The employees of Company A comprise Union A irrespective of occupation (salesmen, engineers, clerks, carpenters, truck drivers, and labourers), and, with few exceptions, only regular employees are eligible for membership. Workers cease to be union members if they leave Company A, if Union A is disbanded, or if Company A ceases to operate. Union A's finances must be raised by members of Union A. Officials of Union A must be regular employees of Company A and are elected by secret ballot. Union A may not take strike action without a secret ballot. No organization of workers can be a union if its objectives are confined to mutual aid or other welfare work or if its principal aim is to engage in political or social movements.

Ninety-four per cent of Japan's unions operate under the enterprise union system (Table 6.1). Other types of union fall into three categories: first, industrial unions; second, craft or occupational unions such as the seamen's union; and third, general unions such as the union of day labourers and unemployed workers.[3]

Table 6.1 Number of unions and union members according to type of union organization, 1975

Type of union organization	Number of unions (basic unit unions)	%	Number of union members	%
Enterprise unions	65,337	94.2	11,361,378	91.1
Craft unions	720	1.0	169,569	1.4
Industrial unions	1,775	2.6	682,728	5.5
Others	1,501	2.2	259,299	2.0
Total	69,333	100.0	12,472,974	100.0

Source: 'Basic survey of trade unions', Ministry of Labour, 1975, in Hanami Tadashi, *Labor Relations in Japan Today*, Kodansha International Ltd, Tokyo, 1981, p. 89.

Although the MOL statistics showing the extent of enterprise unionism are not recent,[4] there are no indications that the percentage distribution of basic unit unions has changed significantly since the ministry conducted this survey in 1975. At this point, classifications of unions used in Table 6.1 ('basic unit unions') and in other data to follow ('labour unions') need some clarification. 'Basic unit unions' are individual unions that are autonomous. Each has its own constitution and negotiates directly with management. Small self-contained unions and each section of a large union (its branches and headquarters) are classed as basic unit unions provided each has such autonomous features. Statistics that refer to 'labour unions' apply to the same unions but the data are dis-aggregated according to different criteria. The data in this instance cover self-contained autonomous unions and, as a single entity, large unions with their headquarters, sections, and sometimes numerous semi-autonomous branches. Under these criteria, in 1981 there were 73,694 basic unions with a membership of 12.4 million workers, and 34,200 labour unions with a membership of 12.5 million (Table 6.2).

175

UNIONIZATION

In absolute numbers, unit unions, labour unions, and union members have increased over the last decade. However, unionization rates have tended to decline steadily in the same period apart from a brief revival following the first oil shock. As shown in Table 6.2, in both 1980 and 1981 the estimated rate of unionization was 30.8 per cent, representing a 4 per cent decrease since 1971.

Table 6.2 Trends in numbers of trade unions, membership, and estimated rates of unionization, 1971–81

Year	Number of unions	Union membership (000)	Estimated unionization rate %
1971	30,500 (62,428)	11,798 (11,684)	34.8
1972	30,818 (63,718)	11,889 (11,772)	34.3
1973	31,674 (65,448)	12,098 (11,967)	33.1
1974	32,734 (67,829)	12,462 (12,325)	33.9
1975	33,424 (69,333)	12,590 (12,473)	34.4
1976	33,771 (70,039)	12,509 (12,374)	33.7
1977	33,987 (70,625)	12,437 (12,293)	33.2
1978	34,163 (70,868)	12,383 (12,233)	32.6
1979	34,112 (71,780)	12,309 (12,174)	31.6
1980	34,232 (72,693)	12,369 (12,241)	30.8
1981	34,200 (73,694)	12,471 (12,355)	30.8

Source: Compiled from Labour Union Basic Survey, June 1981, *Year Book of Labour Statistics*, Ministry of Labour, 1982 and *Japan Labor Bulletin*, April 1982: 5.

Notes: Numbers of unions are data for labour unions, numbers in parenthesis represent data for unit unions.

Unionization rate is estimated by dividing labour union membership at the end of each June by the number of employees as stated in the Labour Force Survey, Bureau of Statistics, Prime Minister's Office.

Union membership is rounded upwards from 0.05.

That unionization has not kept pace with the increase in numbers in the workforce is open to many interpretations. A major contributing factor may be that the percentage share of the workforce occupied by the peripheral workforce is increasing relative to the share occupied by regular workers in large enterprises. Since, in practice, union membership is restricted to regular employees, and since categories of workers unable to join a union have tended to increase as a percentage of the workforce, then this also contributes to declining unionization rates. For example, the numbers of part-timers entering the workforce have been increasing very rapidly.

Repercussions from rationalization in industry should also be taken into account. Rationalization strategies have increased the mobility of workers in the small enterprise sector. As noted, such workers, should they be union members, lose membership when they quit or are fired from a unionized firm. Rationalization has also involved extensive restructuring of sub-contracting (see Chapter 4). Parent companies are giving increasing importance to 'stable labour relations' — criteria that discourage unionization in existing sub-contract firms and in firms hoping to enter a network.

UNIONIZATION, ENTERPRISE SIZE, AND TYPE OF INDUSTRY

The practical difficulties in forming a union increase in intensity as firms decrease in size by numbers employed.

In the light of characteristics of the peripheral environment, it is not surprising that unionization rates decline sharply as firm size decreases. Table 6.3 shows the extent of this decline. These figures also show that unions and unionized workers in the private sector are almost completely confined to Japan's large enterprises. Only in firms with more than 1,000 employees does the unionization rate, at 56.6 per cent, exceed the national average of 30.8 per cent. These large firms employ only 6.6 per cent of regular workers (see Table 2.1). Firms that employ less than 30 account for 47.7 per cent, and for this significant segment of employees the unionization rate is 0.8 per cent.

It is possible under the provisions of the Trade Union Law to have more than one union in an enterprise. Given the difficulties in forming and financing a union in the small-firm sector, it is surprising to find that multiple-union situations occur, if infrequently, in the small-firm sector. According to a Labour Ministry Survey (1977) of 1,700 unionized enterprises, 12 per cent had more than one union (Table 6.4.).

If unionization is looked at in terms of the total private-sector workforce, the contrast between unionization in large and small firms is dramatic (Figure 6.1). Less than 5 per cent of people in

Table 6.3 Number of trade unions and membership by enterprise size, private sector, 1981

Enterprise size (by number of regular employees)	Number of unions (labour unions)	Number of members (labour unions) (000)	Percentage distribution
Total	54,701	8,740	100.0
1,000 or more	15,223	4,930	56.4
300–999	7,524	1,398	16.0
100–299	10,570	1,027	11.7
30–99	12,604	466	5.3
29 or less	5,799	67	0.8
Others	2,981	853	9.8

Source: 'Labour union basic survey', June 1981, Ministry of Labour, 1981, in *Japan Labor Bulletin*, April 1982: 6.

Note: 'Others' includes unions organized by employees of more than two companies (such as general unions) and unions organized in enterprises of unknown size.

Table 6.4 Percentage distribution of multiple unions by size of unionized enterprise, 1977 (%)

Enterprise size	Enterprises with two or more unions
1,000 or more	20.0
500–999	13.0
200–499	12.0
100–199	11.0
30–99	6.0
29 or less	3.0

Source: Data supplied by Fujii Ryuko, Deputy Director, Trade Union Division, Ministry of Labour, interview, 7 January 1983.

Note: The survey is conducted each five years. Results of the 1982 survey were not available at the time these data were obtained.

the workforce are associated with the highly unionized sector of industry. Seventy-seven per cent — those working in firms with less than 100 employees — operate in the sector where unionization is negligible. Of these, more than 57 per cent have jobs in small firms with less than 30 employees, and in this sector of industry, unionization is virtually non-existent.

Low unionization rates in the small-firm sector are reflected

Figure 6.1 Workforce: Japan, participation and unionization rate by enterprise size; number of persons engaged, private, non-agricultural sector as at June 1981 (%)

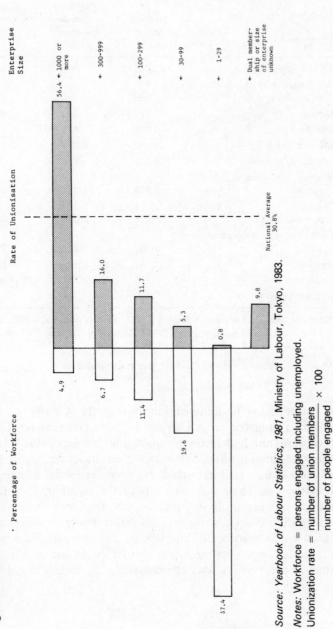

Rate of Unionisation

Enterprise Size
+ 1000 or more 56.4
+ 300-999 16.0
+ 100-299 11.7
+ 30-99 5.3
+ 1-29 0.8
+ Dual member-ship or size of enterprise unknown 9.8

Percentage of Workforce

4.9
6.7
11.4
19.6
57.4

National Average 30.8%

Source: Yearbook of Labour Statistics, 1981, Ministry of Labour, Tokyo, 1983.

Notes: Workforce = persons engaged including unemployed.

Unionization rate = $\dfrac{\text{number of union members}}{\text{number of people engaged}} \times 100$

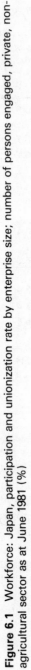

Table 6.5 Unit unions and union members by type of industry, and estimated unionization rates, 1981

Industry	Number of unit unions[1]	Number of union members (000)[1]	Estimated unionization rate (%)[2]
All industries	73,694	12,355	30.8
Agriculture, forestry, fishery, aquaculture	955	88	18.9
Mining	270	45	49.7
Construction	4,025	731	17.2
Manufacturing	19,616	4,024	34.9
Wholesale and retail	6,841	904	9.5
Finance, insurance, and real estate	5,318	1,039	54.4
Transport and communication	15,211	2,001	65.5
Electricity, gas, water, and steam	1,380	232	73.4
Services	14,133	1,843	21.0
Government	5,625	1,403	75.8
Unclassifiable	320	44	—

Source: [1]*Year Book of Labour Statistics 1981*, Ministry of Labour, 1983: 286−7.
[2]'Basic survey of trade unions', 1981, Ministry of Labour, 1981, in *Japan Labor Bulletin*, April, 1982: 5.

Note: '—' indicates that the relevant figure is not available.

in figures showing unionization by industry. Clearly, rates are lower in industries characterized by high frequencies of small businesses and high levels of non-regular labour (Table 6.5). For example, unionization is low in the construction, service, and wholesale and retail industries. However, estimates of unionization rates in Table 6.5 oversimplify the position; they fail to mirror the variations in rates by size that was demonstrated above (Table 6.4). More detailed information on unionization rates within branches of industry by size of enterprise were not available for this research, but a brief discussion on the structures in the construction and manufacturing industries illustrates the point.

The construction industry

The unionization rate of 17.2 per cent in the construction industry needs to be considered in light of characteristics of the industry. It can be assumed that unionization is virtually non-existent for most construction workers, particularly blue-collar sub-contract and contract labour. It will be recalled that this industry has a top-heavy structure and a heavily skewed division of labour. Sohyo respondents point out that:

> There are special problems in the construction industry arising from its structural characteristics. There are a few giant corporations, such as the Kashima Construction family, which has its own member of parliament, and all its workers are unionized. There's a vast number of firms at the bottom with two or three, perhaps four workers, who actually do the installation, sewerage, connection of the water supply, and so on. Between the giant and miniature firms there are a lot of steps, and workers are only organized on the top.
> (Sano and Ogawa, interview, 16 November 1982)

Figures in Japan's 1981 census of establishments (PMO 1982) show that, of the total of 550,000 construction establishments, there are 353 (0.04 per cent) that employ more than 300 employees. In these largely planning and administration centres, 97 per cent of employees are regulars. Employees in these firms come under the official classification of construction and although almost all are white-collar workers, their union would be classified as a construction industry union. The average number of regular employees in each is 567.5, however, in the aggregate, such firms account for a minority (6 per cent) of all regular workers in this industry (PMO 1982). It can be assumed that unionization rates in these large firms are very high, and are at their highest in the 28 giant construction firms that employ 1,000 or more.

Such firms are at the hub of extensive sub-contract networks. The very small firms in the network employ a minimum of administration personnel and otherwise consist of blue-collar workers such as scaffold riggers, carpenters, plumbers, and labourers. On a small scale, the construction industry firm discussed in the previous chapter, Mochizuki Steel Fabrications, is an example of this characteristic of the industry — the

181

separation of white-collar patronage and blue-collar sub-contracting. The census data (PMO 1982) show that 86 per cent of construction firms employ fewer than 30 people but the majority, 70 per cent, employ fewer than 5, who, as noted, are primarily in blue-collar occupations. The average number of regular employees in construction firms that employ fewer than 30 is 5.7 and the smallest firms have only temporaries and day labour.

Irrespective of other control factors, sheer lack of numbers in most firms in this industry makes unionization quite impractical, and for this reason, the estimated unionization rate of 17.2 per cent is misleading.

The manufacturing industry: transport equipment/automobile parts section

Manufacturing, with a unionization rate of 34.9 per cent, provides a second example of the oversimplified picture presented by average rates. In the case of the transport equipment and automobile parts branch of manufacturing, 2 per cent of firms employ more than 300 regulars (PMO 1982). These establishments consist of a mixture of R&D, administration, and production and therefore employ both white- and blue-collar workers. The data also show that 99 per cent of employees in these large firms are regulars, and the average number of regular employees in each is 1,387. These workers make up the majority (66 per cent) of all regulars in this branch of manufacturing. It can be assumed that unionization in enterprises such as these is very high.

The percentage of very small firms (fewer than 5 employees) in this branch of manufacturing is less than is the case in construction — 56 per cent of firms are very small compared with 70 per cent in construction. The rate of sub-contracting, 86 per cent, is also lower than in construction but ranks the highest among all branches of manufacturing (see Table 4.1 above). Only 10 per cent of regular employees work in firms with fewer than 30 regulars. On average, these firms employ 7 regular workers per establishment. The possibility of forming a viable union in these small firms is remote in the extreme, despite the tendency for employment in this branch of manufacturing to be more stable than in construction.

Unionization and sex

The distribution of female workers throughout industry is a further factor to be considered when evaluating average levels of unionization. The ratio of female to male employees becomes particularly significant. Figures in Table 6.5 above show that average unionization rates are low in sectors of industry where the female component of the workforce is known to be high, for example the service industry and the textile and apparel branches of manufacturing (MOL 1983).[5] At the same time, data concerning female unionization rates (Table 6.6), highlight the low female unionization rate compared with the male rate.

This trend does not appear in all the data. For example, in the construction industry, female workers comprise 12.5 per cent of

Table 6.6 Unionization rates, female unionization rates, by industry (establishments of all sizes), 1981

Industry	Estimated unionization rate %	Female unionization rate %
All industries	30.8	27.6
Agriculture, forestry, fishery, and aquaculture	18.9	10.2
Mining	49.7	6.7
Construction	17.2	13.8
Manufacturing	34.9	20.7
Wholesale and retail	9.5	36.7
Finance, insurance, and real estate	54.4	57.1
Transport and communication	65.5	9.7
Electricity, gas, water, and steam	73.4	9.9
Services	21.0	44.4
Government	75.8	34.9
Industries not adequately described	—	27.3

Source: Compiled from 'Trade union basic survey', 1981, Ministry of Labour, in *Year Book of Labour Statistics*, Ministry of Labour, 1983: 286–7.

Notes: Percentage distribution of female union members is obtained by dividing the number of female union members by the total number of members × 100.

regular employees but the female component of union membership is 13.8 per cent. One factor likely to affect this situation is
the tendency for female workers in construction enterprises to be
concentrated in traditionally female occupations in giant, largely
white-collar enterprises. These firms are likely to be highly
unionized. A related and possibly more significant factor may be
the concentration of male construction workers in small and
very small, largely blue-collar firms that are non-unionized.

In the case of the manufacturing industry, it is clear from the
data that female unionization rates are lower than male rates.
Female regular workers comprise 30.4 per cent of regular
employees but only 20.7 per cent of the union membership.
Nevertheless, variations in the structures of branches of
manufacturing have their effect. For example, in the transport
equipment and general machinery branches of manufacturing,
females make up 9.8 per cent and 10.8 per cent of union
membership respectively, and in textile mill production, female
membership accounts for 51.4 per cent of the unionized workforce (MOL 1983: 286–7).

ENTERPRISE UNIONS AND ENTERPRISE SIZE

Of all the factors that affect unionization rates, the size of the
regular workforce in an establishment is critical. Factors such as
type of industry, a worker's occupation, sex, and employment
status affect unionization rates within the unionized firm, but
the number of workers on the job basically determines the
potential for a viable union to be established. The characteristics
of enterprise unionism then come into play with significant outcomes for the industrial relations process. The interaction
between enterprise unionism, firm size, and employment status
affect organization and the distribution of power in the industrial relations process. This occurs in two related ways.

The first stems from the frequency with which workers
become members of the union where they work as distinct from
the frequency with which enterprises and establishments[6] are
unionized. The difference is not clear from the available data.
The following observations indicate the relevance of making
such a distinction. It has been established (Table 6.3) that there
are 15,223 labour unions in the large-enterprise sector of private
industry and that the estimated unionization rate is 56.4 per

cent. These figures apply to the 1,023 enterprises in this sector. The relatively high unionization rate is not surprising. Two trends in these firms operate to maximize unionization. First, some large businesses are virtually 'closed shops'. According to the collective agreement between the union and management of the particular enterprise, all regular employees must join the union or one of several unions in a multiple-union situation (Hanami, interview, 22 December 1982). In a second and stronger trend, there are large establishments where no closed-shop agreement exists but where union membership is expected and almost automatic (Hanami, interview, 22 December 1982).

The same data sources show that among the 150,047 small enterprises (30 to 99 regulars), there are 12,604 unions and the estimated unionization rate is 5.3 per cent. Because of the small numbers on the job, each union would be small and unlikely to be strong enough to negotiate a closed-shop agreement, nevertheless the rate of unionization per unionized small establishment must be considerably higher than 5.3 per cent, otherwise, the unions in these firms would have an average membership of five. This is a possibility that can be confidently rejected. An additional outcome of enterprise unionism in firms of this size is that a relatively higher ratio of non-regular to regular workers inhibits the extent of the union's power base within the company. Clearly, a union's power base is increasingly weakened as more non-unionized employees work alongside fewer union members. The threat, of minimal concern to major unions, becomes increasingly relevant the smaller the firm.

From this perspective, differences in the power base of major and minor unions raise the question of politicization. This issue is dealt with later in this and the final chapter, but a brief observation is appropriate at this point. Quasi-automatic membership operates to enhance the numerical and financial power base of major unions. By contrast, a minor union faces difficulties in establishing and maintaining a base and may even cover a minority of the workers in that firm. This suggests higher levels of commitment to unionization *per se* on the part of minor unions in small firms or minority unions in mutiple-union situations.

This observation is related to the second way in which enterprise unionism, firm size, and employment status interact to affect organization and the distribution of power. Enterprise unionism plays a divisive role by institutionalizing the segmentation of labour organization into enterprise-bound units. The divisive process has a three-fold effect on power relations in industry. First, it establishes powerful 'core' and progressively weaker 'peripheral' unions in the unionized segment of the workforce. Second, it effectively inhibits unionization in the peripheral segment of the workforce. Third, it reinforces the segmentation of core and peripheral labour.

The distribution of unions and union membership dramatically illustrate this process. Although only 15.5 per cent of private-sector employees work in firms employing more than 300 regulars (Table 2.1), these firms account for more than 72 per cent of union members (Table 6.3). In the large-enterprise sector, labour unions are relatively few in number, but they are very large, covering the membership of the headquarters and autonomous branch unit unions. Figures in Table 6.7 show that of Japan's 34,200 labour unions, 337 (1 per cent) have memberships exceeding 5,000 and together these unions account for 44.9 per cent of all union members. At the other end of the spectrum, 21,172 labour unions (61.9 per cent) have less than 100 members[7] and account for 6.7 per cent of all union members.

Table 6.7 Labour unions and membership, by size of membership, 1981

Labour unions by size of membership	Number of labour unions	%	Number of members (000)	%
Total	34,200	100.0	12,471	100.0
5,000 or more	337	1.0	5,599	44.9
1,000–4,999	1,370	4.0	2,884	23.1
500–999	1,537	4.5	1,065	8.5
300–499	2,000	5.8	767	6.1
100–299	7,784	22.8	1,311	10.5
30–99	12,164	35.6	704	5.6
29 or less	9,008	26.3	141	1.1

Source: 'Labour union basic survey', in *Year Book of Labour Statistics 1981*, Ministry of Labour, Tokyo, 1983.

POWER RELATIONS WITHIN ORGANIZED LABOUR

It has already been pointed out that the onus lies with each of Japan's numerous unions to conduct negotiations with management of a firm or management of a division of the enterprise. This responsibility obtains irrespective of whether the union is a self-contained unit union within one firm or is an autonomous branch within the labour union of a large enterprise. This one-to-one relationship also persists as a feature of enterprise unionism despite the existence of large union organizations through which Japan's many unions can liaise. These organizations are the labour unions, national federations of unions in the one enterprise, union federations in particular industries, kindred industry councils, and multi-union confederations. Three of these will be dealt with briefly: industry federations, national trade union centres, and allied industry councils.

Industry federations

Industry federations primarily function as a co-ordinating centre within an industry. At the time of *shunto*, when bargaining on wages and bonuses is on the agenda for the union and management in a firm, federation recommendations to their affiliates are important, but only as guidelines. Industry federations are loose organizations with no direct intervention in the intra-firm discussions that precede and follow *shunto*. Intra-firm discussions independently arrive at collective bargaining agreements (if this is an option) or determine work rules. As Hanami points out, federations are primarily advisory bodies:

> About 80 per cent of them are now advisory bodies. Their functions are restricted to exchanging information and mutual assistance and their decisions are not binding on the affiliated unions. The other 20 per cent are genuine federations whose policy decisions are binding on their affiliated member unions. However, even the latter group is characterized by a rather loose organization. Such lack of authority of the main body over the member unions is caused by the strong independence of the affiliated enterprise unions.[8]
>
> (Hanami 1981: 90–91)

Although affiliation to an industry federation does not diminish the independence of member unions, policy decisions by the federations have an indirect influence on affiliates'

187

deliberations. However, as could be expected, larger unions are in a position to exert considerable influence on federation policy decisions — both economic and political. Sheer weight of numbers of members and access to funds flowing from extensive membership not only give added scope for the operation of the union (including the ability to have full-time paid officials and staff) but increase the union's power advantage in the industry federations:

> The enterprise unions of large firms are bound to exert a great deal of influence on the industrial federations as a result not only of the number of votes they command but also because of their relatively better financial position . . . big firms pay better wages than smaller firms and membership fees are fixed in proportion to each member's income.
>
> (Hanami 1981: 91)

National trade-union centres

In the national trade-union centres, the power game is replicated in a multi-industry situation involving many of the industry federations. Like the federations, national trade-union centres are loose organizations and they have similar policy-making and co-ordinating functions. The autonomy of affiliates is sacrosanct and the influence of the larger affiliates is commensurate with their strength by numbers, finance, and internal unity. There are four such centres. (Their relative strengths are shown in Appendix 5.) The largest is Sohyo (General Council of Trade Unions of Japan) with a total membership of 4.6 million. Domei (Japanese Confederation of Labour) has a membership approximately half that of Sohyo, 2.2 million. Shinsanbetsu (National Federation of Industrial Organizations) and Churitsuroren (Federation of Independent Unions) are the smallest of the confederations, with a membership of 64,000 and 1.4 million respectively. Each of the four national centres has member unions in the public and private sectors. Sohyo's greatest strength comes from its affiliated unions in the public sector. Affiliates to Domei are mainly private-sector unions, and private-enterprise unions also predominate in the other national centres and among non-affiliated and general unions.

Unions not affiliated to the four national centres account for a significant percentage of organized workers (37.4 per cent). This exceeds the affiliated membership of the largest of the national centres, Sohyo (36.6 per cent). Unions in this group, in approximately equal proportions, are: affiliated to umbrella organizations such as the allied industry councils; large independent enterprise unions; and general unions not necessarily based on an enterprise.[9]

Allied industry councils

These councils operate outside the multi-industry national centres, although some of their member unions have dual affiliation with the national centres. There are two main councils, of which the IMF (JC), the Japan Council of Metalworkers' Unions, is the larger.[10] In the same year that the IMF (JC) was established, 1977, a similar allied industry council was formed, the Japan Council of Chemical Industry Workers' Unions, with 500,000 members. The IMF (JC) brings together federations of industry unions in related industries with a total membership of 1.9 million. All IMF (JC) member unions are in the private-enterprise sector. They cover steel workers, workers in metal, machinery and shipbuilding, auto workers, and electrical workers. All but one of its affiliates are among Japan's 20 largest trade unions. (One such affiliate is the Confederation of Automobile Workers' Unions, Jidoshasoren, which has 570,000 members.)

The IMF (JC) is clearly a powerful organization. Together with its affiliates, it is now — in the 1980s — acknowledged as the national pacesetter in *shunto* negotiations, reflecting a decline in Sohyo's earlier leadership. The leadership contest is not only concerned with the relative strengths of these giant organizations, but is a reflection of the ideological differences in the national trade-union centres and the IMF (JC). To a significant extent, the contest also reflects the political persuasion of affiliates to these bodies and some of the divisions generally within the union movement.

Centrist-economic unionism is the dominant philosophy of Domei, which is officially linked with the Democratic Socialist Party (DSP), a minority right-centrist party in the Opposition. The political orientation of the IMF (JC) is, like Domei, centrist-economic unionism. The IMF (JC) asserts its anti-communism and its dedication to the right-centrist union principles of the International Confederation of Free Trade Unions (ICFTU) and the IMF (Geneva). It has no public commitment to any of the Opposition political parties, although its political stance is clear:

> At IMF we don't publicly support any of the opposition parties in government. We are quite strongly represented, however. We have 13 members [in the opposition], 1 in the JSP, 12 in the DSP.
>
> (Seto, General Secretary IMF (JC), interview, 22 November 1982)

Sohyo's political orientation is more complex. At times, it sponsors 'united struggles' on particular issues and campaigns, but otherwise its position is a compromise between moderate and anti-communist unions. Sohyo also carries a heritage of left militancy, and some of its member unions are affiliates of the Japan Communist Party. Sohyo officially supports the Japan Socialist Party (JSP), which is the majority moderate-left party in the opposition in the government.

Although developments in the power relations within organized labour are the direct concern of the major power centres of unionized labour, there are repercussions for Japan's small unions. According to respondents from Sohyo, efforts by right-centrist unions to establish a new national centre based on large private-sector unions will further weaken the power position of the small unions; their voices are already lost in the monolithic federations and national centres that are dominated by giant-enterprise unions:

> Traditionally, big company unions have tended to neglect the needs of those small and medium unions. After long experience of the relationship between large unions and small and medium unions, the smaller unions lack confidence and do not trust the larger unions very much. Their interests do not always coincide. In many cases, the smaller unions are pushed aside.
>
> (Sano and Ogawa, Sohyo, interview, 16 November 1982)

IN SEARCH OF THE PERIPHERAL UNIONS

That major unions are the prime actors in the organized segment of the workforce is to be expected. This feature of unionism is not unique to Japan. What is distinctive is that the action is virtually confined to the large-enterprise sector where the major enterprise unions and the majority of union members are to be found. Before turning to the implications of this situation for minor unions and non-unionized workers, it is appropriate to ask what are the advantages and disadvantages to be gained from the system. From the perspective of an individual union, established and viable, there are advantages. According to a summation by Cole (1971: 227–8) these are four-fold.

First, in mixed white- and blue-collar unions, white-collar workers tend to supply a very high proportion of union leadership.[11] This can mean an increase in the union's knowledge of the affairs of the enterprise and such intimate knowledge may lead to greater bargaining power. It may also result in greater co-operation between management and the union. The second point raised by Cole concerns the maintenance of staff levels. The fundamental purpose of the enterprise union is the retention of members as employees of the firm, and any suggestion of staff reduction is a strong mobilizing issue that contributes to guaranteeing job security for the union's members. His third point is that the employment background of union officials is an advantage. Union officials are usually elected from within the firm, and therefore it is possible to develop close bonds between these leaders and rank and file. Finally, Cole raises the issue of ideology. Enterprise unionism means that the union is based on enterprise consciousness and not on loyalty to the employer or management alone. This, he maintains, makes it possible for the union to think in terms of all employees throughout the enterprise, not merely one branch in one section.

Cole then suggests that, for a union operating under the principles of enterprise unionism, there are three main weaknesses embedded in the system. First, union members tend to be over-dependent on the fortunes of their individual enterprise. This renders union members susceptible to company manipulation. They are subject to pressures such as demands for increased productivity to protect the company and self-imposed wage restraint to avoid bankruptcy. He argues that it becomes difficult under these circumstances for the union to effectively represent the interests of its members as distinct from the interests of the company, that is, to better the company's competitive position and increase its competitive edge. The second disadvantage of the system to an enterprise union is that the presence of both white- and blue-collar workers in the union often contributes to severe internal union conflicts because, like foremen, white-collar workers can be manipulated into supporting company interests. This has a bearing on the propensity for union splits to occur. In this regard, Cole cites Fujita Wakao (1960) in noting that white-collar workers often take the initiative to split from the union and form a second union sympathetic to management (Cole 1971: 228). Finally, Cole believes a weakness of an enterprise union lies in the trade-off that arises from its strong identification with the interests of the enterprise. The enterprise union is usually opposed to opening membership to the company's temporary employees, and often lacks interest in problems outside the company, such as those relevant to national needs or social responsibilities. It is also usual for the enterprise union to be indifferent to the problem of organizing Japan's unorganized workers.

Hanami (1981) looks at disadvantages in the operation of enterprise unions from a different perspective and at factors that tend to hold unions on a short lease. He argues that large unions are, to a considerable extent, dependent on facilities granted by the company. Such privileges often include office space in the company buildings, meeting rooms, telephones, furniture, stationery, sometimes even photocopying services, and the collection of union dues from the payroll (Hanami 1981: 55). He points out that these facilities, granted free of charge by management to the union, symbolize the intimate relationship between them: 'such extensive privileges are more frequently to be found in the larger enterprises, where it may be said without exaggeration that the unions function at the company's expense' (Hanami 1981: 55).

Minor unions operate in their firms on a leash of a different kind, and advantages of the system, as outlined by Cole, are questionable. Minor unions have few, if any, privileges. This may lighten their load of obligation to management, but it adds to other restrictions that control their activities. The major constraints they face, as previously pointed out, lie in their lack of strength in numbers, lack of full-time officials, lack of finance, and lack of solidarity because of the higher labour turnover and higher levels of 'flexible' labour in these smaller firms. The difference in individual union strength in the core and peripheral segments of the workforce is dramatic. There is an average of 12 members in each of Japan's 5,800 labour unions in the small enterprises that employ fewer than 30 regulars (Table 6.3 above).

Clearly the plethora of firms in this environment is unlikely to be able to unionize effectively under the enterprise union system. There are almost 29,000 labour unions that have less than 100 members (Table 6.7 above), and their minor status is predetermined by the prerequisite that each must be self-motivated, operated, and financed.

Unions generally tend to approach management with their problems in the light of their 'enterprise pie' philosophy. Management and unions in the large-scale private sector tend to contend over the share of the pie but co-operate to make the pie larger. In the peripheral environment, if there is contention with management, there is co-operation in the hope that there will be a pie to share.

CONCLUSION

Segmentation of labour organization is an inbuilt feature of enterprise unionism. The system confines and binds labour organization to the enterprise, and in so doing, it is an interlocking mechanism within the structures and processes in Japanese industry that divides workers and stratifies their role in the workforce. The conjuncture of these characteristics — the division of labour, the stratification of labour effort and the segmentation of labour organization — is a crucial factor in the control of articulation of peripheral workers' interests in the management and labour dichotomy.

Enterprise unionism, more so than occupational or industrial unionism, imbues union tactics with particularist and exclusive goals. In so doing, and vested with authority and legitimacy by the state through its labour and related laws, the process inhibits the initiation and execution of broader strategies. Politicization is controlled and power imbalances are sustained not only between unions but between management and labour across the workforce.

The implications of enterprise-union particularism extend

beyond the organized segment of the workforce. Irrespective of the size of the firm and irrespective of whether a union does or does not exist, relations with management are a one-to-one phenomenon which is institutionalized under Japan's labour laws. Each union must negotiate directly with management. Where no union exists, the workforce in each firm must individually communicate with the firm's owner or management. In this way, the central features of the system become as relevant to a non-unionized firm as they are to a unionized enterprise. Moreover, in the organized segment of labour, the one-to-one onus in negotiations is not counterbalanced by the semblance of horizontal organization inferred by the existence of multi-industry or multi-union federations and councils.

Cross-enterprise union structures do not overcome intra-industry or intra-union rivalries or sectional or ideological divisions, rather, they are the arena in which differences emerge and are confronted. Enterprise unionism patently sharpens the containment of centres of union power to Japan's industrial giants and ensures the domination of minor unions in peripheral enterprises. Furthermore, it contributes to the relative expendability of organization among peripheral workers. The enterprise union system thus contributes significantly to the differences between the core and the peripheral sectors of the workforce.

The system also contributes to divisions within the union movement, one aspect of which is the maintenance of powerful major unions at the expense of relatively powerless minor unions. In addition, the segmentation of labour organization embedded in the system reaches out beyond unionism *per se* to affect both the organized and the 'union-free' peripheral segments of Japan's workforce.

That major unions are the prime actors in the organized segment of the workforce, that the action is virtually confined to the large enterprise sector goes far in explaining dominant trends in research. Research in the industrial relations area that concentrates on the large industry unions, national union centres, and allied industry councils fails to address the wider implications of enterprise unionism for minor unions or for non-unionized workers.

Clearly the characteristics of labour organization in Japan have a considerable effect on the articulation of workers' interests. In conjunction with other salient features of working either in the small and medium environment or on a non-regular basis, these characteristics materially influence styles of communication between management and workers and affect the course disputation and conflict will take. The final chapter of this study of the peripheral sector looks at these aspects of the industrial relations process.

NOTES

1. Exceptions are policemen, firemen, and prison guards (Hanami 1981: 102).
2. The list of references is legion. For example, see Cole (1971), Hanami (1981), and Shirai (1983). A useful source (published after the research for this was completed) is Kikuchi Kozo's 'The Japanese enterprise union and its functions' (in Tokunage and Bergmann 1984: 171–94). Other sources used in this profile of unionization were interviews with key actors between September 1982 and March 1983.
3. It is beyond the scope of this book to discuss Japan's industry, occupation, and general unions in depth. Brief reference to two non-enterprise unions has already been made (Chapter 1). The first is a very small union of self-employed homeworkers. Members are full-time male workers and the union covers only homeworkers in one area of Tokyo. In the case of this union, organization may provide some collective strength regarding general conditions of work but, like all homeworkers, members' wages and conditions are determined by contract arrangements with their individual orderers (Fujii, MOL, interview, 8 January 1983). In this sense, their fortunes are tied to the business for which they work. Whether this is a bona fida union under the terms of the Trade Union Law is not known.

The second general union is *Zen'ichijiro*. This is a union of some substance, which covers day labourers. It has 85,000 members — small by Japanese standards. The union is affiliated to Sohyo and to the WFTU (World Federation of Trade Unions). Its members are non-regular workers who work for numerous enterprises, and the union's objective is to improve working conditions for these day labourers and itinerants such as *dekasegi*. Some members of this union are unemployed, and one of the union's main activities is to find employment for these workers, frequently in the construction industry, but also in public works programmes. According to an executive member of the union:

> Some of our work involves trying to organize among day labourers at government employment centres and in the *yoseba* [street labour markets]. We often come into conflict with the *tehaishi* [body hire agents] and *yakuza* [organized criminal groups]. When day labourers get work through those sources, they have no legal protection and are likely to be badly exploited (interview, 22 December 1982).

This union can provide legal protection for its members, nevertheless their working conditions are still determined according to the situation prevailing in the establishment that employs them. These non-regular workers are thus not denied the right to organize but they do not have the capacity to enter a direct union-management relationship where they work.

4. MOL figures for 1975 cited in Hanami (1981) were the only source available at the time of the research for this book.

5. Occupation status — production or salaried workers — may affect unionization rates. This possibility is not pursued in this study. It can be noted that female salaried workers are clearly outnumbered by male salaried workers in all industries. However, there are sections of industry where the percentage of female production workers exceeds that of males: in the manufacture of food and allied products, tobacco products, apparel, and in electrical machinery. The numbers of male and female production workers are roughly equal in precision machinery (MOL 1983: 16–17).

6. Several establishments may be part of one enterprise.

7. IMF, Domei, and Sohyo respondents agreed that a union needed a minimum of 100 members to finance a full-time official and an office worker (interviews, December and January, 1982–3).

8. Figures used in Hanami's analysis are based on the 1976 Basic Survey of Trade Unions, Ministry of Labour.

9. It will be recalled that the union in Daitokogyo gear pump factory is affiliated to Sohyo through a metal trade union, Zen'kin; the union at Ina Sankyo, once a Domei affiliate, is an example of an independent union (see Chapter 5). Regarding non-enterprise-based unions, refer to note 3, this chapter.

10. IMF (JC) is the East Asian Centre of the International Metalworkers' Federation (IMF). The worldwide membership is 14.4 million. The Japan Council has administrative responsibility for the Federation of Korean Metal Workers' Unions, IMF Philippine Council, and IMF Republic of China Committee (ROCC).

11. Cole (1971: 227–8) cites a 1967 MOL survey showing that 47 per cent of unions were combined white- and blue-collar, 21 per cent were exclusively blue-collar, and 32 per cent were exclusively white-collar. Later figures are not available.

7

Communication and conflict

'Communication' is treated in this chapter as the complex range of formal and informal arrangements through which the different interests of management and labour may be aired, resolved, or controlled. The concept of 'conflict' refers to disagreement, protest, antagonism, and confrontation. In other words, conflict is used as a general term referring to the clash of interests in the management–worker dichotomy.

Clearly the issue of class conflict is on the hidden agenda in any examination of industrial unrest. However, it is not the intention to engage in any substantive discussion of class conflict or to reiterate theories of conflict in the industrial relations literature, which were dealt with earlier (Chapter 1). In that discussion, it was pointed out that the literature on industrial relations in Japan emphasizes 'traditional' harmony and consensus in the communication between management and labour. At the same time, there is a section of the literature (mainly the work of the convergence theorists) which sets out to de-bunk the myths in these perceptions. It is also the case that research in the area of conflict from either the classical culturalist or convergence perspectives tends to concentrate on the activities of Japan's large-scale unions. The *shunto* ritual of the unionized sector is frequently analysed but there is little documentation or analysis of other signals of conflict. Because of the importance of the comparative dimension, the following discussion will look at communication and conflict in both the core and peripheral sectors of the workforce. The main question to be considered is the extent to which salient features of the peripheral environment affect these central aspects of industrial relations.

FORMAL COMMUNICATION: THE LEGAL FRAMEWORK

Japan's labour laws, particularly the Trade Union Law, serve to institutionalize exclusivity in the communication between management and labour. Two of the main channels of formal communication are, first, collective bargaining and collective agreements, and second, work rules (rules of employment).

The principal laws that govern the formal procedures are the Trade Union Law (1949) and the Labour Standards Law (1947). Their stated purposes are to establish equal standing for workers and employers in bargaining (Trade Union Law, Article 1) and in reaching agreement regarding working conditions (Labour Standards Law, Article 2). Within an enterprise, it is mandatory for management in the private sector and some sections of the public sector to respond to the initiative of a bona fide union, no matter how small, for collective bargaining. In a collective agreement between management and labour, almost any management decision affecting working conditions in the enterprise can be included. For example, it is management prerogative to build an additional plant, but if employment or working conditions are likely to be affected, such a step is subject to discussion with the union. An application can be made to have the terms of a collective agreement in one establishment of an enterprise extended to include workers who are employed in other establishments of the same enterprise.

The smaller the enterprise, the weaker the trend for labour agreements to include a union shop clause (compulsory union membership). A labour ministry survey of 1,700 labour agreements (1978) showed that 50 per cent had union shop stipulations (Japan Institute of Labour 1979). These occurred in 73 per cent of enterprises employing 1,000 or more compared with 59 per cent of enterprises employing between 500 and 999 workers. The survey report noted that these figures included some agreements in which the wording of union shop clauses was ambiguous. For example, 'all employees shall, in principle, be union members', or 'the dismissal of an employee who leaves the union shall be subject to consultation'. Union shop agreements also frequently include a clause relating to industrial peace. (There are no data available from which to quantify this phenomenon.) In this case also, the wording may be imprecise. To maintain absolute industrial peace, the agreement must specify, for example, that the union agrees that every act of dispute regardless of aim will be refrained from during the term of the agreement. On the other hand, 'yellow dog' clauses in individual employment contracts, whereby the worker agrees not to join a union, are illegal.

There is a high conclusion rate of agreements. In 1981, 54,305 unions covering 9,079,000 members concluded labour agreements, and the conclusion ratio (the number of unions that concluded agreements divided by the number permitted to do so) was 83.5 per cent (*Japan Labor Bulletin*, April, 1982).[1] There are complications when there is more than one union in an enterprise. The Trade Union Law does not establish exclusive jurisdiction or bargaining rights for any one union. If a multi-union situation exists in any one enterprise, each union is entitled to put forward demands. Management must consult with each union although their individual demands or opinions can differ.

The formalization of work rules is a more flexible tactic for management than the procedure of negotiating an agreement.[2] If there are two (or more) unions in an enterprise, management is not required to canvass the opinions of the minor union. It is required to ask only the opinion of the union representing the majority, and if there is no union, a representative of the majority of workers. While the labour laws do not set the agenda for collective agreements, the Labour Standards Law specifies the core of matters that must be covered in work rules (such as starting and finishing times, shift work details, methods of wage determination and payment, and holidays). In addition, as noted previously (Chapter 3), management is free to establish different work rules within the one firm for workers of different occupations or status. Thus, compared with collective agreements, work rules are flexible, cover a narrower range of issues and impinge far less on management prerogative.

From management's perspective, arbitrary 'good management' and work rules are preferable to collective agreements, which are the likely outcome of unionization. It can be expected that this is one factor that motivates management in the peripheral sector to circumvent unionization in their firms. This is not to deny the checks and balances in work rules, whether the firm is unionized or not. Hanami Tadashi, ex-industrial commissioner, is of the opinion that:

the requirement of the Labour Standards Law with respect to work rules provides some guarantees on working conditions, otherwise management has a completely free hand.

(Hanami, interview, 22 December 1982)

Labour laws and the peripheral sector

The brief discussion of work rules and collective agreements above places these methods of communication between management and labour in a legal context. There are four main points to be made concerning the laws in practice in the peripheral segment of the workforce. First, the smaller the firm, the less likely that a union will exist, thus collective agreements are confined to the unionized sector. Second, as noted previously, the majority of firms in the peripheral sector are small in size, and work rules, although they exist in non-unionized establishments, are not obligatory in firms employing fewer than 10 people. Fourth, there are problems with the adequate policing of the Labour Standards Law and the protection it affords,[3] particularly with regard to non-regular workers and to intending entrants into the labour force. Finally, work rules and the stipulations in collective agreements (unless these are extended within an enterprise, as noted above), only apply to the single establishment concerned, in line with the practice of site bargaining over base-up wage hikes and bonuses in the spring and autumn labour offensives (*shunto*). In these ways, Japan's labour laws institutionalize the segmentation of communication and endorse the operating principles of enterprise unionism — principles that entrench work-site orientation and have a discriminatory function with respect to the non-unionized and peripheral segment of the workforce.

FORMAL AND INFORMAL COMMUNICATION MECHANISMS

In addition to formal mechanisms that cover collective agreements and work rules, there are other forms of intra-firm arrangements that buttress enterprise exclusiveness. Two of these are QCs and joint consultation. QCs are an important avenue of communication, and they are covered in a considerable body of literature. (See for example: Shimada 1981; JPC 1981; Littler 1982; *Japan Labor Bulletin* January 1982; Inagami 1983). However, before proceeding with the following discussion on the role and function of joint consultation, some brief observations concerning QCs are relevant.

Quality-control circles

QCs have the potential to bring lower-level management and workers together at shop-floor level or management and workers together at small-firm level. The circles are a form of in-house communication which became established in Japan in the 1960s, the concept originating from the USA. Their aim is to promote co-operation from small groups of workers to achieve improved quality and production. Workers in these groups and in other small-group movements such as the Suggestion System, Zero Defect (ZD), and Cost Reduction are encouraged to talk about problems they face every day in the workplace and to offer suggestions for improvements and innovations.[4]

The percentage of companies with QC and other small group activities varies considerably with firm size. In 1972 and 1977, the labour ministry conducted surveys of the diffusion of small-group activities and suggestion systems. While these surveys confirmed the growth of such groups, they also showed that there was a marked trend for workers' involvement to decrease as firm size declined. The 1977 survey data showed that over 77 per cent of workers in establishments with more than 5,000 workers were involved in QC, ZD, and similar movements compared with only 33 per cent in establishments employing between 100 and 299 workers. The survey covered around 5,000 privately owned establishments, but was confined to those employing 100 or more workers. The situation in smaller firms is therefore unknown.

As to the effectiveness of QCs as a means of communication between management and labour, Slezak, US Labour Counsellor in Tokyo, maintains that there are great disparities:

This depends, I think, on whether they are internally generated or put into place by management, are a sincere two-way communication or primarily a means by which management can prepare the way to do what it intended to do anyway. Some of the earlier QCs may have received their original impetus more from labour than management. Initial enthusiasm, unless kept continually relevant, tends to fall into a stratified, formalistic institution of very little value to either side.

(Slezak, interview, 4 March 1983)

Slezak drew attention to a recent (1982–3) MOL survey of 3,000 enterprises in which there were either QCs or JCs (Joint Consultation Councils). Most of the firms surveyed were small and medium firms. The results showed that 87 per cent of the QCs and JCs felt the activity had no real relevance to what was taking place in the firm:

In other words, the QCs and JCs were basically sounding boards that didn't really have any effect on the actual running of the business: 13 per cent versus 87 per cent. These figures are indicative of the groups' own evaluation that they are *pro forma* exercises rather than real avenues for meaningful discussion. Conversely, about 40 per cent of unions in these enterprises thought the circles and councils were important. That means that more than half (60 per cent) of the unions felt that the small groups basically had no relationship to the way the outfit was being run.

(Slezak, interview, 4 March 1983)

Joint consultation

Joint consultation brings upper management and labour together. This level of interaction has wide ramifications for the industrial relations situation in that it has the potential to involve degrees of information sharing and worker participation. It is an important factor in promoting an internal flow of communication and information about company affairs and employees' problems. It is clear however that joint consultation does not eliminate the demarcation between management and the managed, nor does it bring about the equality in negotiating power inferred in the term 'joint'.

A review of joint consultation strongly suggests differences in its operation between the core and peripheral sectors. Less formal than collective bargaining to which it is frequently linked, the process is a channel for preliminary negotiations leading to collective agreements, particularly in the large-scale sector. For example, prior to *shunto*, wage hikes and bonuses are vigorously examined in joint consultation, and it is at this time that the firm's economic position figures largely in any negotiated trade-offs. As will be seen, joint consultation is sometimes institutionalized through stipulations in collective agreements. This occurs most frequently in the large-scale enterprise sector where, since the mid-1950s, joint consultation has developed as an important ingredient in Japan's industrial relations processes and productivity movement strategy. The productivity movement is co-ordinated by the Japan Productivity Centre (JPC) — a liaison council of leading representatives from government, industry and commerce, and major labour unions.[5] At the outset, the early to mid-1950s, unions were suspicious of the movement, but now most major unions in the private sector participate.

The operative principles of the JPC stress three main points: first, that there is a relationship between improvement in productivity and increased employment; second, that there is a need for co-operation between management and labour in order to increase productivity; and, third, that the fruits of increased productivity should be distributed fairly among management, labour, and the consumer (JPC 1981: 6–8). In line with these principles, in 1980 the JPC took account of Japan's slower economic growth, rapidly ageing workforce, and the effects of the invisible revolution (computerization), which was leading Japan into the information society. It called for 'a concerted effort by business and labour to forge a consensus which is based on deep mutual trust and thorough consultation' (JPC 1981: 6–8).

According to Yamazaki Kichinosuke, Deputy Director of the JPC, consultation is based on the perception of industrial relations in Japan that:

Management and workers are all in the same boat; we sink or swim together. For management, profits are a guarantee of job security and better conditions for employees. Profits have another meaning for the trade unions. When the company's profits guarantee job security, this means job security of the union members and their better conditions.

In our education and training courses for both workers and management, we recommend the company give information to the unions, even secret information, so they trust and believe each other. Neither party likes strikes and workers know exactly what effect, how much money will be lost if they strike.

(Yamazaki, JPC, interview, 10 January 1983)

The disclosure of company trade secrets is a comparatively recent innovation in joint consultation. Suzuki Toshio, Deputy Director, Nikkeiren (interview, 6 December 1982) argues that one reason Japanese industrial relations are flexible in the face of changes in the market is that consultation takes place at the factory level. In this way, consultation within the enterprise is an effective process within Japan's industrial relations:

> Industrial relations is like a big apartment building and each apartment has a fire alarm equal to company level collective bargaining. If this alarm bell rings, everyone says 'Aha! That factory has some problem that may influence others'. In West Germany and the UK negotiations are not made in each apartment but at the higher echelon in the penthouse so if a fire starts it's difficult to recognize [the source], the problem that will inevitably effect, will cause a reaction in the penthouse. It takes a long time, many procedures, and a lot of money to settle the problem. Our system has a different historical and social background. It puts a fire alarm in each apartment, so it is very flexible and sensitive.

(Suzuki, Nikkeiren, interview, 6 December 1982)

Shimada (1981: 24–6) points out that a number of new labour/ management information-sharing practices, particularly joint consultation and QCs, have been developed in successful Japanese industries in the last quarter of a century. According to Shimada, labour leaders in some industries (such as steel, auto, and shipbuilding) attempted to foster new management-labour relations based on closer co-operation with management. This occurred against a background of confrontationist industrial relations and domination by left and communist leaders in the late 1950s. Management supported this new movement, which gradually attracted 'increasingly broader segments of key industries' (Shimada 1981: 24–6). It was in this atmosphere that new management-labour relations were promoted, in which 'intensive interactions between management and labour could take place' (Shimada 1981: 25–6).

Although there is a distinction between formal collective

bargaining and less formal joint consultation, their functions can overlap and, in practice, the separation of issues on the agenda is often not clear. The MOL Communications Survey (MOL, cited in Foreign Press Centre 1978: 32) found that procedures for joint consultations were in some cases stipulated: in establishments with 100 or more employees, 70.8 per cent had some form of labour consultation machinery and 48.1 per cent included this machinery as a stipulation in collective agreement.

Joint consultation is more frequently found in the unionized segment of the workforce. Again referring to the communication survey figures, 71 per cent of all firms surveyed had some form of joint consultation involving management and union officials. However, looking at frequencies by unionization, 83 per cent of unionized firms had a joint consultation system compared with only 41 per cent of non-unionized firms.

Organized information sharing occurs less frequently in smaller firms. This is revealed in a further MOL survey (1978) which looked at labour agreements in 1,700 labour unions in private enterprises (Japan Institute of Labour 1979). On average, 51 per cent of labour agreements in the survey provided machinery for labour-management consultation. However, in enterprises with more than 1,000 workers, the rate rose to 69 per cent. Moreover, the results of the survey underscored the significance of the autonomy of discrete unions; the individual unit unions in large enterprises (headquarters and branch offices or plants) will separately relate with management in regard to mechanisms for joint consultation: 'large enterprises with two plants or more often have joint consultation organs both in headquarters and branch offices or plants' (Japan Institute of Labour 1979: 26).

Union participation in company management through consultation was also covered by the 1979 MOL survey of 1,700 enterprise unions. On management and production issues, management in 13 per cent of cases 'simply make explanations' to the unions; 23 per cent seek opinions from the unions; 56 per cent discuss questions with the unions; 8 per cent need approval from the unions before making a decision; and 2 per cent have a formal agreement that union representatives will participate in corporate decision-making (Japan Institute of Labour 1979: 26–7). The survey results make it clear that joint consultation occurs less frequently as firms become smaller and as the frequency of unionization decreases.

There are other core-peripheral differences in the area of consultation. One difference concerns the composition of consultative meetings.[6] Management and workers usually elect an equal number of representatives, but the proportion of workers' representatives tends to be greater as the size of firms decreases (Japan Productivity Centre 1978, cited in Park 1984: 155). This could be expected in view of the likelihood in small firms that the owner-manager, frequently a working staff member, is able to consult with most of the workers in the firm without the arrangement becoming unwieldy.

A further way in which joint consultation differs according to firm size concerns management intervention in the selection of workers' representatives to meetings. Figures in Table 7.1 indicate that levels of management intervention tend to increase the smaller the firm, although in giant enterprises at plant level the percentage of management appointees is also relatively high.

Table 7.1 Workers' and employees' joint consultation meetings (*rōshi kyōgikai*), representatives appointed by management

Company size (workers)	Company level (%)	Plant level (%)
5,000 or more	—	22.0
1,000–4,999	10.1	1.1
300–999	9.6	4.0
100–299	16.7	24.6

Source: Ministry of Labour, *Rōshi Kommyunikeishon Chōsa Hōkoku* (Report on analysis of labour-management communication), Tokyo, 1978, pp. 88 ff. in 'Trade unions and joint consultations', in *Industrial Relations in Transition*, ed. by Tokunaga Shigeyoshi and Joachim Bergmann, Tokyo: University of Tokyo Press, 1984: 156.

This brings into question the effectiveness of worker participation through joint consultation. Park (1984: 162–3) refers to a recent MOL study that indicates managers regard negotiations with union leaders as less important than their informal contacts with shop stewards and supervisors.[7] Park then cites MOL figures indicating increasing worker dissatisfaction with the system as firms decrease in size (Table 7.2). Thirty-four per cent of workers in very large companies (over 5,000 workers) felt that joint consultation concerning business policy was 'fairly good' compared with only 15 per cent in medium and small firms (employing 100–300 workers). Those 'not at all satisfied' accounted for 34 per cent of the workers surveyed in the very large firms, but 55 per cent in the medium and small category (Park 1984: 162).[8]

Table 7.2 Workers' satisfaction with labour-management system (*rōshi kyōgi-sei*) concerning business policy

Company size (workers)	Fairly good (%)	Not at all (%)	Don't know (%)
5,000 or more	34.0	34.1	31.9
1,000–4,999	22.4	47.4	30.2
300–999	21.6	51.5	26.9
100–299	15.0	55.4	29.6

Source: Ministry of Labour, *Rōshi Kommyunikeishon Chōsa Hōkoku* (Report on analysis of labour-management communication), Tokyo, 1978, pp. 88 ff. in 'Trade unions and joint consultations', in *Industrial Relations in Transition*, ed. by Tokunaga Shigeyoshi and Joachim Bergmann, Tokyo: University of Tokyo Press, 1984: 162.

Park argues that the functioning of joint consultation largely depends on management:

> As long as unions remain in the present state of weak bargaining and organizational capacity, labour-management consultation may remain a matter for the management. The system should therefore be named the 'management information (downward) system'.
>
> (Park 1984: 163)

Park clearly looks at the management/union relationship when making the point that formal consultation in the unionized segment of the workforce may be management-dominated though nominally democratic. It then becomes relevant to raise the issue of informal consultation outside the unionized segment.

COMMUNICATION AND WORKERS' ASSOCIATIONS

Workers' intra-firm societies and associations become increasingly important as channels for interaction between management and labour with the decrease in unionization and formal communication as firms employ fewer workers.[9] Views differ on their function. For example, Yamazaki (JPC executive member) believes that they are a deliberate choice by conservative and inexperienced management:

> One of the main reasons there are so few unions in small and medium firms is that most are individually owned, the president is the owner, they live in small towns where many friends are also owners of small businesses. They have no idea about working with an organized union. To them, a union means 'left wing' or 'communism'. They believe that unions are not useful to management. The union concept is not matured and they cannot understand that the union is a counterpart of the company.
>
> (Yamazaki, JPC, interview, 10 January 1983)

According to Levine, there is undoubtedly a considerable amount of informal collective negotiation within small and medium-scale enterprises via workers' associations:

> it is well-known that the workers form their associations or 'friendly clubs' within the small firms for the purpose of presenting a common front to their employer over terms and conditions of work, even though they do not bother to seek to be qualified as legally recognized unions under the procedures provided for that purpose by the labor-relations [sic] commissions.
>
> (Levine 1982: 25)

Koike (1983) sheds some light on the inverse relationship between frequencies of unions and workers' associations (Figure 7.1). As unionization declines with the decrease in firm size, there is 'an inverse and partially compensating relationship between size of firm and the number of employees belonging to some other employee organization' (Koike 1983: 103–4). Koike estimates that if these 'de facto unions' became qualified as unions, the rate of unionization in Japan would rise to more than 50 per cent. From another perspective, Park (1984) sees the function of these company social groups as being 'strongly converging' towards that of joint consultation. As a result, a workers' association tends to replace the labour union and formal joint consultation, at least in small and medium-sized enterprises (Park 1984: 164).

Figure 7.1 Ratios of firms in which employee organizations exist, by size of firm

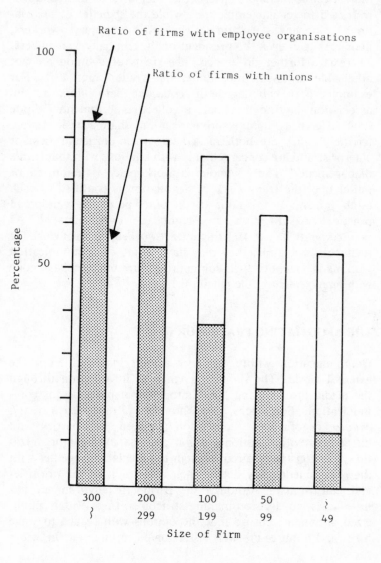

Source: Koike, K., 1981, in Koike, Katsuo, 'Workers in small firms and women in industry', in Shirai, T. (ed.), *Contemporary Industrial Relations in Japan*, Wisconsin: University of Wisconsin Press, 1983: 103.

A major difference between workers' associations and unions lies not only in the informality of the associations but in their more flexible membership criteria. Membership of a union is restricted to regular employees, while the societies or associations can have part-time workers, temporary workers, managers, and even the president of the company as members. There is a further difference. The rights of a union are not applicable to associations under the Trade Union Law. For example, both can engage in collective bargaining, but an association may not negotiate a collective agreement. Despite such differences, unions and associations share a basic characteristic — they are both locked into their particular firm or enterprise and are concerned only with relations with that firm's management.[10] Thus, whether a work place is unionized or union free, the framework of negotiation is confined to each establishment. In this context, the outcome of the widespread practice of sub-contracting cannot be over-estimated. As pointed out (Chapter 4), sub-contract workers in effect work for their firm's patrons; they may have a line of communication with management of their sub-contract firm but they have none with management in the patron firm.

THE NEGOTIATING FRAMEWORK

Communication within the firm is not insulated from the external world. The public exchange of information through the media has a strong input into internal processes of communication. For weeks, even months, prior to each year's *shunto* negotiations, contention between the parties and differences within national union and management organizations are constantly aired through the media as, together with the government, they debate their evaluation of the priorities and constraints.[11] Although the peripheral environment has little access to decision-making structures, these widely publicized arguments ensure that the options with regard to wage hikes and bonuses are well disseminated throughout the wider society.

The options come to the attention of management and labour even in the smallest firms. In addition to the extensive media coverage, the national federations and confederations of employers and unions transmit their diverse arguments to their affiliates and to each prefectural and local chapter, council, and branch. This co-ordinating role, as noted previously (Chapter 6), is one of the major functions of these centres. National management or union federations do not sit at each negotiating table, nevertheless, their arguments and eventual agreements are the unwritten preamble to each agenda when the options reach each firm's bargaining table. It is then that the particular priorities and constraints indigenous to the firm enter the debate.

Examples of this were observed in some of the firms discussed in case studies (Chapter 5). The president of the Mochizuki Steel Company, a non-unionized firm, was waiting on the outcome of *shunto* negotiations before deciding on 'base-up' wage hikes and bonus allocations for his firm. At this time also, the union at the Daitokogyo gear pump plant, affiliated to Sohyo, was having regular meetings to discuss Sohyo's position and publishing details of Sohyo's argument in its regular news sheet. By way of further illustration, the official discussion paper issued by the Federation of All Toyota Unions to its 189 union affiliates (Spring Offensive 1981) states in part:

> *Independent, self-incentive negotiation*
> *is required for each union to reach a satisfactory*
> *agreement with management*

> Owing to the stringent economic environment, it is probable that the management's reaction will be based on the actual business performance of each enterprise. Each union will have to carry out its bargaining on an independent basis according to the actual wage level, livelihood, and service of its members.
>
> (*Union Activities at Toyota*, International Division,
> Federation of All Toyota Unions, 1981: 16)

Hanami (interview, 22 December 1982) maintains that the media play an extremely important role in taking *shunto* beyond the confines of management and union bargaining in the large-scale sector. He argues that *shunto* affects conditions in both the unionized and non-unionized sectors in a situation in which enterprise unionism, as opposed to craft or industrial unionism, is less likely to achieve an equitable distribution of working conditions throughout industry. In Hanami's assessment:

211

Shunto has a total reaction in the unorganized sector, and it is in this context that the role of the media becomes critical. Through bargaining by pattern setters in strongly organized and prosperous industries, a market price — the wage hike for the year — is established, say 6 per cent to 8 per cent. Then smaller enterprises — I'm talking about the organized ones — must follow this pattern more or less. At this point the media is very important. Everyone knows that this year's market price is x per cent. Large and prosperous enterprises agree to, say, x plus per cent wage hikes, others, maybe smaller and less prosperous, settle for x minus per cent.

(Hanami, interview, 22 December 1982)

Even in the non-organized sector, Hanami asserts, management must provide an approximation of the wage equivalent in order to get new workers. This was particularly so in the 1960s and early 1970s with Japan's very fast rate of economic development and serious labour shortage. At that time 'there were about seven job offers for one junior school leaver' and this continued for several years (interview, 22 December 1982). Wages increased very rapidly — small businesses found it very difficult to get labour and had to offer even higher starting wages compared to large enterprises. In this way:

The *shunto* mechanism and our notion arising from it, particularly about the market price of labour, taken together with the function of the media, are very important. Even workers in the very smallest enterprises think — well, we are part of the market therefore we are entitled to a share of the cake somehow.

(Hanami, interview, 22 December 1982)

In reply to an interview question on the flow-on effects of *shunto*, a leading official of Nikkeiren (Federation of Employers' Organizations), put the following management view:

We say, of the small-scale enterprises, the average wage increase should not exceed the total productivity increase. Therefore large-scale industries have a pattern-setting influence, while the smaller firms maintain slightly lower-level increases, taking account of their lower productivity levels.

Differences between the large and the medium/small sector are generally accepted by society. The important point is the small-sector role of the individual proprietor — the president — and his attitude. His attitude and personality have a big influence. He may be very arbitrary, he has a wider freedom to be so.

(Suzuki, interview, 6 December 1982)

The Workers' Association at Mochizuki Steel Fabrication Company (Chapter 5) illustrates this role of the owner/president. In the Mochizuki case (as in the Ōshima Seisakusho and Takamori Company factories in the Ina Valley), decisions regarding conditions may have been benevolent but they were nevertheless arbitrary.

THE NEGOTIATING FRAMEWORK: THE PERIPHERAL SECTOR

Given the focus here on communication, the point made by Hanami and Nikkeiren thus opens up the question of who makes the decision on wages. Notwithstanding the effects of *shunto* in setting the bargaining framework, it is clear that dominance of management in these and other decisions sets the power-relations parameters. This point was pursued throughout the research for this book; respondents were asked how working conditions for workers in the small and medium sector were decided, particularly in the case of non-unionized firms. A selection of their responses is as follows.

Sohyo respondents, Sano and Ogawa, who are responsible for organization among workers in small and medium to small firms, asserted that 'there is no reliable data collection on the determination of wages and conditions for small and medium, non-unionized workers, nor is there any known systematic approach to such data collection' (interview, 16 November 1982). Sano and Ogawa made the following points. The peripheral, non-unionized workers exist in a relatively 'lawless situation'. As the scale of companies and the numbers of employed decrease, so does the frequency of neglect of the provisions of the Labour Standards Law. They gave the example of the situation for part-timers. Even the government officially admits the law is breached. The respondents gave an example.

Research into the conditions of part-timers (conducted by the Administrative Bureau under Nakasone prior to his election as Prime Minister) found that 30 per cent did not receive any annual leave despite the stipulation that they must do so.

The Sohyo officials then agreed with other estimates that workers' associations may function as informal instruments of negotiation between management and non-unionized labour, although they felt this would be unlikely to apply to very small firms:

> Off the cuff, in a non-union shop there is often a friendship, or social association, which might meet to organize social activity. A representative of such an organization often has meetings, talks, with the owner — in a very friendly way, sometimes not so friendly — where questions of wages and conditions will come up. This situation would often apply in the larger of the small enterprises. In the smaller firms, the decisions are arbitrary . . . workers have no choice but to accept or quit.
>
> (Sano and Ogawa, Sohyo, interview, 16 November 1982)

They pointed out that members of workers' associations and societies share entertainment and travel together, and they share in collecting gifts of money for members and their families' weddings and funerals. The owner or the company management often subsidizes these activities:

> In supporting [workers' associations] management tends to absorb any dissatisfaction, resolve any problems before such problems encourage workers to organize a union *per se*. So long as this type of organization stays at the social or friendship level . . . okay. Management is happy to see them established but is particularly careful not to let these friendly associations have contact or affiliation with any outside organization. The attitude of management of small and medium firms is pragmatic in the sense that unionization is inhibited, a friendly one-family atmosphere is promoted, workers are happier and morale is increased.
>
> (Sano and Ogawa, Sohyo, interview, 16 November 1982)

On this question of decision-making structures and working conditions, Hanami saw the situation as one in which the arbitrary decision of management was paramount:

> It's quite simple. When there is no union — even if there is a very weak or very small union that is not able to put its case, it can be ignored by management in small enterprises — management decides working conditions. Even if management consults workers about work rules (and by law he should if there are more than 10 employees), and even if they protest, management can unilaterally make the rules. As a result, for the majority in the unorganized sector — the small and medium sector — management decides. That's the true situation today. Still. If workers object, they can leave.
>
> (Hanami, interview, 22 December 1982)

The Secretary of the International Division of Domei, Sado Masatoshi, also pointed to the arbitrary decisions of management in non-unionized enterprises (interview, 12 January 1983). He noted, however, that there were some controls over management, particularly the perception of unionization as a 'threat'. These controls prompted management concessions of some advantage to workers:

> It must be borne in mind that management of small enterprises always have been and will continue to be fearful of their workers getting together to form unions. It is an important task to spread information to unionized as well as non-unionized workers, to keep them better informed, but it is also important to inform management. Management will try to pass on base-up increases to non-union workers that are similar to those for unionized workers in order to circumvent unionization. The decision is of course an arbitrary one. Management is not ruthless. It is part of the control mechanism to avoid the emergence of trade unions that management listens and then determines wages and conditions. They tell their workers 'you haven't a union but you're getting similar improvements, so what's the point in having a union?'
>
> (Sado, Domei, interview, 12 January 1983)

In making decisions, management in smaller firms are themselves constrained by their dependent status. Lester Slezak noted that little is known about management relations with workers who, in his words, exist in the void:

215

Scholars such as Taira zeroed in on Japan's large enterprises and ignored — took no cognizance of — the bulk of enterprises. Take, for example, the extensive system of subcontracting. This keeps everybody on a very tight rope — they have nowhere else to go. I was naïve enough when I came here two and a half years ago to believe that the *kanban* system meant that if a sub-contractor has labour problems you shut down the whole facility. But workers know that if they interrupt production, the contract is quickly cancelled. Under this system there is no real democracy. Trade union latitude is very much at the beck and call — totally — of the prime user. A sub-contractor, say, has 20 to 30 workers and some self-employed and industrial homeworkers — they have nowhere to go. What are the alternatives for management of small and medium sub-contractors? Many would prefer greater freedom but of these, many have been set up with loan capital, and they are in bond.

(Slezak, interview, 4 March 1983)

Slezak argued that in the short and long term the major problem facing labour is fear. Fear is probably the strongest control mechanism in the management-labour relationship, he maintained, particularly fear that the world economic climate is going to have a negative effect on the export market — the moving force behind the economy. At the core of fear is also the effect on workers of technological advances and the use of off-shore suppliers.[12]

Slezak pointed out that until the end of the 1970s it was an article of faith in unions of big corporations that nobody lost a job as a result of the introduction of high technology. The corporations have been reassuring the unions that displaced workers will have other employment within the enterprise. However:

there has been a gradual but now very perceptible concern that the intervention of these new technologies will in fact result in diminished employment down the line. 'We' now have to find new ways to handle this and this change contributes to fear. Even the slightest improvement on the assembly line means less sub-contract and less sub-sub-contract work, for example for homeworkers. . . . The tail end of the line gets socked every time.

(Slezak, interview, 4 March 1983)

216

COMMUNICATION BREAKDOWN

Problems for labour that are brought about by the technological revolution can be dealt with through conventional channels in the core sector. For example, after three decades of harmonious labour-management relations, an historic agreement with Nissan unions (signed in March 1983) was a direct response to the concern over the effects of technology on the workforce. The dispute involved Jidosharoren, the Federation of Japan Automobile Workers' Unions, which covers unions belonging to corporations in the Nissan group. (Jidosharoren has a total membership of 230,000 and is affiliated to IMF-JC.) What had previously been an 'article of faith' was written into the new Nissan agreement. No workers presently employed by Nissan were to be released or demoted as a result of the introduction of new technologies. Attrition could occur, but workers now employed were for the time being protected. The union was particularly concerned that there should be consultation prior to technological change: no lay-offs, demotion, or wage reductions as a result of the introduction of robots; education and retraining and a fair distribution of the fruits of increased productivity following robotization. The dispute ended when union demands were eventually incorporated into the labour agreements that covered the Nissan group workers.

However, fear related to the effects of new technologies on job security was not the only issue in the dispute. While the union was concerned that the rapid advance of robotization was not going to proceed as smoothly as expected, it was also concerned that management was not keeping to the spirit of agreements on joint/prior consultation (*Japan Labor Bulletin*, December 1982, March 1983). At the union's October 1982 annual convention, it was decided to cease co-operation in the productivity movement because 'management strongly opposes labour-management joint consultation'. The '3 Ps' movement (participation, productivity, and progress) had not worked well because management was neglecting the joint consultation system (*Japan Labor Bulletin*, December 1982).

Problems related to joint consultation were highlighted also by a bitter dispute which occurred in 1982 in the Japan National Railway (JNR), involving management and two of several JNR unions — the National Railway Workers' Union (Kokuro) and a splinter union of the National Railway Locomotive Engineers'

217

Union (Doro). The dispute arose over management's attempts to revise the long-standing 'workplace consultation system'. Japan National Railway authorities wanted a revision, because 'the consultation had deviated from its original purposes and has been used by union members as "kangaroo courts" to try their bosses' (*Japan Times*, 2 December 1982: 2). The two rebel unions (three others had worked out an agreement with management) rejected a management plan for revision on the grounds that it was unacceptable in that it denied them the right to have direct negotiations with management at each workplace. The two unions took the matter to arbitration. This involved the body that has jurisdiction over disputes in public corporations and public enterprises (Koroi), which ruled it could not mediate 'because both sides had not discussed the matter enough' (*Japan Times*, 2 December 1982: 2). Negotiations broke down completely. There was no disruption to JNR services, but until the matter was eventually settled, there were no labour contracts between the two unions and management.

These disputes involving Nissan and JNR unions suggest that any default in consultation procedures that have become customary can precipitate a dispute. Joint consultation can become so deeply entrenched in highly unionized sections of the workforce as to be seen as a 'right'. More importantly, these two disputes are also an indication of the delicate balance between co-operation and disputation despite an array of mechanisms aimed at diffusing conflicting relations within an enterprise.

CONFLICT AND INDUSTRIAL ACTION

As noted at the outset of this discussion, the literature dealing with Japan's industrial-relations situation is dominated by the theme that relationships between management and labour are consensual and strongly influenced by Japanese values. From this perspective, co-operative communication through such mechanisms as joint consultation is seen as a means of avoiding recourse to open conflict. This interpretation is oversimplified, undifferentiated, and misleading. The preceding discussion has shown the differences in incidence and effectiveness of communication mechanisms across the spectrum of the Japanese workforce. In the following analysis of conflict and industrial action, it will be argued that the interaction between Japan's enterprise union system, the relevant laws, and working environment produces not only differences in expressions of conflict through dispute tactics but differences in conflict control. Avenues through which workers are able to communicate in a positive way or express conflict through disputation thus tend to be proscribed by objective circumstances. Where consensual relations appear to exist, they still tend to be more a function of the relative power relations between management and labour than an abiding commitment to a traditional ideology. This perception is supported by an examination of disputation and conflict control.

Conflict and disputation: the legal framework

There is clearly a difference between conflict and disputation. Conflict is an informal state of confrontation and under given conditions has the potential to become a labour dispute. Obviously, conflict can arise at any point across the whole spectrum of core-peripheral enterprises and, in a broad sense, such conflict can result in 'disputes'. In the Japanese situation, formal labour disputes, that is, those to be dealt with under the specified procedures for resolution, can occur only when a union is involved. Although this is not specifically stated, the provisions of the Trade Union Law, for example, make it clear that only unions are involved in formal disputes.[13] The distinction between conflict and dispute was explained by one actor as follows:

> Disputes (*rodosogi*), are official, and are employer versus union. Labour conflicts (*funso*), are not official and can be settled informally.
>
> Disputes are between management and a union, not a labour organization. If there is conflict where there is no union, we do not call this a dispute. There are cases of unions setting up friendship clubs for individual workers to go to for help about their conditions. One example is Zen'kokuippan Rodokumiai, the National Union of General Workers. It's affiliated to Sohyo and its membership covers workers in several enterprises. Another is Zen'ichijiro, the day labourers' union. The unions can be involved in disputes but not the clubs attached to them.
>
> (Fujii, Trade Union Division, MOL, interview, 7 January 1983)

219

As defined by the labour ministry (MOL 1983), a labour dispute is any action by the concerned parties with regard to workers' status, which is accompanied by an act of dispute or for the settlement of which a third party intervenes through conciliation, mediation, or arbitration. The responsibilities of officers attached to MOL (frequently referred to as labour policy officers) at times involve their participation as the third party in resolving formal disputes. In 1980, for example, these officers were involved in 12 out of 299 formal disputes that were resolved through the intervention of a third party (MOL 1982b). However, they are frequently called on by parties in a unionized firm to attempt to diffuse conflict at the informal level and prevent its escalation.

The labour commissions have many diverse responsibilities related to the different interests of labour and management. One of these, for example, concerns disputed interpretations of collective agreements or applications for extensions of their terms to cover workers in another section of the same enterprise or who are covered by a unit union of the labour union involved. A case noted by Fukuda, Deputy Director, Dispute Adjustment Division, Central Labour Commission (interview, 8 March 1983), illustrates this role.

Shitetsuroren — a national union which covers unions of workers in privately owned transport (trains and buses) was involved and therefore the case came under the jurisdiction of the central rather than prefectural labour commission. Unions affiliated to Shitetsuroren in two small bus companies in Hokkaido found that one company offered a ¥10,000 wage rise, while the other offered ¥8,000. The two unions, each with their own labour agreements, came to the Central Labour Commission for a ruling on parity.[14]

A further role of the labour commissions is to interpret what constitutes a 'proper' (legal) industrial action and what constitutes an 'unfair labour practice'. (The parties concerned can choose whether the case will go to the commissions or to Japan's courts.) Sympathy strikes and political strikes are ruled to be illegal, that is, not proper industrial action, the former by the Tokyo District Court (1975), and the latter by the Supreme Court (1973). The rationale for this is that the purposes of such disputes are outside management authority. For this reason also, political strikes are deemed to have been 'settled', and are quantified in this way (Fukuda, Central Labour Commission, interview, 8 March 1983).

Industrial action involving production control is also illegal (Supreme Court ruling, 1950). By definition, production control is an industrial action by which a union, in order to gain its objectives, seizes the workplace, its facilities, and materials. The union runs the business and refuses to accept the employer's directions. In the post-war period and prior to the 1950 Supreme Court ruling there were many such cases (see Moore 1983). Thus there are legal restrictions and prohibitions that determine 'proper' industrial action.[15]

Briefly, improper industrial actions include wild-cat strikes, acts that can cause bodily harm or threaten the maintenance of safety machinery, deliberate production of defective goods, sabotage, and blocking non-striking workers from entry to a workplace or access to equipment. Interpretation of what constitutes an improper industrial action is needed in cases where tactics otherwise acceptable are deemed to have been carried to excess (see for example, Hanami 1981). Examples are: the wearing of union armbands that may embarrass customers (as witness the Hotel Okura case, discussed below); pasting up so many posters that glue has to be removed by paid labour; mass applications for leave; and excessive go-slow tactics.

The Hotel Okura case illustrates neatly how conflicts can be transformed into disputes, and shows the distinction between 'improper industrial actions' and 'unfair labour practices'. The 'improper act' on the part of the union occurred in 1970, when members of the Hotel Okura union wore their union armbands during working hours to display the union's demands for wage increases. Six union leaders were penalized a half day's pay. This case was raised with the labour commission which ruled that management's penalties on union leaders was an unfair labour practice. The supreme court 12 years later, in 1983, upset this ruling after years of argument in lower courts. The higher court ruling on the case was that the union's activity was not 'proper' industrial action and management's imposition of penalties was therefore not an unfair labour practice. This case, as discussed with the director of the Dispute Adjustment Division (Fukuda, Central Labour Commission, interview, 8 March 1983), illustrates a legal aspect of dispute settlement — that disputes are not solely confined to labour commission jurisdiction. Fukuda explained:

221

We are asked to step in, and we check the facts and the precedents. We make a judgement — literally this is not regarded as an 'adjustment' but *shinsa* — 'examine and judge'. We interpret nuances. When a case such as this goes to the courts, many delicate differences would become apparent. In manufacturing, armbands are tolerated, but in banks and hotels, the judgement suggests the action would embarrass and alienate people in the company from customers, *fuyukai*.

(Fukuda, interview, 8 March 1983)

Thus the labour commissions and the courts act when it is claimed, as in the opening gambit of the Hotel Okura case, that 'unfair labour practices' have been committed by management.

UNFAIR LABOUR PRACTICES

The original concept of unfair labour practices came from the US Wagner Act (1935), which was a protective measure for unions against management. In the US, however, the Taft-Hartley Act (1947) introduced measures whereby the employer could also claim protection — in this case from unfair practices on the part of the union. This extended idea of unfair labour practices in the US does not exist in Japanese law. Nevertheless, in some circumstances, again citing the Okura case, management may be successful in having an act of dispute ruled to be improper, thereby invoking legal protection against a designated union.

There are, in general terms, three categories of unfair labour practices, as summarized by the Japan Institute of Labour (1979). In the first category, management discriminates against an employee by discharging him for taking part in union activities. Such unlawful discharge is also null and void according to civil law. A 'yellow-dog' employment contract — a worker undertaking not to join a union — is also null and void. A second type of unfair labour practice occurs if management refuses to take part in collective bargaining. The third type of unfair labour practice occurs if management attempts to control or interfere with the organization or management of a union. Examples of this are paying the wages of union officials or striking workers or giving excessive financial assistance or facilities to the union.

With regard to redress in the case of claims of unfair dismissal, refusal to bargain, and interference in union affairs, plaintiffs have the choice of taking the issue to either the labour commissions or the civil courts. There is the right of appeal, and an appeal against a commission ruling can be lodged with a civil court. If final judgement is in the union's or worker's favour, management must reinstate the dismissed worker or workers and pay wages retroactively, management must participate in collective bargaining, and management must publicly apologize to the union and agree to discontinue interference. The plaintiff may be a union, an individual union member, or an individual worker who, for example, has been dismissed for attempting to establish a union.

Unfair labour practices: the peripheral sector

It would seem at first sight that in the unfair labour practice at last there is scope for action for workers in Japan's non-unionized peripheral sector. The average case, however, takes well over 600 days to process through the labour commission (Matsuda 1983: 182). There is always the possibility that litigants will appeal to a higher and then still higher court, and 'one could easily assume that it might take decades for a dispute involving an employer's unfair labour practice to be resolved once and for all' (Matsuda 1983: 184). The Hotel Okura case, a case in point, took twelve years to be finally resolved.

The prospect of lengthy (and costly) litigation is a strong disincentive for minor and minority unions or individual workers to pursue a perceived industrial malpractice on the part of management. According to Sado (Domei):

A worker might be dismissed as undesirable because, for example, he tried to start a union. He can take his case to the courts or the commission, but this seldom happens. These cases commonly take up to four years to be settled, sometimes much longer. Long delays frequently happen if the union concerned is influenced by the communist element. The labour commission tends to consider this brings confrontation into the case, that the Japanese Communist Party always has class conflict uppermost in mind. A compromise is very difficult to achieve because of the Communist Party's rigid class struggle

223

approach. In addition, their demands are very difficult for management to accept. Such cases very often drag on for years. This is unlike cases in which we [Domei] are involved. Our philosophy is that industrial relations problems should be decided by direct management and labour negotiation. If we are involved in a dispute, the case tends to be settled quickly.

(Sado, interview, 12 January 1983)

The number of cases of unfair labour practices has remained around 1,000 to 1,500 annually since the peak industrial unrest in 1974–5 (Fukuda, interview, 8 March 1983; Matsuda, 1983).[16] This consistency contrasts with strike frequencies, dealt with below, which show a decline over the same period, but tend to fluctuate. The most 'troublesome' area is the small and medium sector (Matsuda 1983; Fukuda, Central Labour Commission, interview, 8 March 1983; Hanami, interview, 22 December 1982). Matsuda (1983) researched this aspect of conflict and found two trends: first, looking at unions involved in cases of unfair labour practices, the majority of cases involved minor unions and minority unions in a multi-union situation; second, compromise or a swift resolution was particularly remote when minority unions were involved. This finding is not surprising given the likelihood that cases that reach the courts and commissions involve only the most determined and committed litigants who persist despite the disincentives.

Perceived unlawful dismissal or other inequities[17] are at times unable to be confronted by conventional industrial action due to the absence of a union or union support. Such a situation can produce other forms of protest. As Sado pointed out:

On occasions, if one worker claims unfair treatment, sympathetic outsiders, sometimes the Japanese Communist party, form an association to help the worker. They picket and so on. This isn't a true union, and this is conflict — not a dispute.

(Domei, interview, 12 January 1983)

It is not uncommon for outsiders to give support by forming an *ad hoc* association or protest committee. Such groups may then organize demonstrations, pickets, poster paste-ups, petitions, and the distribution of leaflets aimed at publicizing the issue and embarrassing the management concerned.[18] If the issue is substantial, applications will be lodged with the Police Traffic Branch for permits to stage a march. Such actions are at times successful in obtaining informal settlement of the issue in dispute. This form of action is not outside the law provided life and property are not endangered. The support group, however, has no formal status, settlement is a private arrangement and, throughout the exercise, the group does not have the protection that is afforded to unions with their institutionalized rights and special access to legal redress.

DISPUTATION AND STRIKES

Characteristics of disputation and strikes in Japan are dealt with only briefly here,[19] nevertheless several observations, because of their relevance to the core-peripheral dichotomy, need to be raised. First, the majority of disputes are settled by direct negotiation between management and labour. Of the disputes 'adjusted' by a third party, mainly the labour commissions, the vast majority are dealt with by conciliation, particularly disputes in the private sector. Some are settled by mediation and relatively few go to arbitration (PMO 1982b; Fukuda, interview, 8 March 1983).

The overall picture of disputation in Japan is biased due to trends in the public sector. The majority of disputes (not involving work stoppages) and also the majority of brief disputes are in the public sector, particularly in the public utilities where industrial action is extensively restricted. For example in 1980,[20] Sohyo, with its base in the public sector, was involved in 72.7 per cent of disputes accompanied by dispute action, and accounted for 83.3 per cent of all disputes of less than half a day (PMO 1982b; see also Appendix 7: 'Labour disputes by principal labour unions, 1980'). Disputes involving Domei, Shinsanbetsu, Churitsuroren and other labour unions, who operate mainly in the private sector, were involved in the remaining 27.3 per cent of disputes and 16.6 per cent of the short strikes. Data for other years show similar trends. As has been noted, higher levels of militancy in the public sector may be due in part to the long-standing demand for 'restoration of the right to strike'. This demand is a strong politicizing factor. Hanami believes that if government workers were given the right to strike, disputation would decrease markedly, and 'workers in the JNR [Japan

National Railways] would behave themselves much better' (interview, 22 December 1982).

But what of the private sector, and in particular, the small and medium sector? One point to be noted is the range of issues involved in disputes (MOL 1983). Irrespective of enterprise size, wages and allowances are by far the major issues in all disputes. Of the array of other problems and demands, disputes in large enterprises tend to be related to the conclusion or overall revision of agreements. Disputes in the small and medium enterprises are less concerned with this question than with workers' security — retirement and continuity of employment — for example, closure or reduction of business operations and, in the small firms, discharge or the re-instatement of discharged workers.

Of particular interest is the data concerning strike frequencies. The data here (Table 7.3) indicate that disputation tends to be higher in the mid-range of enterprises by size than in either large enterprises or very small firms, thus forming an inverted U-shaped curve. Of 2,766 private enterprises involved in disputes (accompanied by dispute tactics), 57 per cent were medium in size. Almost 10 per cent involved firms with less than 30 employees. This means that about 67 per cent of firms involved in disputes were in the small and medium sector. Of course, because of the sizes of these firms, the numbers of workers involved was small — less than 25 per cent of the total.

The interesting pattern that emerges from the figures in Table 7.3 is the level of industrial turbulence in firms of the medium to medium-small range. There are literally millions of firms in the peripheral sector, and from this perspective, the number of enterprises in which strikes occur is relatively small. From another perspective, the incidence of disputes is surprisingly high, given that unionization rates in this sector are extremely low and that unionization is a prerequisite for dispute action. It can be assumed that industrial unrest is at times sufficiently intense in unionized medium to small-medium firms to override the difficulties and restraints facing such unions.

The inverted U-shaped curve of disputation by size of the enterprises involved is not pursued here in depth — it is a phenomenon that invites further research. However, some explanation for the relatively low dispute rates at either end of the spectrum may lie in salient characteristics of the core-peripheral continuum. In the large-scale sector, it is not

Table 7.3 Enterprises in which labour disputes occurred by size of enterprise, employees involved, private sector, 1981

Size (number of employees)	Number of enterprises	%		Number of employees involved	%	
Total	2,766	100.0		468,987	100.0	
Large						
5,000 or more	115	4.2 ⎫		92,984	19.8 ⎫	
1,000–4,999	258	9.3 ⎬ 30.5		121,528	25.9 ⎬ 71.2	
300–999	470	17.0 ⎭		119,694	25.5 ⎭	
Medium						
100–299	797	28.8 ⎫		80,039	17.1 ⎫	
30–99	780	28.2 ⎬ 57.0		31,157	6.6 ⎬ 23.7	
Small						
29 or less	274	9.9	9.9	3,398	0.7	0.7
Not classified	72	2.6		20,187		

Source: Compiled from *Year Book of Labour Statistics, 1981*, Statistics and Information Department, Minister's Secretariat, Ministry of Labour, Tokyo, 1983.

Note: Including disputes beginning during the period as well as those brought forward from the previous period.

surprising that disputation is relatively low. There are relatively few giant corporations, which in part accounts for the fact that only 4 per cent of all striking enterprises in the data were in this size category. But there are other significant factors to be taken into account. Unions are well organized; management and unions are well established and experienced. At the same time, there is a strong tendency for unions in the large-scale sector of private enterprise to be committed to economic rather than ideological unionism and to be aligned with non-militant union federations and confederations (see Chapter 6). An equally important factor, perhaps more so, is that working conditions are sufficiently good and job security sufficiently secure, that a 'weight-off' unions process takes place. In other words, there are fewer issues of potential contention in large enterprises than in firms in the medium and small sector. Related to this is the greater frequency of internal communications machinery in large that can function to maximize co-operation and minimize conflict. In this environment, the short strike by a powerful union is a salutory warning to management.

In the mid-range of enterprises by size, the positive aspects of the management and labour relationships and conditions of employment begin to deteriorate sharply: less experienced management and unions, a wider range of problems for unions to cope with, and less effective internal mechanisms for communication. The situation in these companies suggests a heightened potential for conflict and a reduced capacity of both parties to reach an acceptable compromise. The likelihood of disputation may also increase due to greater politicization — a commitment to unionism *per se* where unionization is less automatic than tends to be the case in large enterprises.

In small and very small firms, features of the working environment discussed in earlier profiles of the peripheral sector have a strong input into low dispute frequencies. Low rates of disputation are consistent with estimates of circumstances in which small unions operate. In addition, not only is unionization minimal, thereby reducing the option of taking formal dispute action, but familial ties and closer locality and community links, particularly in rural areas, make open conflict less socially acceptable. There is a further factor. The separation of management and labour is not so distinct; blue-collar management often works side by side in an informal atmosphere with other workers, family members, the nominally self-employed, and day labour. If there is a union, its strength within the firm is minimal despite the fact that, so far as problems for labour are concerned, these tend to be maximized. The 'weight-off' unions process starting in larger enterprises reaches the end of the line.

From a variety of perspectives, respondents confirmed the trend for conflict, expressed in many diverse forms, to be higher in medium and small-medium firms. The reason, according to Hanami, is 'quite clear':

In large enterprises, unions are already well established and they can bargain without going into a dispute or struggle. Therefore the most troublesome area is among firms employing between 100 and 200 workers. The unions [in firms of this size] lack experience and when they have demands they tend to take action . . .

My hypothesis is this. A union must of course have discipline. If a union exists but is not firmly established — is rather fragile — it lacks this discipline. It has no mass support among employees. If the union is not very well organized or strong, membership perhaps covers a minority. It lacks power, it lacks finances. Such a union cannot go on strike, not a normal type of strike. So in this case, the union members tend to resort to different forms of protest, like the wearing of the union badge and the *hachimaki* [headband]. Since there are a lot of non-union members working in the firm, union members have to stay in the workplace and make a noisy sort of protest. If they went on strike, the company could carry on at a reduced scale with the non-union employees.

You will find that most of the noisy protest cases occur in these small firms, or in the public sector where strikes are prohibited.

(Hanami, interview, 22 December 1982)

The respondents from Sohyo, referring to the low rate of disputation in large enterprises, noted that most disputes and strikes are concentrated around *shunto*, mainly on issues of wage increases, hours, and retirement pay. But they also talked of non-*shunto* disputes:

These disputes are due in particular to industrial reorganization, that is, rationalization, which is taking place on a massive scale. Smaller firms cannot escape the effects of this nationwide trend. Workers are often shifted from one section to another, one establishment to another, must frequently change jobs, or are retrenched. It often happens that management singles out union leaders and members, making their situation more difficult than it is for other workers . . . this behaviour can cause workers to challenge management.

(Sano and Ogawa, interview, 16 November 1982)

The Sohyo officials argued that the fact that strikes are decreasing does not mean disputation and conflict are decreasing. Conflict and dissatisfaction are increasingly being shown through wearing union badges and *hachimaki*. Also more union meetings are being held, many in the lunch break. Other forms of protest are used more frequently than staging large strike action. Moreover:

229

People's attitude or approach to strikes is still backward, and workers strike with a sense of guilt, hesitancy. The social atmosphere says that strikes are undesirable, and although strikes are not a crime, some people look at them as if they were. Strikes are of course illegal in the public sector, and society is upset when they do occur in this area. This sort of social pressure tends to discourage workers from organizing a strike.

(Sano and Ogawa, interview, Sohyo, 16 November 1982)

The respondent from IMF (JC) was asked what could be done in a non-unionized workplace if, for example, a worker's wages were below the minimum or working conditions were unsafe:

In small enterprises it's take it or leave it. According to management, you can leave any time. There is no protection without a union. You can go to, say, the labour commission, but many people don't bother, they just look for another job. If there's enough inspectors, there's some protection under the Labour Standard Law, but there aren't enough. As to strikes, unions in small companies can't afford it. A recent MOL study of working conditions showed that 90 per cent of unions in the small companies in the survey had no strikes over the past five years.

(Seto, interview, 8 November 1982)

These diverse views support the conclusion that the rights and opportunities open to unions cannot be freely exercised across the workforce — unions are constrained by the conditions in which they operate. In the peripheral segment of the workforce, the likelihood of minor unions mounting a formal dispute is remote, lacking as they are in full-time officials or clerical staff, and hard put to finance a strike. Their funds are very limited because of their small membership and because membership fees, at between 1 per cent and 2 per cent of wages, are based on workers' wages that are considerably lower than those paid to workers in larger firms. Minor unions lack union security (compulsory unionism agreements), and a strike would not mean 'one out, all out', but 'one out, some out'. As a result of such a lack of solidarity, there is the strong possibility that a strike, more so a long strike, will encourage management to break the strike by supporting the formation of a second union or, more frequently,

230

to neutralize its effects by employing non-regular labour to fill any shortfall in the productive workforce.

Equally important to minor unions is the trend for few small Japanese firms to be completely independent of larger firms and for a majority to operate under a sub-contract relationship. This can mean that the mere formation of a union may put the firm or the sub-contract relationship at risk. The risk of severance from a network is multiplied if any of the few unions in existence protest or stage a strike. The workers concerned would be acutely aware of this situation, and the likelihood of becoming unemployed would tend to weigh heavily against the desire to try for a short-term victory through a strike. In the face of inhibitions such as these, that strikes do occur in the small and medium-small sector with relative frequency suggests a high level of commitment — a point raised previously (Chapter 6) concerning politicization in the union movement.

Despite all of these difficulties in a unionized situation, it is clear that, of all forms of workers' organization, a union is still in the most advantageous position to raise grievances within an enterprise and through external legal machinery. In order to have access to the rights available to unionized workers, workers could form a union, otherwise an association or society could adjust its membership and limited welfare aims to conform to the requirements of the Trade Union Law (Article 23). As has been pointed out, however, many obstacles stand in the way of these options.

From this perspective, establishing a union in what was once a non-union firm is of itself a manifestation of conflict. Each year well over a thousand unions appear and disappear (Sado, Domei, interview, 12 January 1983). The phenomenon is no doubt partly due to new business entries and exits. Research into when, where, and why these unions are disbanded and established may indicate other factors: their disbandment related to increasingly insurmountable difficulties in remaining viable; their formation related to conflict in previously non-unionized firms. The new union of timber workers, referred to in the news bulletin of the Daitokogyo Company Union (Chapter 5), is a case in point.

The segmentation of labour organization in its legal and negotiating framework directly affects the access to power of workers in conflict situations. Large unions in large enterprises have ready access while non-unionized workers in the peripheral sector are almost powerless.

231

CONCLUSION

This chapter set out to look at the communication and conflict aspects of industrial relations in both the core and peripheral sectors. The focus was on the formal and informal contact between management and labour as interest groups operating within legal and negotiating frameworks. In this sense, communication and conflict were dealt with as aspects of one phenomenon — the process through which management and labour interact. The context was set in earlier chapters, which looked at the structures and processes within which management and labour operate. The discussion that ensued was approached from the perspective of the relative power position of the parties.

In Japan's large enterprises, major unions have the capacity to seek and find somewhat effective channels of negotiation and to constrain management up to (but not including) areas defined as being inviolably within management prerogative. Each is in a relatively advantageous position to negotiate the terms of work practices (work rules) or collective agreements and resolve problems through institutionalized communication mechanisms such as joint consultation. Each major union is also better placed when the gap between management and workers' interests changes qualitatively from agreement to dispute. The union is able to seek redress in cases of the perceived abuse of agreements or standards established in various industrial laws of the country, and to resort to formal disputation including work stoppages. By institutionalizing arrangements between the parties (for example collective agreements), such unions impose a degree of constraint on management in their enterprise and a degree of constraint upon themselves.

Arbitrary arrangements are the order of the day in the majority of firms in Japan's private sector — its small firms. If a worker does not accept the terms, he can quit. If he is fired, his capacity to seek reversal in the courts is severely limited. The minor unions that exist are ill-equipped to give support or initiate industrial action around the issue. Moreover, the circumstances under which people work in the peripheral sector virtually preclude unionization. As a result, binding collective agreements, formal protest and 'proper' industrial action are scattered though not infrequent phenomena. The capacity for non-regular workers in the large- or small-scale sectors to engage in institutionalized forms of communication or disputation is minimal if not totally non-existent, and additional constraints on workers stem from contract and sub-contract labour's inferior position in the patron/sub-contractor relationship.

However, there are indications that, where unionization exists in medium and medium-small firms, there is a higher level of militancy and commitment to unionism *per se* than in either large enterprises (quasi-automatic membership) or small firms (familial relations and welfare/social organizations of workers). In this context, the entry of a newly formed union may be an indicator of workers' perceptions that a union will provide them with formal access to management and will also give some protection in disputes with management. The exit of a union may indicate that its members are unable to maintain viability in the face of demonstrable barriers.

In the non-organized segment of the workforce, workers are relatively powerless. Their potential to organize, to articulate their interests, and to use even mildly effective avenues for expression of dispute and conflict are circumscribed. Unlike more regulated and organized workers in the core sector of industry, peripheral workers are inhibited by the constraints inherent in unstable employment and contract labour.

Features of the peripheral environment such as these, together with the general segmentation of labour, affect the processes within which management and labour operate. They have a crucial input into styles and frequencies of negotiating machinery and disputation, and in defining the means of access to conventional forms of expressing conflict. The segmentation of labour and labour organization precipitates a situation in which power is distributed unequally among sets of actors. More importantly, given the decreasing capacity of workers to organize or articulate their interests along the peripheral continuum, the relative effectiveness of workers to set the agendas or bargain at the negotiating table diminishes as their workplace becomes more remote from the core industrial sector.

Relationships in the management and labour dichotomy are subject to a network of direct and indirect controls that are engendered by the conjuncture of three major factors: the division and deployment of workers, the stratification of workers' labour effort, and the segmentation of labour organization. The autonomy of relations in each enterprise means that the interaction between management and labour is exclusive. The autonomy of each enterprise and each union means that from the largest to the smallest enterprise union, each set of actors interacts under separate circumstances. The perception of members of a union is that they have more in common with their management than with union members in other firms or with other workers. The segmentation of labour and the fragmentation of organized labour induce this contradiction of class interest.

It remains to evaluate this situation in the broader context of Japan's industrial relations and interpretations in the literature.

NOTES

1. Agreements are valid for a maximum period of three years. If the term of validity is not stipulated, either party can give written notice (minimum 90 days) of termination. In negotiating an agreement, clauses relating to the working relationship between management and the union (union activities in the enterprise and bargaining procedures) must conform to the Trade Union Law. Other matters in the agreement concerning working conditions must conform to the Labour Standards Law. Stipulations in collective agreements take precedence over conditions set out in the firm's work rules.

2. Registered work rules have no fixed term of validity. They can be changed frequently, or retained indefinitely.

3. Clauses in collective agreements and work rules must conform to the range of labour laws, such as those concerning labour standards, health and safety, women and minors, employment security and so on.

4. In many cases competition between groups and companies is stimulated by a 'suggestion quota' system. In response to an interviewer's question, Dore commented that QCs at their best are very impressive but that others suffer from over-enthusiastic management: 'The factory next door has 2,346 improvement suggestions and we have only 2,222, we must improve our record!' (Dore 1983: 1).

5. The Japan Productivity Centre developed from a suggestion in 1953 from officials of the United States Government's Technical Aid Program. The concept of a concerted productivity drive was supported by Japan's four major business organizations: Federation of Economic Organizations (Keidanren), Federation of Employers' Associations (Nikkeiren), Chamber of Commerce and Industry (Nissho), and Committee for Economic Development (Keizai Doyukai). Despite initial opposition from most unions, the JPC was launched in 1955 with tripartite participation.

Background to the development of the productivity movement and joint consultation is derived from an interview with Yamazaki Kichinosuke, Deputy Director of JPC (10 January 1983), and documents that he supplied, in particular, *Productivity Movement in Japan*, JPC, Tokyo, 1981, pp. 6–8.

6. It will be recalled that in the Daitokogyo gear pump factory, consultation involved upper management and lower management, with the union as a third party (Chapter 5).

7. Shimada maintains that there are several major elements in a 'complex fabric of information flow' in Japanese industrial relations. In addition to QCs and Joint Consultation Councils, he includes the role of first-line supervisors, who are the 'pivotal point between management and rank-and-file workers'. In the transmission of information, first-line supervisors play a dual role as 'lowest-level management and top leaders at the workshop' (Shimada 1981: 25–6).

8. According to the 1977 Communication Survey (Foreign Press Centre 1978), 90 per cent of workers (blue and white collar) wanted to know their companies' corporate policies and financial positions, 88 per cent wanted to play some part in the forming of company policies. Management attitudes to these questions are not indicated in available reports of that survey.

9. For example, there was an informal type of consultation at Mochizuki Steel between management and the self-employed sub-contract workers belonging to the Mochizuki Workers' Association (Chapter 5).

10. The charter of the workers' association at Mochizuki Steel illustrates this point. The association's focus was on the company, irrespective of the fact that its members were not employees but permanently employed sub-contract labour.

11. Shimada argues that the mass media (TV, newspapers, and magazines) should be included in the complex 'fabric of communication channels'. In his view:

The fact that the four major nationwide newspaper companies issue 20 million newspapers which report essentially identical news twice a day in the country where the total number of households including singles is only 35 million eloquently suggests the breadth and intensity of information flows.

(Shimada 1981: 26)

12. Tokunaga (Tokunaga and Bergmann 1984: 49–50) cites research by Denkiroren (Federation of Electrical Machine Workers' Unions) which showed that the average wage of employees in this industry in Asian firms (affiliated to Japanese enterprises) was one-fifth that of domestic wages. More importantly, Denkiroren's data showed a rapid increase in employment of overseas workers.

13. The relevant laws and official statistics refer only to 'parties to the dispute', 'management and workers' organization', 'dispute participants', or 'disputes between capital and labour'. The conclusion that the workers' side in a formal dispute is represented by a union is nevertheless inescapable.

For example, in the total number of disputes in 1980 (4,376 strikes, lockouts, and slowdowns), the principal labour unions involved are listed as follows: Sohyo, 72.7 per cent; Domei, 5.1 per cent; Shinsanbetsu, 0.5 per cent; Churitsuroren, 2.6 per cent; and Other, 19.0 per cent (PMO 1982b). Although these statistics do not define 'other', labour union surveys that deal with the principal labour unions note that 'other' refers to unions that are not affiliated to any of the above four major organizations.

The Trade Union Law (1949) makes it clear that only unions are involved in formal disputes: each union must include a clause in its constitution to the effect that no strike will occur unless voted for in a secret ballot by union members or by union delegates who are elected by secret ballot:

> no strike action shall be started without the decision made by secret ballot either directly by a majority of members voting or directly by a majority of delegates voting, elected by secret ballot directly by members.
>
> (Trade Union Law, Article 5:2 [8])

14. To take a hypothetical case, the structure of the Canon group of enterprises illustrates this function. The labour commission could be asked to extend certain stipulations in the collective agreement in one Canon group company to similar workers in other unionized companies in the group. However, an act of dispute involving any of these enterprises invokes a more complex procedure, which is discussed below, because not all companies in the group are unionized (see Appendix 6: 'Group Structure: Canon').

15. Some qualifications and restrictions have been mentioned previously (Chapter 6). For example, in public corporations and national enterprises, no union or closed shop is allowed, there are special restrictions on matters subject to negotiation and on the use of the bargaining system, strikes are prohibited, and disputes must go to arbitration. Advance notice of a dispute is required if the action is in the public utilities. Public servants, national and local, cannot conclude collective agreements, strikes are prohibited, there is no provision for unfair labour practices although there are guarantees against discrimination for participation in an employee organization and its legal activities. Wages and conditions come under the jurisdiction of the National Personnel Authority which makes recommendations for Cabinet consideration and the authority also presides over matters of discriminatory treatment and disciplinary action taken against employees.

An analysis of conflict in the public sector is outside the scope of this discussion. Nor will dispute settlement procedures be discussed in depth. These questions are dealt with elsewhere, for example Hanami (1979, 1981), Matsuda (1983), and Japan Institute of Labour (1979).

16. For an analysis of cases before the courts involving management and labour, see Matsuda (1983).

17. Claims concerning abuses of the Labour Standards Law are a matter for the criminal courts, not the labour commissions or the civil courts. Abuses are reported to the police department. Data concerning this aspect of industrial relations were not available. This could be an interesting aspect of industrial relations for future research.

18. For a discussion on manifestations of conflict in Japan see, for example, Levine and Taira (1979, 1980); Hanami (1981); Sugimoto (1975); Matsuda (1983).

19. For relevant data, see PMO 1982b; MOL 1983.

20. Figures for 1980 are used here because of the bias in 1981 figures caused by the notable increase in disputes in that year. The increase was largely in response to the Cabinet's rejection of National Personnel Authority (NPA) recommendations for wage increases in the public sector.

Conclusion

The purpose of this book is to examine the relatively unknown segment of Japan's private sector workforce — its peripheral workers — and industrial relations in that sector. A subsidiary purpose was to assess the implications of this information and analysis for the broader interpretation of industrial relations in Japan.

The central argument pursued is straightforward: industrial relations in Japan's peripheral workforce tends to be controlled directly and indirectly through structures and processes of Japanese industry in its social context. These controls become more indirect and less formal and institutionalized as firm size and workers' employment status decline. They also become more coercive. This argument was well supported in the main body of the work, but the research and analysis suggested a greater complexity than the argument implies. This is clear in the analysis of the findings, which are set out following a brief recapitulation of the main areas of investigation. These areas were:

1 To investigate the main features of the structure of the workforce in the peripheral sector of industry, namely, the working environment of workers in small and medium firms and workers employed on a non-regular basis.

2 To investigate the impact of two dominant processes — sub-contracting and technological innovation — on workforce rationalization in this sector.

3 To investigate how the segmentation of labour relates to labour organization in Japan, and, looking at the core and peripheral sectors in comparative terms, how the role and nature of labour organization relates to the phenomenon of enterprise unionism.

4 To investigate the peripheral interactions and the power relations of management and labour in the process of communication and conflict.

5 To assess whether there is a relationship between the type of management and labour relations that exist in the large-enterprise sector and the type that exists in the peripheral sector and, if so, its nature.

6 To discuss what the research and analysis suggest for the literature on industrial relations and, in particular, the literature on industrial relations in Japan.

INDUSTRIAL RELATIONS AND THE PERIPHERAL ENVIRONMENT

The first area of investigation concerned the industrial environment of workers in small and medium firms and those employed on a non-regular basis and the possible effects of this environment on industrial relations. It was found that for such workers, as discussed in Chapters 2 and 3, the following features are virtually assured: their permanent exclusion from the regular workforce of the giants of industry and powerful restraints on their potential for organization and the articulation of their interests. Thus their input into the interaction of the major power groups is minimal despite the fact that these workers represent by far the largest segment of the labour force.

Even given these virtually immutable characteristics, there is a particular dynamism in this segment of the workforce. The further Japanese firms are located in scale from the core sector of industry, the greater the percentage of workers involved. The pyramid shape of this phenomenon, with the large-scale sector and a small segment of the workforce at the apex and the small-firms sector with a large number of workers at the base, is virtually unexplored in the context of industrial relations. In that context, it is not difficult to establish that decreasing levels of wages, benefits, general working conditions, and job security affect increasing numbers of workers as the firms for which they work become smaller or less viable. Moreover, casual and contract labour increases, more family members are involved, and more blue-collar managers work alongside their regulars and casuals. At the same time, there is considerable mobility in this sector, which involves the movement of retired personnel from large enterprises into smaller firms, changing jobs, and entre-preneurship — all of which are linked to a constant turnover of business. Paralleling these trends, there is the greater involve-ment of female and older workers and workers with a lower education level towards the extremity of the continuum. While such factors may represent a reduced access to better paid and more secure jobs with higher skills, they do not of themselves impair workers' ability to establish a workers' interest group to negotiate with management. The organizing potential of these workers is frustrated when conditions in the smaller firms, which tend to employ them, militate against any attempt to establish a strong and effective negotiating mechanism.

The extent to which barriers to labour organization exist is inversely related to firm size: lack of time to give to organization (which must be outside working hours), lack of funds to mount a self-supporting and active union, a small workforce from which to draw support, familial relations with management, and strong community/industry links, notably in the rural sector. More importantly, the analysis of characteristics of the peripheral workforce strongly suggested that, since the peak of Japan's high growth period, the gap between the core and peripheral sectors is increasing. At the same time, within the peripheral sector itself there are indications that the gap between medium enterprises and small to very small firms is widening. In this dynamic segment of the industrial workforce, given the enterprise-bound determination of working conditions and labour organization in Japan and the lack of regulation in the peripheral sector, two trends are at work. First, the relative power of workers to have an input into the industrial relations agenda diminishes as firms become smaller, and second, the gap between the extremes is tending to widen.

RATIONALIZATION AND THE PERIPHERAL WORKFORCE

The rationalization of the workforce, specifically, the impact of the sub-contracting practice and technological innovation, was the second area investigated. As discussed in Chapter 4 and illustrated in the case studies in Chapter 5, the pyramid organization of work and workers adds new dimensions to the picture painted above. Work that is not cost-effective is separated from the parent company and given to outside firms. In the process, the parent and sub-contractor relationship produces asymmetry in dependency, with a plethora of small firms inevitably vying for the opportunity to survive in the network. The parent company has control over the selection of contractors in this array of competing firms. It is in a position to require compatibility with new production schedules and techniques such as the *kanban* system with requirements of precision, fast delivery, low cost, and laid-off stock inventories. In addition, the parent company expects stable labour relations from its sub-contractors. In a highly competitive milieu, sub-contractors have little recourse but to transmit such demands and expectations to their workers. Acceptance and transmission of parent company specification is a matter of survival for each sub-contractor, while for the patron, who may depend on sub-contracting *per se*, it is immaterial which of an array of sub-contractors is prepared to supply according to parent control.

Two interesting observations can be made on the analyses of the research into sub-contracting and the use of contract labour. The first, noted but not pursued in depth, is that the pronounced imbalance in parent company and sub-contractor relationships in Japan has had a politicizing effect. In many industrialized societies, managements of small and medium businesses, as a special interest group, take a position similar to that of managements of large enterprises in their approach to labour. In Japan, however, a lobby has emerged, small yet strong enough to have an input into protective legislation, consisting of managers and owners of medium and small businesses who challenge the excessive power of 'big business'. The ideology underlying their 'us' and 'them' perception is an ambivalent mixture of self-protection and protection of peripheral workers' interests.

The second observation concerns the use of sub-contract and contract labour and Japan's workforce rationalization: control over the segmentation of labour and control over integration of the work done by labour. The sum of all the parts in one final product is the physical symbol of the centralization of power and the decentralization of work and labour. The widespread use of this style of rationalization in Japan underscores its significance as a control mechanism. It is a process that vests considerable power in large-enterprise management, which could be aptly called the final assembly power.

LABOUR ORGANIZATION AND SEGMENTATION OF THE WORKFORCE

Inevitably, this situation and the main characteristics of the peripheral workforce environment in general are related to the third area of investigation — the relationship between segmented labour and the nature of labour organization in Japan.

The relationship, in synthesis, lies in enterprise unionism. This evaluation does not ignore the cause and effect complexities in this relationship, but accepts the existence of the phenomenon of enterprise unionism and takes cognizance of the implications of the system.

An assessment of enterprise unionism, discussed at length in Chapter 6, was approached through two perspectives: first, its implications for the unions in Japan's private-sector enterprises and second, its implications in the broader area of labour organization.

From the first perspective, enterprise unionism as a system of labour organization brings legal protection, institutionalized privilege, and bargaining advantage to an enterprise union, but at the same time there is a trade-off. Each of Japan's 74,000 unions is perforce sensitive to its particular enterprise environment. Each is constrained to act primarily in the interest of the enterprise in addition to the interests of its membership and their retention in employment in that company. This has a divisive effect in that labour organization for Japan's 12 million organized workers is severely fragmented. More importantly, against this background of fragmentation, the level and priorities in constraints on unions' purposes change with the status of the company. Minor unions have legal protection but little negotiating muscle with respect to their members' interests or job security within their enterprises as a result of their small numbers, their lack of experienced and full-time officials, and their likely lack of solidarity within the firm. Additional controls are strong if their firm has a tenuous hold on business viability or has financial or sub-contract dependency on a larger enterprise or patron — controls that vary with levels of viability and dependency. Moreover, within the organized segment of the workforce, the voice of minor unions is virtually unheard and the development of a core- and peripheral-union dichotomy is assured.

From the second perspective — the broader context of Japan's industrial relations — the implications of enterprise-based labour organization are far reaching, and the effects extend beyond the organized sector. The system is as relevant to non-unionized firms as it is to unionized firms. For example, by default, the protection, privilege, and advantage associated with organized labour are denied to workers in Japan's largely non-unionized and non-regulated sector. Enterprise unionism, as set out in law and as practised in its organizational structure, pre-empts the diffusion of unionization to workers in peripheral firms and non-regular workers. The operation of enterprise unionism militates against politicization and the initiation of broader union movement strategies that may cover issues of concern to non-unionized workers. Such disenfranchised workers, through lack of regulated organization (workers' associations have no legal force), have little capacity themselves to express their interests in these issues or to have them placed on the agendas of major industrial unions and union federations. As to non-unionized workers' interaction with management, this too is site-bound under the impact of enterprise unionism. The imbalance of power between the parties is crucial in circumstances in which the workforce in each firm communicates or comes into conflict with management in a decentralized, devoluted pattern of workers' interaction with management.

COMMUNICATION AND CONFLICT: THE CORE AND PERIPHERAL SECTORS

This imbalance of power relations is also crucial in the fourth area of investigation: the interaction between management and labour as expressed through formal and informal avenues of communication and conflict. These phenomena were assessed in comparative terms, juxtaposing the core and the peripheral sectors in their legal and negotiating frameworks.

There are significant differences in these areas between the two sectors. It was pointed out, for example, that although bargaining is guaranteed, the formalization of a collective agreement is not an option in a non-unionized firm. Work rules must comply with basic standards, but because of the few employed in their workforce, almost 6 million small private enterprises (89.8 per cent of all establishments), are specifically excluded from any legal obligation to formalize such rules. Bargaining and collective agreements, work rules, joint consultation, and decisions to strike are matters for each enterprise or firm and at this point the power relationship between the parties is a paramount factor. Joint consultation can only be institutionalized in a unionized firm through stipulation in collective agreements, otherwise it occurs informally and sporadically. While enterprise joint consultation is not confined to unionized firms, this form of communication occurs less frequently as firm size decreases and, at the same time, management appointment of workers' representatives to consultative meetings tends to increase.

Management in the peripheral sector is largely free from the constraints imposed by unionization and the formal communication it entails. However, other factors work to constrain managements in their interaction with their workers: for example, the need to attract and retain skilled workers, the need to respond to the pressures that flow from an unequal power relationship with a patron in a sub-contract relationship, and the desire to forestall unionization. An informal and indirect discipline is also embedded in the setting of a market value for labour. At least in the area of base-up wage increases and bonus levels, management is influenced by the dissemination in the wider society of the agreements between the major actors in the large-scale sector. However, such constraints on management exist in a laissez faire sub-market of the Japanese workforce, where the whim and individual response of management is the final arbiter.

Moreover, both management and labour in the peripheral sector are acutely aware of their competitive industrial environment and the expectations that are generally associated with the lower status of their small workplace. Entrepreneurship is a gamble, and the graduate has only one opportunity to enter the core sector of industry — to achieve the higher status and elite expectations associated with working for the giants of Japanese industry.

The consensus of respondents, supported by case studies (Chapter 5) and macro-data, was that decision-making is arbitrary in the vast majority of firms in the peripheral sector. Formal communication is minimal and conflict is frequently expressed outside the legal framework. Workers who object to arbitrarily set working arrangements can quit. Redress for discriminatory treatment by management or for abuses of basic standards is hardly an option (though a right) because of the lack of institutionalized support, and litigation is costly and prolonged. Formal dispute action is the province of a unionized firm. The threat of forming a union demonstrates a conflict situation in a non-unionized firm.

Nevertheless, relative powerlessness is also a characteristic of minor unions. Moreover, the smaller the union, the less its resources and solidarity in the firm, and the greater the fragility

244

of its negotiating position. When these circumstances are meshed with increasingly unstable employment and poor alternative job prospects, a process of weight-off larger unions occurs.

Large unions tacitly accept the problem dumping to smaller firms that accompanies managements' rationalization of work and workers. Indeed, such rationalization is in part undertaken to externalize labour problems and to extract maximum advantage from the regulated and unregulated dichotomy in the workforce.

THE CORE-PERIPHERY DICHOTOMY

The fifth area investigated in this research was concerned with possible links between processes of interaction between management and labour in the core segment of the workforce and between management and labour in the peripheral segment. There is an assumption here, of course, that there is a difference, and the research and analysis found this assumption to be justified.

The relationship between management and labour in large enterprises is controlled through structures and processes of industrial production, but these are formal and institutionalized. Relations in the peripheral sector are also controlled by such structures and processes, but there is a strong tendency for these to be informal and non-institutionalized. The dichotomy is between regulated and non-regulated sectors and is directly associated with the segmentation of labour and the segmentation of labour organization.

This has different outcomes with respect to the distribution of power between management and labour in each sector. On the one hand, the degree of imbalance of power between management and labour in the large enterprise sector is institutionalized through checks and balances and the operation of the law, and it commands a good deal of acceptance among the actors. On the other hand, the imbalance of power between management and labour in the peripheral sector is more extreme, indeed, some actors have no access to power, and checks and balances operate less directly and more arbitrarily, without legal sanction. At the same time, there are almost no alternative channels for articulation of workers' interests.

Moreover, since this dichotomous situation derives directly from the segmentation of the industrial structure and labour organization, the nature of management and labour relations in the peripheral segment of the workforce is strongly influenced by the repercussions of enterprise unionism and the operation of enterprise unions in the core segment of the workforce. For example, in the same way that the peripheral sector of industry acts as a buffer for the large-scale sector in times of economic fluctuation, so the unregulated patterns of industrial relations act as a buffer and a protector for industrial relations in terms of relationships and conditions of work obtaining in the large enterprise sector. This advantage exists for the core workforce to the disadvantage of the peripheral workforce.

Within the peripheral continuum, as the size of firms decreases and workers' status declines, so imbalances of power increase. The peripheral segment of the workforce is thus not one undifferentiated protector and insulator, but one that relays problems for workers to the extremities of that segment as represented by casual, itinerant, contract, and the definitively expendable workers. The main body of this work reveals this phenomenon.

THE RESEARCH FINDINGS AND THE LITERATURE

The final area of enquiry pursued in this analysis was an evaluation of the implications of the research findings in the context of the relevant literature (Chapter 1). The implications are compelling. The first point to note is that, with few exceptions — notably studies of stratification in the workforce — the literature is inadequate in its treatment of the issues raised throughout this book. While the importance of Japan's secondary industrial sector is acknowledged, the problems of the workforce in that sector are not pursued. This skew goes far in pointing to a basic weakness in pluralist approaches to industrial relations research — the failure to examine the dichotomy of regulated and unregulated segments of the workforce and analyse the relationship between them. The vast bulk of the literature assumes that a focus on major interest groups, the large-scale sector, and regular employees covers the most important or only significant elements of the industrial relations scene. However, the majority of enterprises and workers in Japan do not fit neatly into the resultant conventional model. Admittedly, it is widely acknowledged that enterprise unionism in Japan is a crucial institution, nevertheless, the literature stops short of recognizing that enterprise unionism sets the framework for the operation of industrial interaction throughout the *total* workforce.

A second point to note is that many issues of central concern in the literature have not been dealt with in this study. For example, the *nenko* system, QCs, and concepts such as welfare corporatism were not ignored, but were not explored. It could be argued that there are control mechanisms inherent in these areas, and that, in view of the power-relations perspective adopted throughout this work, they warranted deeper discussion. However, to a significant extent they are irrelevant in the peripheral context, and to give them the attention they generally attract in the conventional literature would divert discussion from the book's central purpose.

A final point to raise is that, again, with few exceptions, the literature is restricted in scope. It is dominated by debates that revolve around entrenched perceptions that are self-perpetuating because they prescribe the research parameters. This assessment is particularly applicable in the literature dealing with Japan, where a major debate revolves around the convergence hypothesis. This debate finds its chief expression in an obsessive concern with examining aspects of the Japanese model from pro-model to anti-model positions. This in turn gives rise to two related debates: the cultural specificity of '*the*' Japanese system, and the continuity or otherwise of traditional and pre-industrial values. These debates are not directly addressed in the main body of this work. However, this concluding chapter has something to say about them.

THE RESEARCH FINDINGS AND MAJOR DEBATES IN THE LITERATURE

With regard to the convergence hypothesis, it seems that the Japanese economic system and its industrial structures produce a dichotomous industrial-relations situation. From an economic perspective, this may be efficient. In the long term, the outcome is obscure. From the perspective of the workers involved, there are severe trade-offs. If industrial relations in Japan is different from industrial relations in other advanced industrial societies, the difference lies in the extent of the extremes observable between the core and peripheral sectors. If it is similar, this is observable in comparisons of discrete aspects. For example, pyramid sub-contracting is not unique to Japan. However, it is a crucial process in Japanese industry, highly developed and refined as an integral part of a total production process. In Japan's highly competitive situation, human resource dependency is diversified and the patron is able to exert strong if indirect control over external workteams. A second example lies in the use of casual and contract labour. This strategy is not unknown elsewhere, but it is fine-tuned in Japanese employment strategies to minimize the core, higher wage component of the workforce in an enterprise and maximize the expendable, lower wage (or lower contract labour cost) component either within or external to the enterprise. In a third example, a range of relationships from streamlined collective bargaining to arbitrary and familial relations is not unique to Japan. However, the gap between the poles is extreme in Japan, and is accentuated by the almost complete concentration of unions in the large enterprise sector. In a broad assessment of the convergence hypothesis, it can be said that industrial relations in Japan is less an example of the logic of industrialism as the logic of the competitive free enterprise system.

Further, far from being a pluralist system with a rough balance of power among interest groups, industrial relations in Japan is dichotomous, with starkly different outcomes in the core and peripheral sectors. This has been discussed at length in earlier chapters. It can be repeated, however, that the difference in outcomes is directly related to the effects of a regulated situation in the core sector, albeit decentralized, and an unregulated situation in the peripheral sector that is compounded by the increasing expendability of workers along the continuum in that sector.

The issues raised above are relevant to the implications of the transportability debate. Industrial relations in Japan is largely controlled by the segmentation of labour and labour organization that is the outcome of its industrial structures and processes. These features are integrated into the economic, industrial, and social environment. Elements of the compound cannot be transferred and be expected to operate with similar results. Clearly, the whole is not amenable to transfer. In this context, the social environment assumes a particular significance.

Reference to the social environment raises issues central to a further debate in the literature, particularly that dealing with Japan: the continuity of traditional and pre-industrial values. The foregoing comments on major debates lead to an assessment of continuity which gives traditional and pre-industrial values only a minor role in industrial relations in Japan. Where consensual relations appear to exist, they tend to be more an outcome of the relative power relations between management and labour than a residual commitment to traditional values. Clearly, some of these values exist. For example, they emerged in analyses of the familial relations in very small firms and in the case studies, and suggested strong large-enterprise/small-firm and urban/rural dichotomies. Such traditions and values in the industrial relations context do not permeate society equally across the spectrum.

The literature that places stress on the continuity of traditional and pre-industrial values imbues the concept of continuity with the status of an ideology, not only for scholars but for the actors. In this sense, the ideology of continuity is extremely important. This is the paradox: the persistence of the ideology, not of its own accord but reiterated and assumed to be reality, is as powerful as the reality of the industrial structures and processes which are the subject of this book. It seems that this synthesis of perception and reality gives 'Japanese-ness' to the industrial-relations situation in Japan.

In this way, the significance of the distinctive Japanese festival of the 47 samurai — recounted in the introduction to this work — becomes apparent. Japanese cultural tradition tends to obscure more pragmatic features of the society — the complex web of controls that influence the process of interaction between management and labour. These processes involve people such as those in the festival crowd. By adopting a power-relations framework, it has been possible to evaluate the relationship between homeworkers making festival souvenirs and the orderers who commission the work; between day labourers maintaining and cleaning the streets and subways near the temple — the site of the festival — and the *tehaishi* who recruit them, sometimes from among part-time farmers; between the sub-contract worker making parts for radios, cassette players, and cameras carried by festival onlookers and the managements of their sub-contract firm; and between the sub-contractor and his patron, and so on.

By focusing on the peripheral sector, this book has assessed the relationship between an elite and the majority of Japan's workforce who, to paraphrase Enright, work beyond the corporate fence:

> The garden is not a garden,
>   it is an expression of Zen:
> The trees are not rooted in earth, then:
>   they are rooted in Zen.
> And this tea has nothing to do with thirst:
> It says the unsayable.
> And this bowl is no vessel:
>   it is the First
> And the Last, it is the Whole.
>
> Beyond the bamboo fence are life-sized people,
> Rooted in precious little, without benefit of philosophy,
> Who grew the rice, who deliver the goods, who
> Sometimes bear the unbearable.
> They too drink tea, without much ceremony.

Tea Ceremony, D. J. Enright, quoted in Strong (c. 1975)

Appendices

JAPANESE RESPONDENTS

Ministry of Labour

1 Sato Ginko, Director, Women Workers' Division, Women's and Youth Workers' Bureau: 7 January 1983.
2 Hiromi Kazuo, Director, Employment Measures Division, Countermeasures Department for the Ageing: 26 January 1983.
3 Deputy Director, Employment Measures Division, Day Labourers' Department: 26 January 1983.
4 Fujii Ryuko, Deputy Director, Trade Union Division, Labour Policy Bureau: 7 January 1983.
5 Fujii Kiyoko, Director, Home Workers Division, Labour Standards Bureau: 8 January 1983.

Prime Minister's Office

6 Funatsu Y., Director, Labour Force Statistics Division, Statistics Bureau: 17 January 1983.

Ministry of International Trade and Industry

7 Sakamoto Harumi, Director, Small and Medium Enterprise Agency: 8 March 1983.
Ozawa T., Director, Sub-contracting Division of the Small and Medium Enterprise Agency: 8 March 1983.
Director, Bankruptcy Division of the Small and Medium Enterprise Agency: 8 March 1983.

Central Labour Commission

8 Fukuda K., Division Head, Labour Disputes Adjustment Division: 8 March 1983.

Department of Foreign Affairs

9 Personnel of Oceania Division, European and Oceania Affairs Bureau: 6 December 1982.

Japan Institute of Labour

10 Professor Kuwahara Yasuo, Senior Research Associate, Lecturer Hosei and Yokohama Universities: 12 October 1982, 8 November 1982.

Management and employer organizations

11 Yamazaki Kichinosuke, Deputy Director, Japan Productivity Centre, Industrial Relations Department: 10 January 1983.
12 Japan Chamber of Commerce (Nissho) (telephone): 6 January 1983.
13 Suzuki Toshio A., Deputy Director, International Division, Japan Federation of Employers' Association (Nikkeiren): 6 December 1982.
14 S. Inoue, Chairman, Labour Problems Committee, Japan Federation of Small and Medium Enterprise Management Associations: 1 February 1983.

Labour organizations

15 Sano Akira, Department Director, and Ogawa, M., Organizer, Bureau of Social Organization, General Council of Trade Unions (Sohyo): 16 November 1982.
16 Sado Masatoshi, Director, International Division, Japan Confederation of Labour (Domei): 12 January 1983.
17 Seto Ichiro, General Secretary, Japan Council of Metalworkers' Unions (IMF-JC): 8 November 1982.
18 Kato Masuo and senior executives, Day Labourers' and Unemployed Workers' Union (Zen'ichijiro): 22 December 1982.
19 General Secretary, National Federation of Low Income Earners and Health and Welfare Protection Associations: 12 March 1983.

Political parties

20 Senator Kuroyanagi Aira, Director, International Affairs Bureau, Komeito: 17 January 1983.
21 Kato Masanori, Assistant Director, International Affairs, Komeito: 16 February 1983.
22 Ide Hiroshi, Member International Commission and Central Committee, Japanese Communist Party: 1 March 1983.

Academics

23 Professor Hanami Tadashi, Dean, Law School, Sophia University, Chairman, International Legal Studies, author *Japanese Industrial Relations*, etc.: 22 December 1982.
24 Professor Eguchi Eiichi, Senior Lecturer, Economics Faculty, Chuo University: 16 February 1983.

25 Professor Ikeda Masayoshi, Faculty of Economics, Chuo University: 25 January 1983.
26 Professor Kato Yūji, Economics Faculty, Senshu University: 13 January 1983.

Case studies

27 Daitokogyo Manufacturing Company, Tokyo, medium-size firm, gear pump manufacture. President of the firm; secretary of the firm's labour union: 1 February 1983.
28 Mochizuki Steel Fabrication Ltd, Chiba Prefecture, medium-size firm, steel girder manufacture, construction industry. President and staff members; Chairman of Mochizuki Steel Company Workers' Association: 1 February 1983.
29 Ina Sankyo, Nagano Prefecture, large-size firm, precision machinery manufacture, electronic industry. Member of board of directors; section heads: 24 February 1983.
30 Oshima Seisakusho, Nagano Prefecture, small/medium firm, sub-contracting firm for Ina Sankyo above. President; senior manager; five female employees, permanent part-time agro-industrial workers: 25 February 1983.
31 Takamori Company, Nagano Prefecture, small/medium firm, sub-contractor, electrical appliance parts manufacture. President; consultant; senior administrator; two female employees, permanent part-time agro-industrial workers: 25 February 1983.

Non-Japanese respondents

32 Garth Hunt, Labour Attaché, Australian Embassy: 5 October 1982, 8 December 1982, 14 March 1983.
33 Lester P. Slezak, Labour Affairs Counsellor, US Embassy: 4 March 1983.
34 Jon Woronoff, American author, *Japan's Wasted Workers*, etc.: 17 January 1983.
35 Professor Gregory Clark, Australian lecturer, Sophia University, journalist: 14 January 1983.
36 Michael Byrnes, correspondent, *Australian Financial Review*: 19 October 1982.
37 Walter Hamilton, correspondent, *Australian Broadcasting Commission*: 19 October 1982.
38 Ken Merrigan and Ian McArthur, correspondents, *Herald and Weekly Times*: 30 September 1982.
39 Charles Smith, Far East Editor, *London Financial Times*: 9 February 1983.
40 Greg Dodds, Director, Australia-Japan Foundation: 12 February 1983.
41 T. J. Nevins, US, Managing Director, Labour and Human Resources Consultant: 24 January 1983.

Appendix 2

Figure A2.1 Japan: regions and prefectures

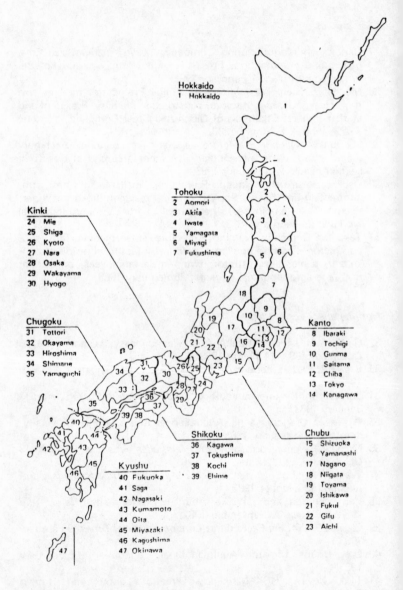

Hokkaido
1 Hokkaido

Tohoku
2 Aomori
3 Akita
4 Iwate
5 Yamagata
6 Miyagi
7 Fukushima

Kinki
24 Mie
25 Shiga
26 Kyoto
27 Nara
28 Osaka
29 Wakayama
30 Hyogo

Chugoku
31 Tottori
32 Okayama
33 Hiroshima
34 Shimane
35 Yamaguchi

Kanto
8 Ibaraki
9 Tochigi
10 Gunma
11 Saitama
12 Chiba
13 Tokyo
14 Kanagawa

Shikoku
36 Kagawa
37 Tokushima
38 Kochi
39 Ehime

Kyushu
40 Fukuoka
41 Saga
42 Nagasaki
43 Kumamoto
44 Oita
45 Miyazaki
46 Kagoshima
47 Okinawa

Chubu
15 Shizuoka
16 Yamanashi
17 Nagano
18 Niigata
19 Toyama
20 Ishikawa
21 Fukui
22 Gifu
23 Aichi

Source: Foreign Press Centre, Tokyo, 1982.

Appendix 3

Table A3.1 Japanese corporate board members with union leadership backgrounds, 1981

	Total	Manufacturing	Non-manufacturing
Number of firms responding			
1 Total number of firms responding	313	180	133
2 Number of firms with board members who were union leaders	232	136	96
Ratio 2/1	74.1%	75.6%	72.2%
Number of board members			
3 Total number of board members	6,121	3,314	2,807
4 Number of board members with union leadership background	992	523	469
Ratio 4/3	16.2%	15.8%	16.7%

Source: Report of the Committee for the Study of Labour Questions, Nikkeiren, 1982: 6.

Appendix 4

Figure A4.1 Comparison of automobile manufacture structure, Japan-US: structure for company A in Japan

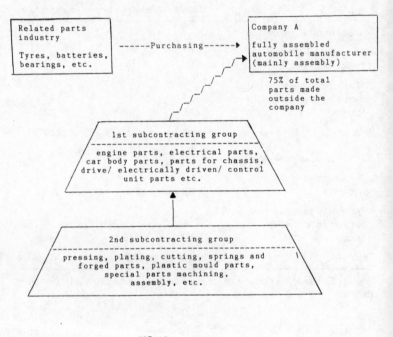

Source: 'Report on the roles played by small and medium enterprises in production specialization', Small and Medium Enterprise Agency, commissioned in January 1980 by Small and Medium Enterprise Research Centre, in Ikeda Masayoshi, 'Special Characteristics and Actual Conditions in Japan's Smaller Enterprises', Tokyo: Chuo University, 1982, unpublished.

Notes: 1 Subcontracting rate 1978:

$$\frac{\text{Purchasing costs} + \text{sub-contracting (including processing) costs}}{\text{Total production costs}} \times 100$$

2 Among the first sub-contracting enterprises, the parent company is not necessarily one company.

Figure A4.2 Comparison of automobile manufacture structure, Japan-US: structure for company B in US

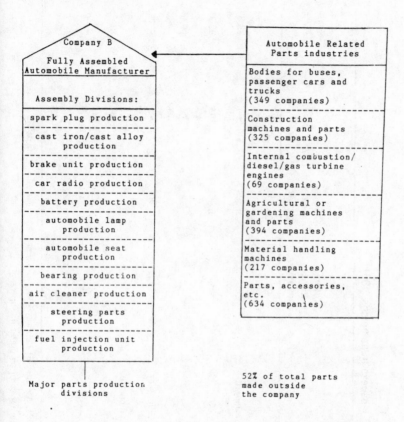

Source: 'Report on the roles played by small and medium enterprises in production specialization', Small and Medium Enterprise Agency, commissioned in January 1980 by Small and Medium Enterprise Research Centre, in Ikeda Masayoshi, 'Special Characteristics and Actual Conditions in Japan's Smaller Enterprises', Tokyo: Chuo University, 1982, unpublished.

Notes: 1 Subcontracting rate 1978:

$$\frac{\text{Purchasing costs} + \text{sub-contracting (including processing) costs}}{\text{Total production costs}} \times 100$$

2 Among the first sub-contracting enterprises, the parent company is not necessarily one company.

257

Appendix 5

Table A5.1 National organizations of Japanese trade unions, 1981

National organization	Affiliated industrial organizations	Affiliated unit unions	Membership (000)	Of which	
				Private sector %	Public sector %
Total	95	34,200	12,471 (100.0%)		
Sohyo (General Council of Trade Unions of Japan)	50	6,594	4,569 (36.6%)	32.3	67.7
Domei (Japanese Confederation of Labour)	31	5,951	2,182 (17.5%)	92.7	7.3
Shinsanbetsu (National Federation of Industrial Organizations)	4	81	64 (0.5%)	99.9	0.1
Churitsuroren (Federation of Independent Unions of Japan)	10	964	1,391 (11.1%)	99.9	0.1
Major unions not affiliated with four national centres	–	3,138	1,758 (14.1%)		
Other umbrella organizations	–	8,394	1,837 (14.7%)	94.7	5.2
Purely independent unions	–	9,327	1,067 (8.6%)		

Source: 'Basic survey of trade unions', 1981, Ministry of Labour, 1981, in Japan Labor Bulletin, April 1982.

Note: Numbers in brackets represent percentages of all union members.

Appendix 6

Table A6.1 Group structure: Canon, unionized, and non-unionized companies, 1982

Unionized companies

Union membership	Company	Remarks
Canon Workers' Union, 14,000 members Ota-ku, Tokyo	Canon, Tokyo	Manufacture of office equipment, cameras, medical equipment, etc.
	Canon Sales (Canon's share: approx. 50%)	Domestic sales of above products (100% for Canon)
Canon Electronics Workers' Union 1,600 members Saitama Prefecture	Canon Electronics (Canon's share: 50% plus)	Manufacture and sales of cameras, magnetic heads, etc. (70% for Canon)
Canon Seiki Workers' Union 150 members	Canon Seiki (Canon's share: 50% plus)	Manufacture and sales of micro-motors, pressed products (30% for Canon)
Canon Seiko Workers' Union 200 members	Canon Seiko (Canon's share: 50% plus)	Manufacture of cameras and flashes, etc. (100% for Canon)

Council of Canon Workers' Unions, total membership: 16,000.

Non-unionized companies, other suppliers:

Company	Number of employees	Remarks
Oita Canon, Oita Prefecture	150 employees	Producing camera parts
Shinkosha, Yokohama	200 employees	Producing parts for office equipment and cameras
Daiichi Seiki Kogyo, Itabashi-ku, Tokyo	250 employees	Producing copy machine parts

Source: Supplied by International Metalworkers Federation, Japan Council (IMF-JC) following interview, Tokyo, 8 November 1982.

Note: This structure includes only major companies in the group.

Appendix 7

Table A7.1 Labour disputes by principal labour unions, 1980

	Total disputes	%	Accompanied with dispute acts					
			Total	Strikes over half a day	Lockouts	Strikes for less than half a day	%	Slowdowns
Total	4,376	100.0	3,737	1,128	10	3,038	100.0	37
Sohyo	3,180	72.7	2,879	594	4	2,532	83.3	18
Domei	222	5.1	97	70	2	32	1.0	3
Shinsanbetsu	20	0.5	20	7	—	14	0.5	1
Churitsuroren	114	2.6	101	65	—	74	2.4	5
Other	840	19.2	640	392	4	386	12.7	10

Source: Statistics and Information Department, Minister's Secretariat, Ministry of Labour, *Japan Statistical Yearbook 1982*, Prime Minister's Office, Tokyo, 1982.

Notes: Data are based on the Statistics of Labour Disputes. *Total disputes* refer to the disputes accompanied with dispute acts and those unaccompanied with dispute acts but mediated by a third party. *Workers affected* are the total workers under the control of dispute parties and *workers involved in dispute acts* are those who are actually engaged in dispute acts. The sum of each kind of dispute act does not add to the total because a dispute accompanied with more than two kinds of acts is counted in each act, while they are counted once in the total.

Bibliography

ENGLISH-LANGUAGE MATERIAL ON JAPAN

Note: Japanese statistics published with English headings and reports officially translated into English are included.

Government material is listed under 'Japanese Government'. Ministries are listed alphabetically under this heading.

Ministry Reports/Survey Summaries published by the Japan Foreign Press Centre are listed under 'Foreign Press Centre' in chronological order.

Japanese organizations as author are listed under their names in English translation.

Material supplied during interviews is not included unless referred to in the text.

Abegglen, J. C. (1958) *The Japanese Factory*, Glencoe, Ill.: Free Press.
Asahi Evening News (January 1982–March 1983), Tokyo: English-language edition.
Benedict, R. (1946) *The Chrysanthemum and the Sword*, New York: Houghton Mifflin.
Bix, H. P. (1978) 'Leader of peasant rebellions: Miura Meisuke', in Hyoe, M. and Harper, T. J. (eds), *Great Historical Figures in Japan*, Tokyo: Japan Culture Institute, 243–60.
Chalmers, N. (1980) *Japanese Perspectives on Australian Industrial Relations*, Brisbane, Australia: Centre for The Study of Australian-Asian Relations, Griffith University.
Clark, G. (c. 1979) 'Japan as a model for US reindustrialization', supplied by G. Clark, publication details unknown, 267–83.
Clark, G. (1982) 'Japan in Asia: a cultural comparison', *Asia Pacific Community*, no. 17, Summer, 60–70.
Clarke, R. (1979) *The Japanese Company*, New Haven, Conn.: Yale University Press.
Cole, A. B. (1959) *Political Tendencies of Japanese in Small Enterprises*, New York: Institute of Pacific Relations.
Cole, R. E. (1971) *Japanese Blue Collar: The Changing Tradition*, Berkeley: University of California Press.
Cole, R. E. (1979) *Work, Mobility and Participation: A Comparative Study of American and Japanese Industry*, Berkeley: University of California Press.
Committee for Economic Development (Keizai Doyukai) (1979) *A Vision of the 21st Century: The Quest for Industrial Restructuring*, Tokyo: The Committee.
Cook, A. H. (1966) *An Introduction to Japanese Trade Unionism*, Ithaca, New York: Cornell University Press.
Crawcour, E. S. (1977) *The Japanese Employment System: Past*

Present and Future, Canberra: Australia-Japan Research Centre, ANU.

Daikichi, I. (1973), trans. Ronald Morse, 'Japan's grass-roots tradition: current issues in the mirror of history', *Japan Quarterly*, XX (1), 82–6.

Doi, T. (1978) *Anatomy of Dependence*, Tokyo: Kodansha International.

Dore, R. P. (1973) *British Factory — Japanese Factory: The Origins of National Diversity in Industrial Relations*, London: Allen and Unwin.

Dore, R. (1983) 'Interview with Ronald Dore', *Economic and Trade Bulletin*, 15, June, 1–2, 11–12, The Australia-Japan Economic Institute.

Embassy of the United States, Tokyo (1982) 'Annual Labor Report: Japan 1981–2', Tokyo: unpublished report.

Foreign Press Centre (1978) *Labour Problems and Industrial Relations*, Japan: The Centre.

Foreign Press Centre (1980) *Basic Statistical Survey on Wage Structure: Results of the 1979 Survey on All Industries, Ministry of Labour*, Japan: The Centre.

Foreign Press Centre (1981a) *Summary of Results from Fiscal Year 1981 Survey on Employment of Female Workers in Enterprises, Ministry of Labour*, Japan: The Centre.

Foreign Press Centre (1981b) *Research and Study Concerning Influences of Microelectronics on Employment: Results of the Survey on Labour Statistics by Occupation in Fiscal Year 1980, Ministry of Labour*, Japan: The Centre.

Foreign Press Centre (1982a) *Wage Structure of the Manufacturing Industry: Summary of Findings of 1981 Survey, Ministry of Labour*, Japan: The Centre.

Foreign Press Centre (1982b) *Fiscal 1981 Annual Report on Agricultural Trends: Part 1. Summary of Agricultural Trends, Ministry of Agriculture, Forestry and Fishery*, Japan: The Centre.

Foreign Press Centre (1982c) *Summary of 1981 Survey on Living Condition(s), Ministry of Health and Welfare*, Japan: The Centre.

Fujii, Kiyoko (1982) 'Industrial homework in Japan', in *Seminar for Public Administration Officers 1982: Outline of Lectures*, Tokyo: Government of Japan, 44–52.

Furuya, Ken'ichi (1980) 'Labour-management relations in postwar Japan: their reality and change', *Japan Quarterly*, 27 (1), 29–38.

General Council of Trade Unions of Japan (Sohyo) (1981) *This is Sohyo: Japanese Workers and their Struggles*, Tokyo: The Council.

General Council of Trade Unions of Japan (Sohyo) (1984) 'ME and Changes in Structure of Employment and Work', Tokyo: The Council, unpublished.

Glazer, N. (1974) 'From Ruth Benedict to Herman Kahn: the postwar Japanese image in the American mind', *Bulletin* (The International House of Japan), 32, April, 1–38.

Gluck, C. (1978) 'The people in history: recent trends in Japanese historiography', *Journal of Asian Studies*, XXXVIII (1), November, 25–48.

Hanami, Tadashi (1979) *Japanese Industrial Law*, The Netherlands: Kluwer.

Hanami, Tadashi (1981) *Labor Relations in Japan Today*, Tokyo: Kodansha International Ltd.

Hanami, Tadashi (1983a) 'The function of the law in Japanese industrial relations', in Shirai Taishiro (ed.), *Contemporary Industrial Relations in Japan*, Wisconsin: University of Wisconsin Press, 161–77.

Hanami, Tadashi (ed.) (1983b) *Viability of the Japanese Model of Industrial Relations*, Kyoto: International Industrial Relations Congress, 28–31 March.

Hancock, K., Sano, Y., Chapman, B., and Fayle, P. (eds) (1983) *Japanese and Australian Labour Markets: A Comparative Study*, Canberra: Australia-Japan Research Centre, ANU.

Ikeda, Masayoshi (1979) 'The sub-contracting system in the Japanese electronic industry', in *Engineering Industries of Japan*, Tokyo: Economic Research Institute (KSK), Japan Society for the Promotion of [the] Machine Industry, no. 19, 43–71.

Ikeda, Masayoshi (1982) *Special characteristics of and actual conditions in Japan's smaller enterprises*, Tokyo: Chuo University, unpublished.

Ikehata, Keiji (1982) 'The frontline of robotization', in *Industrial Robots: Their Increasing Use and Impact*, Japan: Foreign Press Centre, 3–11.

Inagami, Takeshi (1983) 'QC circle activities and the suggestion system', in *Highlights in Japanese Industrial Relations*, Tokyo: Japan Institute of Labour, 65–8.

International Metalworkers' Federation, Japan Council (IMF-J-C) (1982) *Annual Survey: Wages and Working Conditions 1981*, Japan: The Council.

Ishida, Hideo (1977) 'Exportability of the Japanese employment system', *The Japan Industrial Relations Research Association*, Tokyo: Japan Institute of Labour.

Ishida, Takeshi (1980) *The Integration of Conformity and Competition: A Key to Understanding Japanese Society*, Japan: Foreign Press Centre.

Itō, Hiroshi (1973) *Japanese Politics: An Inside View*, Ithaca and London: Cornell University Press.

Itō, Takkichi (1963) 'The high growth of the Japanese economy and the problems of the small enterprises', *The Developing Economies*, 1 (2).

Jacoby, S. (1979) 'The origins of internal labor markets in Japan', in *Journal of Industrial Relations*, Berkeley: University of California Press, 18 (2), 184–96.

Japan External Trade Organization (JETRO) (c. 1981) *Promotion of Small and Medium Enterprises in Japan*, Japan: The Organization.

Japan: Federation of All Toyota Workers' Unions International Division (1981) *Toyota's Working Conditions; Union Organization and Operation; Union Activities at Toyota*, Japan: The Federation.

Japan Federation of Employers' Associations (Nikkeiren) (1981)'Small and medium enterprises', paper presented at ILO/Danida Inter-Regional Assistance to Employers' Organizations, Asian and Pacific Employers' Round Table, Tokyo, 1–8 December, Geneva: International Labour Office (ILO).

Japan Federation of Employers' Associations (Nikkeiren) (1982) *Report of the Committee for the Study of Labour Questions*, Tokyo: The Federation.

Japan Institute of Labour (1985) *Changing Patterns of Industrial Relations*, Tokyo: The Institute.

Japan Institute of Labour (1979) *Japanese Industrial Relations: Series 2*, Tokyo: The Institute.

Japan Institute of Labour (1983) *Highlights in Japanese Industrial Relations*, Tokyo: The Institute.

Japan Labor Bulletin (1982, 1983, 1984) Tokyo: Japan Institute of Labour.

Japan Productivity Centre (1981) *Productivity Movement in Japan*, Tokyo: The Centre.

Japan Productivity Centre (1982a) *The Micro-electronics (ME) Revolution and Labour-Management Relations*, Tokyo: The Centre.

Japan Productivity Centre (1982b) *Indices 1982, National Economy, Business Management and Productivity*, Tokyo: The Centre.

Japan Productivity Centre (1984) *Strategies for Productivity: International Perspectives*, New York: The Centre, unpublished.

Japan Times (January 1982-March 1983) Tokyo.

Japanese Confederation of Labour (Domei) (1981) *Trade Unions in Japan, June 1981*, Japan: The Confederation, unpublished.

Japanese Federation of Electrical Machine Workers' Unions (Denki Roren) (c. 1981) *This is Denki Roren*, Tokyo: The Federation.

Japanese Government: Ministry of Agriculture, Forestry and Fisheries (1982) *The 57th Statistical Yearbook of the Ministry of Agriculture, Forestry and Fisheries, Japan, 1980–81*, Tokyo: Statistics and Information Department, The Ministry.

Japanese Government: Ministry of Foreign Affairs (1982) *Small Businesses in Japan: Underpinnings of Economic Vitality*, Japan: The Ministry.

Japanese Government: Ministry of International Trade and Industry (1981) *White Paper on Small and Medium Enterprises 1981*, Tokyo: The Ministry.

Japanese Government: Ministry of International Trade and Industry (1982) *White Paper on Small and Medium Enterprises in Japan 1982*, Tokyo: The Ministry.

Japanese Government: Ministry of International Trade and Industry, Small and Medium Enterprise Agency (1980) *Survey of Actual Condition of the Sub-contracting Industry, 1979*, Japan: The Agency.

Japanese Government: Ministry of Labour (1980a) *Labour Administration in Japan*, Tokyo: The Ministry.

Japanese Government: Ministry of Labour (1980b) *Labour Laws of Japan 1980*, Tokyo: The Ministry.

Japanese Government: Ministry of Labour (1981) 'Preliminary Report on Results of Basic Survey on Labour Unions 1981', Tokyo: Secretariat, Statistics and Information Department, unpublished.

Japanese Government: Ministry of Labour (1982) 'The recent industrial dispute situation (from results of the 1981 Industrial Disputes Statistical Survey Annual Report)', Tokyo: Statistics and Research Bulletin, Welfare Statistics Bureau, unpublished.

Japanese Government: Ministry of Labour (1983) *Year Book of Labour Statistics 1981*, Tokyo: Minister's Secretariat, Statistics and Information Department.

Japanese Government: Prime Minister's Office (1980) *1979 Employment Status Survey*, Japan: Statistics Bureau.

Japanese Government: Prime Minister's Office (1982a) *1981 Establishment Census of Japan, vol. 1*, Japan: Statistics Bureau.

Japanese Government: Prime Minister's Office (1982b) *Japan Statistical Yearbook 1982*, Japan: Statistics Bureau.

Japanese Government: Prime Minister's Office (1982c) *Annual Report on the Labour Force Survey 1981*, Japan: Statistics Bureau.

Japanese Government (1982) *Seminar for Public Administration Officers in Women's Problems 1982 Fiscal Year: Outline of Lectures*, Japan: Government of Japan.

Kamata, Satoshi (1982) *Japan in the passing lane: an insider's account of life in a Japanese auto factory*, translated and edited by Akimoto, T., New York: Pantheon Books.

Karsh, B. and Cole, R. E. (1968) 'Industrialization and the convergence hypothesis: some aspects of contemporary Japan', *Journal of Social Issues*, 24 (4), 45–64.

Kato, Yūji (1980a) 'Patterns of labour use in Japan', Tokyo: Senshu University, unpublished.

Kato, Yūji (1980b) 'Problems of unemployment and poverty in Japan', Tokyo: Senshu University, unpublished.

Koike, Kazuo (1973) 'Who regulates "on-the-job problems"', *Japan Industrial Relations Research Association*, Tokyo: Japan Institute of Labour.

Koike, Kazuo (1983) 'Workers in small firms and women in industry', in Shirai Taishiro (ed.), *Contemporary Industrial Relations in Japan*, Wisconsin: University of Wisconsin Press, 89–115.

Kōshiro, Kazutoshi (1980) 'Perceptions of work and living attitudes of the Japanese', *Japan Quarterly*, 27 (1), 46–55.

Kōshiro, Kazutoshi (1983a) 'The quality of working life in Japanese factories', in Shirai Taishiro (ed.), *Contemporary Industrial Relations in Japan*, Wisconsin: University of Wisconsin Press, 63–87.

Kōshiro, Kazutoshi (1983b) 'The employment effects of microelectronic technology', *Japan Labor Bulletin*, 22 (3), 4–8, Tokyo: Japan Institute of Labour.

Kuwahara, Yasuo (1985) 'What does the increase of temporary workers bring to the Japanese employment system', *Japan Labor Bulletin*, February, 5–8.

Levine, S. B. (1958) *Industrial Relations in Postwar Japan*, Urbana: University of Illinois Press.

Levine, S. B. (c. 1979) 'Industrial relations in Japan: some cross-national comparisons', paper presented at Seminar, Australian National University, Canberra, unpublished.

Levine, S. B. (1982) 'Japanese industrial relations: an external perspective', paper presented at International Colloquium on the Comparative Study of Japanese Society, Queensland, Australia, unpublished.

Levine, S. B. and Taira, Koji (1977) 'Labour markets, trade unions, and social justice: Japanese failures?', *Japanese Economic Studies*, 5 (3), Spring, 66–95.

Levine, S. B. and Taira, Koji (c. 1979) 'Conflict and co-operation in Japanese industry: is there conflict?', paper, Griffith University, Australia, unpublished.

Levine, S. B. and Taira, Koji (1980) 'Interpreting conflict: the case of Japan', in Martin, B. and Kassalow, E. M. (eds), *Labour Relations in Advanced Industrial Societies*, Washington, DC: Carnegie Endowment for International Peace, 109–16.

Littler, C. R. (1980) 'Internal contract and the transition to modern work systems: Britain and Japan', in Dunkerley, D. and Salaman, G. (eds), *International Year Book of Organization Studies, 1979*, London: Routledge & Kegan Paul, 157–85.

Littler, C. R. (1983a) 'Japan and China', in Feuchtwang, S. and Hussein, A. (eds), *The Chinese Economic Reforms*, London: Croom Helm, 121–47.

Marsh, R. and Mannari, H. (1976) *Modernization and the Japanese Factory*, Princeton, New Jersey: Princeton University Press.

Masaaki, Imai (1982) 'From Taylor to Ford to Toyota: *Kanban* system another challenge from Japan', *Japan Economic Journal*, 30 March, 12.

Masutada, Imaizumi (1982) 'Business Nippon: Japan's Quality Control systems', *Asahi Evening News*, Japan: 22 December, 6, English-language edition.

Matsuda, Yasukiko (1983), 'Conflict resolution in Japanese industrial relations', in Shirai Taishiro (ed.), *Contemporary Industrial Relations in Japan*, Wisconsin: University of Wisconsin Press, 179–203.

Matsushita, Mitsuo (1980) *Administrative Guidance and Economic Regulation in Japan*, Brisbane, Australia: Asian Studies Association of Australia, Third National Conference.

Matsuzawa, Tetsunari (1985) '*Yoseba* (street labour markets), the struggles of day labourers, and the structure of oppression in Japan', paper read at the Fourth National Conference, Japan Studies Association of Australia, Melbourne, May, unpublished.

Moore, J. (1974) 'The Japanese worker', *Bulletin of Concerned Asian Scholars*, 6 (3), September/October, 35–47.

Moore, J. (1983) *Japanese Workers and the Struggle for Power 1945–1947*, Wisconsin: University of Wisconsin Press.

Mouer, R. and Sugimoto, Yoshio (eds) (1980a) *Social Analysis Special*

Issue: Japanese Society — Reappraisals and Directions, Australia: University of Adelaide.

Mouer, R. and Sugimoto, Yoshio (1980b) *Some Questions Concerning Commonly Accepted Stereotypes of Japanese Society*, Australia: Australian National University.

Muto, Ichiyo (1984) 'Class struggle on the shopfloor: the Japanese case (1945−84)', *AMPO*, 16 (3), 38−49.

Nakagawa, Keiichiro (ed.) (1979) *Labour and Management*, Tokyo: University of Tokyo Press.

Nakane, Chie (1970) *Japanese Society*, Berkeley: University of California Press.

Nakayama, Ichiro (1975) *Industrialization and Labor-Management Relations in Japan*, Tokyo: Japan Institute of Labour.

Nevins, T. J. (c. 1981), 'Managing poor performers out of your company'; 'Discharge with strategically phrased work rules'; 'Hire marginal employees as temporaries on contract with separate work rules'; *Japan Times* series.

Nevins, T. J.(1982) 'Labor on a leash? A look at Japanese enterprise unions', *Tradepia International*, no. 12, 8−11.

Ōkōchi, Kasuo, Karsh, B., and Levine, S. B. (1973) *Workers and Employers in Japan: The Japanese Employment Relations System*, Tokyo: Tokyo University Press.

Ouchi, W. (1981) *Theory Z, How American Business Can Meet the Japanese Challenge*, Reading, Mass.: Addison-Wesley.

Park, S. J. (1984) 'Labour-management consultation as a Japanese type of participation: an international comparison', in Tokunaga, Shigeyoshi and Bergmann, Joachim (eds), *Industrial Relations in Transition*, Tokyo: University of Tokyo Press, 153−67.

Patrick, Hugh (ed.) (1976) *Japanese Industrialization and Its Social Consequences*, Berkeley: University of California Press.

Patrick, H. and Rosovsky, H. (eds) (c. 1976) *Asia's New Giant*, Washington: Brookings Institute.

'Progress of technological innovation in the Japanese machine industry and sub-contracting manufacturers' (1982) in *Engineering Industries of Japan*, Tokyo: Economic Research Institute (KSK), Japan Society for the Promotion of [the] Machine Industry, no. 22, 1−21.

Roberts, B. C. (1979) *Towards Industrial Democracy: Europe, Japan and the US*, London: Croom Helm.

Rohlen, T. P. (1974) *For Harmony and Strength: The Japanese White-Collar Organization in Anthropological Perspective*, Berkeley: University of California Press.

Sano, Yoko (1983) 'Women in the Japanese workforce', in Hancock, K., Sano, Yoko, Chapman, B., and Fayle, P. (eds), *Japanese and Australian Labour Markets: A Comparative Study*, Canberra: Australia-Japan Research Centre, 435−57.

Shalev, M. (1980) 'Industrial relations theory and the comparative study of industrial relations and industrial conflict', *British Journal of Industrial Relations*, XVIII (1), 26−43.

Shimada, Haruo (1980) *The Japanese Employment System*, Japanese Industrial Relations Series no. 6, Tokyo: Japan Institute of Labour.

Shimada, Haruo (1981) 'Japanese perceptions and expectations of industrial relations', paper presented to Conference: Trading with Japan: The Industrial Relations Factor, Monash University, Australia, unpublished.

Shimada, Haruo (1983) 'Japanese industrial relations: a new general model? A survey of the English-language literature', in Shirai, Taishiro (ed.), *Contemporary Industrial Relations in Japan*, Wisconsin: University of Wisconsin Press, 3–27.

Shirai, Taishiro (1983) 'Characteristics of Japanese managements and their personnel policies', in Shirai, Taishiro (ed.), *Contemporary Industrial Relations in Japan*, Wisconsin: University of Wisconsin Press, 369–82.

Steven, R. (1983) *Classes in Contemporary Japan*, Cambridge: Cambridge University Press.

Strong, K., 'Tanaka Shōzō: Meiji hero and pioneer against pollution', address given to the Council Chamber of the Law Society, 8 February, London: Publication details and year unknown.

Sugimoto, Yoshio (1975) 'Surplus value, unemployment and industrial turbulence', *Journal of Conflict Resolution*, 19 (1), March, 25–47.

Sugimoto, Yoshio and Mouer, R. (1979) *Japanology: A Methodological Deadend for Theories Assuming Uniformity Among the Japanese*, Brisbane: Griffith University.

Sugimoto, Yoshio and Mouer, R. (1981) *Japanese Society: Stereotypes and Realities*, Melbourne: Japanese Study Centre.

Tanaka, Yuki (1985) 'Japan's nuclear gypsies', paper read at the Fourth National Conference, Japan Studies Association of Australia, Melbourne, May 1985, unpublished.

Tan Hong, W. (1977) *The Development of Industrial Relations in Japan*, Paris: Organization for Economic Cooperation and Development (OECD).

Tokunaga, Shigeyoshi (1983) 'A Marxist interpretation of Japanese industrial relations with special reference to large private enterprises', in Shirai, Taishiro (ed.), *Contemporary Industrial Relations in Japan*, Wisconsin: University of Wisconsin Press, 313–30.

Tokunaga, Shigeyoshi and Bergmann, J. (eds) (1984) *Industrial Relations in Transition: The Cases of Japan and the Federal Republic of Germany*, Tokyo: University of Tokyo Press.

Trade Union Movement in Japan (1981) Tokyo: Japanese Conference of Trade Unions for Promotion of a United Front (Toitsu Rosokon).

Tsurumi, Kazuko (1975) 'Yanagita Kunio's work as a model of endogenous development', *Japan Quarterly*, XXII (3), 223–38.

Ujihara, Shojiro (1965) 'Japan's laboring class: changes in the postwar period', *Journal of Social and Political Ideas in Japan*, 3 (3), 60–7.

Vogel, E. F. (1971) *Japan's New Middle Class*, 2nd edn, Berkeley: University of California Press.

Vogel, E. F. (1979) *Japan as Number One: Lessons for America*, Cambridge: Harvard University Press.

Whitehill, A. M. and Takezawa, Shin'ichi (1968) *The Other Worker. A Comparative Study of Industrial Relations in the United States and Japan*, Honolulu: East-West Centre Press.

Woronoff, J. (1982a) *Inside Japan, Inc.*, Tokyo: Lotus.
Woronoff, J. (1982b) *Japan's Wasted Workers*, Tokyo: Lotus.
Yomiuri Shinbun (20 January 1983), Tokyo.

JAPANESE-LANGUAGE MATERIAL ON JAPAN

Chūshō kigyōka dōyūkai zenkoku kyogikai (National Association of
Managers of Small and Medium Firms) (c. 1981) *Chūshō kigyō ni
okeru rōshi kankei no kenkai* (Opinions on labour-management
relations in small and medium industry), Japan: The Association.
Kato, Yūji (1980, 1982) *Gendai nihon ni okeru fuantei shūgyō rōdōsha*
(Workers in unstable employment in contemporary Japan), vols 1
and 2, Tokyo: Ochanomizu shobō.
Chūō daigaku keizai kenkyūjo (ed.) (1982) *Kengyō nōka no rōdō to
seikatsu shakai hoshō: Ina chiiki no nōgyō to denshi kiki kōgyō jittai
bunseki* (The work of part-time farm households and social welfare
[social security]: an analysis of farming and the electronic equipment
industry in the Ina Region), Tokyo: Chūō daigaku shuppanbu.

GENERAL ENGLISH-LANGUAGE MATERIAL

Armstrong, P. J., Goodman, J. F. B., and Hyman, J. D. (1981)
Ideology and Shop-floor Industrial Relations, London: Croom
Helm.
Averitt, R. (1968) *The Dual Economy*, New York: Norton.
Barrett, B., Rhodes, E., and Beishon, J. (eds) (1975) *Industrial
Relations and the Wider Society: Aspects of Interaction*, Middlesex:
Collier Macmillan.
Bendix, R. (1967) 'Tradition and modernity reconsidered', *Comparative Studies in Society and History*, 9 (3), 292–346.
Bendix, R. (1974) *Work and Authority in Industry: Ideologies of
Management in the Course of Industrialization*, Berkeley: University
of California Press.
Bendix, R. and Lipset, S. M. (eds) (1966) *Class Status and Power*, New
York: Free Press.
Beynon, H. (1973) *Working for Ford*, Middlesex: Penguin.
Braverman, H. (1974) *Labour and Monopoly Capital*, New York:
Monthly Review Press.
Burns, T. (ed.) (1969) *Industrial Man: Selected Readings*, Middlesex:
Penguin.
Child, J. (ed.) (1973) *Man and Organization*, New York: Allen and
Unwin, Halstead Press.
Clegg, H. A. (1970) *The System of Industrial Relations in Great Britain*,
Oxford: Basil Blackwell.
Clegg, H. A. (1975) 'Pluralism in industrial relations', *British Journal
of Industrial Relations*, XIII (3), 309–16,
Clegg, H. A. (1976) *Trade Unionism under Collective Bargaining*,
Oxford: Basil Blackwell.

Cox, Robert W. (1971) 'Approaches to a futurology of industrial relations', *International Institute of Labour Studies*, 8, 139–64.

Crouch, C. (ed.) (1978a) *State and Economy in Contemporary Capitalism*, London: Croom Helm.

Crouch, C. (1979b) *The Politics of Industrial Relations*, Glasgow: Fontana.

Doeringer, P. B. (1981) *Industrial Relations in International Perspective*, London: Macmillan.

Donovan Report (1968) Royal Commission on Trade Unions and Employers' Associations, London: HMSO.

Dunlop, J. T. (1958) *Industrial Relations Systems*, New York: Henry Holt.

Dunlop, J. T., Harbison, F. H., Kerr, C., and Myers, C. A. (1975) *Industrialism and Industrial Man Reconsidered*, Princeton, N.J.: Inter-University Study of Human Resources in National Development.

Edwards, P. K. and Scullion, H. (1982) *The Social Organization of Industrial Conflict*, Oxford: Basil Blackwell.

Edwards, R. C. (1975) 'The social relations of production in the firm and labor market segmentation', in Edwards, R. C., Reich, M., and Gordon, D. M. (eds), *Labor Market Segmentation*, Lexington: Heath and Company, 3–26.

Edwards, R. C. (1979) *Contested Terrain*, London: Heinemann.

Edwards, R. C., Reich, M., and Gordon, D. M. (eds) (1975) *Labor Market Segmentation*, Lexington: Heath and Company.

Flanders, A. (1975) *Management and Unions*, London: Faber and Faber.

Fox, A. (1971) *A Sociology of Work in Industry*, London: Macmillan.

Fox, A. (1973) 'Industrial relations: a critique of pluralist ideology', in Child, J. (ed.), *Man and Organization*, London: Allen and Unwin, 185–233.

Fox, A. (1974) *Beyond Contract: Work, Power and Trust Relations*, London: Faber and Faber.

Friedman, A. L. (1977) *Industry and Labour: Class Struggle at Work and Monopoly Capitalism*, London: Macmillan.

Gordon, D. M., Edwards, R. C., and Reich, M. (1982) *Segmented Work, Divided Workers: The Historical Transformation of Labour in the United States*, Cambridge: Cambridge University Press.

Gospel, H. F. (1983) 'Managerial structures and strategies: an introduction', in Gospel, H. F. and Littler, C. R. (eds), *Managerial Strategies and Industrial Relations*, Surrey: Heinemann, 1–24.

Gusfield, J. (1967) 'Tradition and modernity: misplaced polarities in the study of social change', *American Journal of Sociology*, 72, 351–62.

Haraszti, Miklos (1978) *A Worker in a Worker's State*, translated by Wright, M., New York: Universe Books.

Hill, S. (1974) 'Norms, groups and power: the sociology of workplace industrial relations', *British Journal of Industrial Relations*, XII, 213–35.

Hyman, R. (1975) *Industrial Relations: A Marxist Perspective*, London: Macmillan.

Hyman, R. (1977) *Strikes*, 2nd revised edn, Glasgow: Fontana.

Hyman, R. and Brough, I. (1975) *Social Values and Industrial Relations*, Oxford: Basil Blackwell.

Ingham, G. K. (1970) *Size of Industrial Organization and Work Behaviour*, Cambridge: Cambridge University Press.

Kerr, C. (1964) *Labor and Management in Industrial Society*, New York: Doubleday and Co.

Kerr, C., Dunlop, J. T., Harbison, F. H., and Myers, C. A. (1960) *Industrialism and Industrial Man*, Cambridge: Harvard University Press.

Littler, C. R. (1982) *The Development of the Labour Process in Capitalist Societies*, London: Heinemann.

Littler, C. R. (1983b) 'A comparative analysis of managerial structures and strategies', in Gospel, H. F. and Littler, C. R. (eds), *Managerial Strategies and Industrial Relations*, Surrey: Heinemann, 171–96.

Littler, C. R. (ed.) (1985) *The Experience of Work*, Aldershot: Gower.

Littler, C. R. and Salaman, G. (1985) 'The design of jobs', in Littler, C. R. (ed.), *The Experience of Work*, Aldershot: Gower, 85–104.

Marx, Karl (1859) *A Contribution to the Critique of Political Economy*.

Moore, B., Jr (1966) *Social Origins of Dictatorship and Democracy*, Middlesex: Penguin.

Paci, M. (1981) 'Class structure in Italian society', in Pinto, Diana (ed.), *Contemporary Italian Sociology*, London: Cambridge University Press, 206–21.

Palmer, G. (1983) *British Industrial Relations*, London: Allen and Unwin.

Parker, S. R., Brown, R. K., Child, J., and Smith, M. A. (1981) *The Sociology of Industry*, 4th edn, London: Allen and Unwin.

Piore, M. J. (1975) 'Notes for a theory of labour market segmentation', in Edwards, R. C., Reich, M., and Gordon, D. M. (eds), *Labor Market Segmentation*, Lexington: Heath and Company.

Poole, M. (1976) 'A power analysis of workplace labour relations', *Industrial Relations Journal*, 7 (3), 31–43, London: Mercury House.

Russett, B. (1984) 'Dimensions of resource dependence: some elements of rigor in concept and policy analysis', *International Organization*, 38 (3), Summer, 483–99.

Salaman, G. (1984) *Work Organization and Class Structure*, New York: M. E. Sharpe, Inc.

Williams, A. (1984) *Power Conflict Control: Recurring Themes in Industrial Relations Theory*, Palmerston North, New Zealand: The Dunmore Press.

Woodward, J. (1965) *Industrial Organization: Theory and Practice*, London: Oxford University Press.

Woodward, J. (1970) *Industrial Organization: Behaviour and Control*, London: Oxford University Press.

Acknowledgements

I acknowledge with gratitude the support and assistance of colleagues and friends in Japan and Australia who contributed to the production of this work. For their encouragement and advice, I would like to thank in particular Alan Rix, Nancy Viviani, Michael Quinlan, Jack Sherrington, and Craig Littler, and, for their painstaking efforts, Jeff Russell who produced the index and Chris Nicholson who sub-edited the final text.

The generous assistance I received during my research in Japan in 1982 and 1983 was invaluable. I am deeply grateful to Suzuki Hideo, Ian McArthur, and personnel of the Australian Embassy in Tokyo for their help, and to those I interviewed, for their patience with my questions and keen interest in the research. I would like to acknowledge my special debt to Ikeda Masayoshi who made it possible for me to meet with and talk to some of the workers in small urban and rural plants — the major actors of this book.

My greatest debt is to my daughters Gillian, Janet, and Kathleen. They had an unwavering faith that this book could be written and backed their faith with practical help.

Index

Abegglen, James C., 22, 25, 27, 34
'Administrative Guidance', 60, 74n6, 91
Aged/Ageing, 36, 37, 38, 99, 203: within large firms, 54; and mid-career hiring, 54, 57, 98; as a problem in small/medium firms, 54–5; and rural sector, 87; unemployment as a problem within, 98
Agriculture (see Rural sector)
Agro-industrial workers, 2, 77: changes in employment trends, 84; distribution of, 84; employment stability of, 88–9; female role, 84–5; as part-time entrepreneurs, 84–5, 87–8; as part-time workers, 67–8, 84; (see also Ina Sankyo; Ōshima Seisakusho; Takamori Tshushin; Rural sector)
Ainu, The, 37
Allied Industry Councils, 189
Arubaito (part-time student workers) (see Workforce)
Australia: and 'body-hire system', 136n4; and Japan trade relations, 137n11; and laissez faire approach to industrial relations, 44n1
Australian National Times, 137n7
Automation, 130

Benedict, Ruth, 22
Bix, Herbert B., 35
Blue collar management, 166
Blue collar workers, 23, 90, 145, 165, 166, 168, 181, 182, 184, 192, 235n8: job mobility, 63–4, 67; as managers, 228, 239

Boards of Management: ex-trade union leaders on, 101–2
Body-hire, 118, 136n4: (see also Oyakata; Tehaishi)
Brecht, B., 35
Britain, 25, 28, 97: level of sub-contracting in, 109; and laissez faire approach to industrial relations, 13

Canada, 97
Canon group, 236n14
Central Labour Commission, 220–2
Churitsuroren (Federation of Independent Unions), 188, 225, 235n13
Clegg, H. A., 15, 170
Cole, Robert E., 23, 166, 191–2, 196n11
Collective agreements, 198–9, 203, 210, 232, 234n3, 243
Collective bargaining, 11, 202, 210, 223, 243: enterprise unions and, 198
Communication, 198–209, 210–18
Comparative studies of industrial relations, 24–7
Conflict: definition of, 10–11, 197, 219; marxist approach to, 11, 13–14, 22; in the peripheral sector, 106; pluralist approach to, 9–15; unitary approach to, 9–10; (see also Fujii, Ryuko, Trade Union Division, MOL)
Construction industry: employment in, 48, 78–80; and female unionism, 183–4; role of contract labour within, 41; sub-contracting as part of, 110; and

273

unionization, 180–2; (see
also Mochizuki Steel
Fabrications Limited)
Cook, Alice S., 22
Corporate paternalism, 29
Cost reduction, 201
Cox, Robert W., 25–6
Crawcour, E. S., 30–1

Daitokogyo Company
Employees' Union, 148,
150–2
Daitokogyo Manufacturing
Company: benefits of
specialization, 147; relations
with sub-contractors, 147–8,
166, 168; relations with
union, 148–50, 167, 235n6;
structure of, 146–8;
workforce of, 146–7; (see
also National Association of
Managers of Small and
Medium Enterprises)
Daitokogyo Union news
bulletin, 152–4
Dekasegi (seasonal workers)
(see Workforce)
Democratic Socialist Party
(DSP), 189
Dependency theories, 18, 170
Differentials (see Wages)
Discrimination, in employment,
38
Disputes: conflict as a basis
for, 221; definition of,
219–20; frequency of, 226,
235n13; in large firms,
227–9; and the private
sector, 226; public sector
dominance of, 225;
resolution of, 225–31; role
of labour commission in,
220–1; in small/medium
firms, 226, 228; strikes as
part of, 220, 221, 225–31;
union role in, 230–1; (see
also Proper industrial action;
Unfair labour practices)
Dispute Adjustment Division,
Central Labour Commission,

4, 220–2
Domei (Japanese Confederation
of Labour), 188–9, 215,
223–4, 225, 235n13; (see also
Sado, Masatoshi)
Dore, Ronald P., 23–7, 29, 30,
234n4
Dunlop, John T., 11–12, 22,
24

Education: as factor in
employment, 53–4, 57–9;
(see also Large firms; Small
and medium firms; Wages;
Women)
Eguchi, Eiichi, 42, 44n5
Electrical machinery and
equipment manufacture, 48,
79–80
Engineering Industries of
Japan, Economic Research
Institute (KSK) (see KSK
report)
Enterprise unionism:
advantages of, 132, 191,
193–4; definition of, 184;
disadvantages of, 191–4;
extent of, 174–5; and
segmentation of labour,
185–6, 193–4; (see also
Unions)
Eta, 37

Family workers (see Workforce)
Farmers: and ageing, 87;
decline in numbers of, 84–6;
as enterprise owners, 87–8;
and movement to wage
labour, 84–5; and part-time
work, 84, 87; role in
workforce, 87–9; (see also
Rural sector)
Federation of All Toyota
Unions, 211
Federation of Employers'
Associations (see Nikkeiren)
Federation of Independent
Unions (see Churitsuroren)
Federation of Industrial
Homeworkers' Union, 96

Productivity Centre)
Yoseba (street labour markets),
39, 41

Zaibatsu (industrial cartels), 40
Zero Defect (ZD), 133, 201